Near and Far Waters

Near and Far Waters

The Geopolitics of Seapower

Colin Flint

STANFORD UNIVERSITY PRESS
Stanford, California

Stanford University Press
Stanford, California

© 2024 by Colin Flint. All rights reserved.

No part of this book may be reproduced or transmitted in any form or by any means, electronic or mechanical, including photocopying and recording, or in any information storage or retrieval system, without the prior written permission of Stanford University Press.

Printed in the United States of America on acid-free, archival-quality paper
Library of Congress Cataloging-in-Publication Data
Names: Flint, Colin, 1965- author.
Title: Near and far waters : the geopolitics of seapower / Colin Flint.
Other titles: Geopolitics of seapower
Description: Stanford, California : Stanford University Press, [2024] | Includes bibliographical references and index.
Identifiers: LCCN 2023048606 (print) | LCCN 2023048607 (ebook) | ISBN 9781503639645 (cloth) | ISBN 9781503639812 (paperback) | ISBN 9781503639829 (ebook)
Subjects: LCSH: Sea-power. | Geopolitics.
Classification: LCC V25 .F55 2024 (print) | LCC V25 (ebook) | DDC 359/.03--dc23/eng/20231117
LC record available at https://lccn.loc.gov/2023048606
LC ebook record available at https://lccn.loc.gov/2023048607

Cover design: Derek Thornton / Notch Design
Cover art: Shutterstock and Wikimedia Commons

To the educators and students of redbrick and public universities

CONTENTS

List of Illustrations		ix
Preface		xi
Introduction	The Geopolitics of Seapower	1
One	What Is Geopolitics?	11
Two	Strong and Weak Countries and Stories of Geopolitical "Threats"	26
Three	The Rise and Fall of Seapowers	39
Four	The Geopolitics of Near Waters and Far Waters	61
Five	The Geopolitics of Primary-Subsidiary Trade	85
Six	The Geopolitics of Innovation	106
Seven	The Visions behind Force Projection	124
Eight	No Island Is an Island	140
Conclusion	The Gathering Storm Clouds of War	160
Acknowledgments		173
Suggested Readings		175
Notes		177
Index		213

LIST OF ILLUSTRATIONS

Figures

1.1	The virtuous cycle of seapower	18
4.1	The process of force projection in near and far waters	63
7.1	Rostow's stages of economic growth	131
8.1	The role of islands in force projection	141
C.1	The nonvirtuous cycle of seapower	163

Maps

1.1	Sea lines of communication and choke points	20
2.1	China's Belt and Road Initiative	31
2.2	Post–Second World War US global military alliances	33
3.1	Imperial concessions in China	53
3.2	Operation Ocean Shield	58
4.1	Dutch near waters	65
4.2	Dutch far waters	67
4.3	Destroyers for Bases and US near waters	72
4.4	The voyages of Admiral Zheng He	79
4.5	China's nine-dash line	83

5.1	Dutch Brazil	89
5.2	The British Empire	91
5.3	The Japanese Empire	93
5.4	The corridors of the Belt and Road Initiative	102
6.1	The Heligoland-Zanzibar Treaty	119
6.2	The world's busiest container ports	121
8.1	The Greenland-Iceland-United Kingdom (GIUK) gap	149
8.2	The Acheson perimeter and the nine-dash line	155

PREFACE

One of my early childhood memories, surprisingly vivid, is of standing in the Canterbury branch of a W. H. Smith's bookstore flicking through a young adult's history book bringing the exploits of British naval hero Horatio Nelson and the Napoleonic-era missions of the Royal Navy to life. The book was visually appealing, and the storyline had enough ingredients of an adventure story that I was hooked. But it wasn't just the atmosphere conjured up by the book that made it appealing. I knew it was tugging at strings within me that were being formed and made taut by the pervasive salesmanship of English nationalism. Though I was holding the book sometime in the early or mid-1970s, there was a pitch that England still ruled the waves.

The personal appeal of this story was encouraged by the fact that I lived near what was at the time the busiest ferry port in the world. Seeing the boats leave and enter Dover harbor reinforced a sense of the naturalness of my country's global connections across the sea. And I was a boy and had my moment of fascination with things military. My bedroom wall was covered with posters featuring outlines of the ships of the Royal Navy fleet and the badges of each ship. I recall a poster of a painting of armed planes, probably Buccaneers, taking off from an aircraft carrier. Once a year it got real when my parents took me to "Navy Days" at Portsmouth Naval Base, where the youth, and more than a few excited parents, were allowed to clamber through ships, submarines, and helicopters. The day ended with a demonstration by the Royal Marines showing their ability to use force to resolve some minor crisis or other. For a few years I was intoxicated by the myth of British naval power.

But life takes you on different paths, and I wasn't pulled toward studying seapower even after I found my way to academia. I wasn't studying geopolitics at all. And oddly enough, I, and most of my fellow political geographers, weren't studying war much. The terrorist attacks of September 11, 2001, changed that for me and for the subdiscipline of political geography. After 9/11, I scrambled to change my class syllabi. I searched for edited volumes covering the geography of war. There were two, both outdated. One focused on the Cold War and the other on the Israel/Palestine conflict.[1] As political geography strove for relevance, my colleagues and I shifted our focus to war, mainly to the new War on Terror.[2]

Around this time a couple of professional opportunities came my way. I was invited to write a textbook called *Introduction to Geopolitics*.[3] I also became coeditor of the journal *Geopolitics*. Suddenly my writing, teaching, and professional duties were all about geopolitics, and I had many colleagues as fellow travelers. The textbook and the coeditorship led to invitations to give talks and attend workshops across the globe. Several times a year I found myself on an airplane flying over oceans to talk about geopolitics. It was exciting and I felt privileged. But I was also uneasy. Why?

The individual opportunities were the result of a global resurgence of interest in the word *geopolitics*. From being a topic largely ignored by geographers it had become a focus of our discipline.[4] And this was not just the case for geographers. Academics in other disciplines, commentators in newspapers, and public intellectuals were all using the word. With this interest in the subject, I should have been anything but uneasy. But the word *geopolitics* had been invented and become part of everyday language in the buildup to the First World War.[5] The new interest in the word, the interest that was paying for my globetrotting, seeing exciting new places, and meeting interesting people, could also be a sign that the world was on course for another round of major wars.

And what is this word *geopolitics*? It was being bandied about more frequently, yet with a lack of understanding that was also troubling. *Geopolitics* is usually used to refer to world politics, but the term has a more sinister edge. People tend to think of "world politics" as a normal and largely peaceful state of affairs, with some ongoing conflicts but nothing to get worried about for those living in the relative safety of the US, Europe, Australia, or Japan. Somehow saying *geopolitics* rather than *world politics* suggests a more dangerous situation and is used to draw attention to threats that require what is deemed just and reasonable military action. In other words, *geopolitics* is often used when talking about actual or impending war and is used to justify "our" use of force. That too was the general tone of the use of the word in the buildup to the two world wars.

As a geographer I had another nagging concern. The term *geopolitics* was used without any sense of what was meant by the *geo-*.[6] The geography of geopolitics was usually absent; *geo-* was just a synonym for *world* when we say "world politics." Sometimes the understanding of geography in geopolitics was very old-fashioned. It was a sense that geography determined national destiny. The term *geopolitics* was often used to take away choice from politics and send a message that war was inevitable. In this meaning, it was used to justify arguments that military expenditures and the use of military force were somehow predestined because we can't escape geography. Yet war or no war is a matter of choices and not the fact that a country has, say, a Pacific coastline!

That raises another question: Whose choices? Geopolitics is closely associated with statesmanship—the sense that decisions of war are in the hands of a political elite, usually predominantly men.[7] I was first rattled by this notion in an office hour I spent while teaching at Penn State University. A student came to see me to ask for help understanding some idea or other from the class. I tried my best to explain and show how it related to his future in the world. But he shrugged his shoulders and said, "I'm just a kid from Pittsburgh." I wanted to shout, "But I'm just a kid from Dover!"

This book is, perhaps, also the result of that conversation. Geopolitics is something that we are all involved in; it's not the preserve of "statesmen." When I was a kid from Dover, influential political and media messages, which included that book about the exploits of Nelson and encouragement to picture myself in the operations room of a Royal Navy destroyer, led me down the path toward a flag-waving nationalism and commitment to the military. I have come to believe that it is important that people of all social standings and nationalities understand geopolitics in a way that does not motivate us to fight wars.

I aim to provide an understanding of geopolitics that isn't so simple and so nationalistic but is hopefully still accessible. I do so by taking the *geo-* of geopolitics seriously while recognizing that my childhood fascination with seapower was based on something real and important. The topic that developed out of my fascination was the role of the projection of power across the world's oceans.[8] Learning from past patterns of naval power helps us understand why the moment we live in is one step on a potential path toward global war. And by recognizing this historical moment, all of us can think of and act on alternatives to such a war.

By "all of us" I mean people beyond academic and policymaking elites. As Jack Lawson, Durham miner turned peer and Clement Attlee's secretary of state of war, said: "I held that no man needs knowledge more than he who is subject to those who have. That if there is one man in the world who needs knowledge, it is he who does the world's most needful work."[9] I hope this book engages those recognized by Jack Lawson (if we can excuse the gendered language of his time) as doing the world's "needful work" while being subject to the whims of those who claim to have knowledge. Academics, such as myself, need to create knowledge of geopolitics that addresses the needs of everyday people and try to put it across in everyday language.

I recognize the appeal of nationalistic stories and the urge to see a threat and rally around the flag. Geopolitics has encouraged us to act that way. But by thinking of geopolitics in a different way we can see why country is pitted against country, how strong countries try to dominate weak countries, and how by so doing they may get dragged into global wars with other strong countries. To be forewarned is to be forearmed.

INTRODUCTION

The Geopolitics of Seapower

> Command of the sea has frequently passed from one nation to another, and though Great Britain has continued longer in possession of the superiority than perhaps any other nations did, yet all human affairs are subject to great vicissitudes.
>
> BRITISH GOVERNMENT REPORT OF 1727[1]

What Is Seapower and What Is It Meant to Do?

The opening quote for this chapter is three centuries old. It illustrates that seapower has been a constant part of world politics, that the relative ability of countries to act as seapowers waxes and wanes, and that seapower is a particular type of geopolitics that has been a key cause of global war.[2]

Seapower is the possession and use of large and effective military and merchant fleets to achieve interests and goals.[3] In a virtuous cycle,[4] economic wealth can be used to build seapower, and seapower can be used to increase wealth. Four attributes of the sea are vital in this cycle: the sea as a resource; the sea as a means of trade; the sea as a means of information flows; and the sea as a dominion or something that can be controlled.[5] To control the sea requires wealth generated from commercial and information flows across the oceans. The wealth created through maritime trade is used to build up the military naval strength that is used to secure trade. Merchant and military naval strength need each other, and strength in one allows for building up strength in the other.[6]

Perhaps surprisingly, the importance of seapower is a question of what happens *onshore*. This has been recognized in terms of military strategy: as Sir Julian Corbett observed, "Since men live upon the land and not upon the sea, great issues between nations at war have always been decided—except in the rarest cases—either by what your army can do against your enemy's territory and national life, or else by fear of what the fleet makes it possible for your army to do."[7] Seapower has been used to project power by transporting and disembarking armies to fight on land.

Seapower is even more important in making favorable onshore economic conditions for powerful countries. In a world in which certain countries have been labeled "failed states," navies are seen as "defending the system indirectly by what they do *from* the sea rather than *at* sea. They are defending the *conditions* for trade rather than trade itself."[8] This has been the case throughout history.[9] To understand why requires thinking about the "system" as a set of global economic relations that are unequal and designed to benefit the powerful to the detriment of the weak.[10]

Powerful countries have used seapower to create economic, political, and military conditions in weaker countries that have benefited the powerful;[11] it is part of the broader foreign policy of a powerful country that connects industrial strategy for the domestic economy with a need to maintain economic relations with weaker countries. An element of seapower is the geopolitical policing of the seas as a means of passage for global commerce.[12] Underlying the pattern of global trade is the geography of production and consumption, or the where and how of what is made and sold. It is this economic geography that seapower tries to create and keep steady by controlling the seas to influence what happens ashore.

Technological change over the centuries results in new ways to use force at sea. Further, strategic decisions depend on matters of timing in the geopolitics of the rise and fall of powerful countries. For example, decisions to precipitate a decisive sea battle (such as the Second World War's Battle of Midway in May 1942 or, over one hundred years earlier, the Battle of Trafalgar in October 1805) or to seek commercial control via blockades (as in the Battle of the Atlantic in the Second World War) were made within the context of global war. Yet though tactics and technologies may change, the broad goal to control the oceans for economic and strategic gain has been a historical constant.[13]

This book highlights the geography of seapower as an ever-changing struggle to gain control of near waters or far waters. Near waters are those parts of the oceans close to a country's shoreline. Far waters are those parts of the oceans across the horizon and neighboring the shorelines of other countries. One country's near waters are another country's far waters, and vice versa.

Mainstream understandings of geopolitics are inadequate for understanding what drives periods of competition over near and far waters. Geopolitics as the term is commonly used is more precisely classic geopolitics: a way of thinking that became prominent in the late nineteenth century. It is a realist understanding of the world that creates knowledge from a national perspective. It criticizes the actions of other countries while promoting the military actions of one's own. Classic geopoliticians are advocates for the foreign policy of one country. They are not critical analysts of global processes or history, though they often cloak their agenda-setting work in theory. The subject matter of geopolitics is a poorly defined "national interest" that is primarily about the possession of territory and resources. It advocates for national strength and preparation for war through the construction of a world of "us versus them." It has been the intellectual justification for competition and war for well over a century.

Classic geopolitics is a poor explanatory framework because it focuses on political and military relations. A fuller understanding of geopolitics requires a political economy framework that identifies economic dynamics as the engine for interstate competition. Furthermore, the scope must move beyond the traditional focus on "great powers" and consider a web of global relations that constantly creates a grossly unequal world. Global economic relations connect us, rather than divide us. However, the way countries maneuver within an unequal global economy often requires military strength that extends over the horizon. "National interest" is a matter of global calculations and force projection.

Geopolitics is not about possessing one's own national territory and resources. Rather, it is extraterritorial in its attempt to control access to others' resources. Seapower has been, and remains, the means to project force, access resources in other countries' territories, and secure trade routes. Understanding geopolitics as selfish behavior within a web of global relations suggests that the pursuit of "national interest" is probably going to result in war. Considering the structure within which countries act is a necessary step to considering the type of political change needed to prevent future wars. Otherwise, we will continue with the national mythmaking that makes "our" ambitions and might right, and "their" *similar* might and ambitions wrong.

The next chapter introduces geopolitics as a mixture of economic, political, and military competition. It requires thinking about what we mean by the geography of geopolitics. Giving serious thought to the "geo-" in geopolitics helps us connect global economic patterns as the underlying reason for global trade and the need for seapower in the competition for near and far waters.[14] Recognizing that the economic pattern is based on inequality and competition leads us to understand why the struggle for the control of near and far waters may lead to global war. And history provides us with lessons on how these struggles have played out in the past and may happen again.

The Value of History

History can provide a map to help us understand and make decisions within the current geopolitical situation. That is not to say that the map is perfect or that we are destined to follow similar pathways. But similar historical contexts are likely to provide countries with similar hopes and opportunities, as well as similar fears and limitations.[15] Understanding the similarity in historical contexts across centuries provides insight into current geopolitics even though the technologies of commerce and war have changed.

The historical contexts that are particularly useful are those in which a country that has been the dominant power starts to decline and is faced with challenges to its ability to project power.[16] In the modern era only three countries provide useful comparisons: the Netherlands in the 1600s; Great Britain from the late 1800s through the Second World War, and the United States from the 1970s to the present. These three countries were the most powerful countries in the world, what we will call hegemonic countries or hegemons. Their economic, political, military, and cultural prowess was not exclusive or unchallenged, but it was large enough for a period of time to dominate global economics and politics.[17] These three countries played host to the most advanced economies of the time, and their cities were the locations of the world's most important and profitable businesses.[18] These businesses led the world in innovation. Their societies were the most open and were the venues for the newest thinking about politics. They were the most tolerant countries in the world.[19]

Despite this tolerance and openness, these countries exported violence across the globe. They were the world's strongest naval powers. They could wage war across the globe, and their merchant navies dominated world trade.[20] The navies of these countries connected parts of the world producing essentials inputs to the industries back home. The navies also made possible the export of the products made at home to customers across the globe. The economic connections required the country to be present within the borders of other countries—especially the weaker ones. This presence used to take the form of different types of colonialism or imperialism. More recently control has taken the form of the creation of client states. It has always involved the use of violence.

The seapower of these countries is best thought of as a historical process, rather than something static. They gained control of their near waters and then projected power into far waters. In other words, they established a presence in the near waters of other countries. This presence was established using force. It went hand in hand with the creation of global trade networks. Violence abroad and economic outposts enabled the cities back home to thrive. This is the lesson from the histories of how and why the Netherlands, Great Britain, and the US established themselves as global and military powers.

But the most pertinent lessons come from how these three countries lost their global dominance. Over time, these countries faced challenges to their economic strength, their military prowess, and the resonance of their political and cultural messages. The causes and consequences of these challenges may be found in the geographic arenas of near and far waters. Other countries, those who had little choice but to accept the presence of the powerful country within their near waters, saw an opportunity to reassert their control. The hegemonic country faced a situation it found unusual—a situation in which its projection of seapower was limited. As this process continued, new seapowers emerged. The far waters that the hegemonic country had operated in quite freely became venues of tension and conflict. The situation worsened to the extent that the hegemonic country's own near waters became the far waters of other countries.

The Netherlands and Great Britain have both experienced a history in which their ability to project seapower from their near waters to far waters diminished, and their concern had to switch to the protection of their near waters. The move from the projection of power into far waters to protection of near waters in light of the projection of others has, in the past, resulted in global war. These past contexts are worthy of study given the contemporary geopolitics of challenges to the United States in its far waters of the western Pacific, China's assertion of control of its near waters, and China's growing presence in far waters. Are we indeed heading back to the future—a future that looks much like past historical contexts that were the precursors to global war?

The Logic of the Book

Many of today's warnings about the risk of war between the US and China concentrate on islands in the South China Sea.[21] Thinking about conflicts over islands as a potential cause of global war is merely looking at the tip of the iceberg. Islands do play an important role in competition between countries because of the strategic value of their location in near/far waters. But to understand why requires looking below the surface to the economic competition and relations that have proven to be the historic driving force leading to global war. Economic competition is based on unequal relations between rich and poor/strong and weak countries. Classic geopolitics has largely ignored economic relations and the role of weaker countries. By drawing attention only to the tip of the iceberg, it has been able to create an "us *versus* them" view of the world that promotes military responses. Looking under the surface shows that geopolitics is more a matter of "us *and* them," and that there are many "thems" rather than a single military foe.

The wealthiest countries in the world try to host the newest, most advanced, and most profitable economic activities.[22] Businesses create supply networks to support these industries that connect to the world's poorer countries to gain access to raw materials and components.[23] There is competition over this access as the supply of the inputs is limited and preferential treatment is desired. Countries become involved by providing military and diplomatic resources to establish and protect business arrangements. This involvement requires the projection of naval power from near waters to far waters. Countries may compete for access in the same far waters, and their presence may be challenged by countries who identify these parts of the ocean as their own near waters. Control of islands is a crucial part of the struggle for control over near and far waters.

The countries making the world's newest and most profitable products have an interest in promoting free trade. This interest also requires access across the world's oceans and into the near waters of other countries. This becomes another source of competition and potential conflict over access to far/near waters that may involve controlling islands.

The outbreak of global war over islands in near/far waters, driven by economic motives, is best thought of as the culmination of a developing process. As a country becomes more powerful, it tries to control its near waters by excluding the influence of other countries. These other countries may have seen these self-same waters as their far waters. The process of gaining control of near waters involves a combination of diplomacy and force that has often led to war. Once a country has gained control of its near waters, it may try to gain access to far waters/other countries' near waters. Such projection of power is driven by the need to secure access to key inputs (defined below as the generative sector) and to markets. Over time countries may resist this presence in their near waters and attempt to deny access in what the dominant country has come to see as its far waters. The strategic value of islands is heightened in these moments of conflict over access and access denial, or the projection of seapower and resistance to that projection.

Key Concepts

Making sense of the history of seapower, its connection to economics, and the potential for global war requires understanding a few key concepts.

Seapower

Seapower is a country's combined military and merchant navy strength.[24] The classic geopolitics view of the world sees a big difference between continental-oriented countries and maritime-oriented countries. In this argument, landpowers are expected to have a large-standing army, and this tends to make authoritarian, rather than democratic, politics more likely. The argument also claims that their economies are more likely to be agricultural and their culture more inward-looking. On the other hand, seapowers look toward trade and industry for their economic success and support navies rather than large armies. The result is more democratic, outward-looking, and open societies.[25]

This traditional labeling of landpowers and seapowers rings true to some extent but does not help us explain why tensions over parts of the world's oceans and islands may lead to global war.[26] Instead of seeing landpower versus seapower as the persistent geopolitical friction, we need to explore why countries seek to become seapowers and why they come into conflict with other maritime-oriented countries in the process. That requires understanding patterns of global inequality, the geography of rich and poor countries.

Primary and Subsidiary Countries

It is common sense that some countries are more powerful and wealthy than others. The geopolitics described in this book is one in which more powerful countries project their seapower and, relatedly, attempt to exclude countries from their coastal waters and territory. It is no coincidence that the countries projecting seapower are also the wealthier ones. The more powerful and wealthy countries are defined as *primary* and the weaker and less wealthy ones as *subsidiary*.[27] The global inequality between primary and subsidiary countries has been a permanent feature of modern world history, is likely to continue, and is the underlying reason for the geopolitics of seapower.[28]

Hegemony

The most powerful primary country at a given time is called the hegemon or hegemonic country, and its period of dominance is called *hegemony*.[29] Seapower, or more generally the ability to project power across the globe, has been a crucial part of the rise and fall of hegemonic powers.

Generative sector

Primary and subsidiary countries are tied to each other through economic and political connections. These connections are the reason for, and the means of, the projection of seapower. One of the most important set of relations, and the one that has in the past been a cause of war, is known as the *generative sector*—or the subsidiary countries that are the location of the raw materials essential for highly profitable manufacturing in primary countries.[30] Creating the links between the generative sector and primary countries has, in the past, been a source of tension and conflict. More discussion of the concepts of primary and subsidiary countries, hegemony, and the generative sector follows in the next chapter.

Primary countries have competed over the creation of the generative sector by developing and applying seapower. There is a geography to the projection of seapower, and it is the focus of this book.

Near Waters and Far Waters

The geography of seapower boils down to competition over near and far waters. Near waters are those parts of the ocean close to a country's shoreline that it believes it needs to secure to protect it from invasion or blockade. Far waters are those shorelines across the ocean. Of course, one country's near waters are another country's far waters. For example, the Caribbean Sea is a near water for the US and was once a far water for Great Britain.

Exerting control over one's own near waters is a fundamental security concern for a country. Once a country has control of its near waters it may gain the ability to project power across an ocean and create a presence in far waters. These far waters would be another country's near waters.[31] For example, during the Second World War the US secured its Pacific near waters and then projected power into western Pacific far waters, which were the near waters of China and Japan.

In the seventeenth and eighteenth centuries countries defined their effective reach from their coastline by the "cannon shot rule"—defined as three or four nautical miles.[32] Today, a version of near and far waters exists in international law and is generally adhered to. Near waters are legally defined in Part V of the United Nations Convention of the Law of the Sea (UNCLOS) as an Exclusive Economic Zone (EEZ),[33] the area of ocean "beyond and adjacent to the territorial sea" for two hundred nautical miles from the coast. Article 56 of UNCLOS gives coastal states sovereign rights within their EEZ, including the right to explore, exploit, and conserve and manage natural resources, "whether living or non-living," of the waters, the seabed, and the subsoil, including the production of energy from "water, current and winds." Countries may also establish "artificial islands, installations and structures" within their EEZ. The EEZ is an economic asset to a country, and such assets, plus the coastline, can be defended and exploited through defensive and extractive structures. Islands have their own EEZ. Hence the value for countries to claim islands, perhaps far from their coastline, as their sovereign territory. For example, the British claim to the Falkland Islands in the South Atlantic is an extension of the country's sovereignty into another hemisphere.

Those parts of the ocean not within an EEZ are identified in Part VII of UNCLOS as "High Seas."[34] Article 87 of UNCLOS gives coastal and landlocked countries the right to the freedoms of navigation, overflight, the laying of submarine cables and pipelines, fishing, and scientific research in the high seas. Countries have the right to build structures on the high seas, though the practical difficulties are a challenge except in shallow waters. Disputes over which maritime areas count as EEZs and which countries can claim sovereign rights to them have, unsurprisingly, resulted in court cases. The most important recent one was the July 12, 2016, ruling of the Permanent Court of Arbitration at The Hague. The Court agreed with the Philippines, who had brought the case, that China had no legitimate claim to the South China Sea because of a history of control. This case was part of the geopolitical tensions over island sovereignty and over China's construction of islands from existing reefs, discussed in chapter 8. In this instance, the legalities of EEZs and the High Seas were a feature of near-water/far-water geopolitics.

However, far waters and near waters are not precise geographic areas or legal terms. They are a matter of the perception of countries. The extent of near waters depends on a country's ability to secure waters relatively close to its coastline and its perception of threats to that area. The extent of far waters depends on the country's definition of interests beyond the horizon and its related need to develop an economic and military presence in that region. Since the UNCLOS agreement, a country has a legal term to define its near waters, but a country may have a strategic sense of near waters beyond its EEZ. In turn, though a country may define far-waters interests near the coastline of a country, it must now be conscious of violating the sovereign rights of EEZs.

Near and far waters are fuzzy areas that are defined by the actions and desires of countries, and not by lawyers. Control of near and far waters is a historical process rather than a definitive definition of boundaries. The control of near and far waters is a matter of competition, as rising and existing powers try to reach beyond their near waters and extend into far waters, while wrestling with the concern that another power may be in their near waters. The US grappled with this issue in the late 1800s, and the matter was addressed in the writing of Alfred Thayer Mahan.[35] Since the 1980s China has been expanding its naval reach from its coastline to near waters and now into far waters.[36]

Considering geopolitical competition over near and far waters requires understanding the relations between stronger and weaker countries, hegemony, and the generative sector. Classic geopolitics is not fit for this task. What understanding of geopolitics is? That's the topic of the next chapter.

ONE

What Is Geopolitics?

Geopolitics is one of those words we often see without thinking about what it actually means. Sometimes it is used as a synonym for *national security* or *international politics*.[1] When it is used more thoughtfully it is usually in reference to the role of geography in international politics. This role of geography could simply be something like how mountains form a defensive barrier between two countries, or the issues facing a land-locked country like Nepal.[2] Another example would be how Hawaii's location plays a role in the US's naval strategy. In other uses geopolitics is invoked to claim that some things just don't change. This is the argument that certain parts of the world will always be in turmoil because they are geographically "destined" to be so.[3]

More care and precision are needed when thinking about geopolitics. The term *geopolitics* has been around since the late 1890s. Since the 1980s scholars have been trying to rethink how the word is commonly used.[4] Why? Because classic geopolitics is designed to justify war from the perspective of just one country.

The Problems with Classic Geopolitics

The way classic geopolitics makes us look at the world will always lead to more wars. It is designed to conclude that the wars are necessary and to tell us how "we" can win them. All countries create their own geopolitics. Hence there are as many "we's" as there are countries in the world.[5] The geopolitics of the most powerful countries go a long way in defining the geopolitics of weaker countries. Powerful countries use classic geopolitics to put them at the center of the world's politics and to make claims that their fights are necessary and morally just.[6] By doing this, classic geopolitics sees the world as consisting of a whole bunch of "thems." Many of these "thems" are seen as threats to "us." Classic geopolitics is the foundation for a realist world of competition and the survival of the fittest.[7]

The classic conception of geopolitics that emerged in the late nineteenth century is *not* a good way to figure out the world's problems. It was not even designed for that purpose. Classic geopolitics is part of the problem and not the solution. It was designed to make an argument for why and how a particular country should compete with other countries. Different scholars proposed geopolitical ideas to make their own country stronger and more likely to win wars.[8] They usually hid these national security strategies behind impressive scholarly ideas. For example, the famous and influential British academic and member of parliament Sir Halford Mackinder wrote a grand history of how Eurasian tribes had waged a civilizational battle against the peace-loving trading peoples on the western coast of the European continent.[9] But it was just a way of arguing that Britain needed to counter a Russian threat by maintaining its empire. Mackinder's sleight of argument was that by ruling "the Heartland," a large and central portion of Eurasia, the Russia Empire controlled vast amounts of resources and had an overwhelming "geostrategic advantage."[10] To deal with what he cleverly identified as an unfair geography, Mackinder argued Britain had little choice but to be imperial. The grand world history was merely a policy for empire cloaked in academic language. And it was written in a way that could bring the British public along in agreement.

Captain Alfred Thayer Mahan is the classic geopolitician who is most renowned for promoting seapower as a crucial part of foreign policy. Writing in the late 1800s, he was a public intellectual. He was promoted to the rank of rear admiral in 1906 (along with all other naval captains who had served in the Civil War). He died in 1914. His seminal work is *The Influence of Sea Power upon History, 1660–1783*, published in 1890. The book is a good illustration of how classic geopoliticians make their argument. It is a long book, over five hundred pages, that gives a seemingly authoritative, yet very selective, global history. The book covers just 120 years of history. I suspect that most people just read the opening chapter entitled "Discussion of the Elements of Sea Power." The oceans are introduced as a "highway" or "commons" to enable commerce. Yet the world is not a peaceful place, so protection of commercial fleets and refuge in a network of ports is needed. The success of a country in becoming a seapower is, for Mahan, "less determined by the shrewdness and foresight of governments than by conditions of position, extent, configuration, number and character of their people,—by what are called, in a word, natural conditions."[11]

Hence, the favorite explanatory trick of classic geopoliticians is revealed early in the book: the idea that the ability of a country to rise to the status of a seapower is determined by physical geography rather than political and military actions. Despite Mahan's complaint that seapower had not been discussed as part of "general history,"[12] his emphasis upon geographic determinism allowed him to play down the different forms of violence required in the pursuit of seapower when outlining his framework. Of course, these forms of violence are explicit or implicit in the history that follows in the next four hundred-plus pages. But the key message is that US history is both determined by "natural" conditions and in need of a *national will* to move from continental isolationism to oceanic intervention. Finally, the blessings of "natural" physical features, and the benefits of national character, must be put into action through the "Character of the Government," or the "intelligent will-power" of political elites that can create policies seeking the advantages of commerce and naval power.[13] In other words, the US government must wake up, smell the coffee, and see the economic benefits of being a seapower.[14]

The same use of geopolitics continued after the Second World War. In Cold War geopolitics, both sides described a simple ideological battle of "us" versus "them" and marked out vast swathes of the world (called "blocs") that were either "ours" or "theirs." A simple division of the world into landpowers and seapowers was reinvigorated from the writings of Mackinder and Mahan. The idea of continental powers (referring to the Soviet Union) competing against maritime powers (referring to the US) had been crucial to Mackinder's worldview.[15] US Cold War theorists used it to portray the Soviet Union as despotic and expansionist, and thereby a threat to world peace. The US and its allies were identified as peaceful commercial countries (also echoing Mahan) who just wanted to get along.[16] The Soviet Union was simplified as a violent landpower. The US was an evidently peaceful seapower, with its violence involved in projecting power into far waters ignored or portrayed as defensive actions against the aggressive landpower.

Cold War geopolitics continued with the rhetoric of describing different parts of the world in different ways to justify different policies.[17] Its bipolar view of the world was used to argue for the necessity of massive nuclear arsenals.[18] US geopoliticians described countries as if they were dominoes to justify the carnage of the Vietnam War.[19] The domino theory was readily accepted by the US public during the war. But how would you react if people in another country thought your own was as simple and as passive as a token used in a game? Later politicians, commentators, and academics gave meaning to the War on Terror by describing an "Axis of Evil" between three countries (Iran, North Korea, and Iraq) that had little in common and no shared interests.[20]

Classic geopolitics is written by people with the interests of their own country in mind. Their ideas are appealing because they simplify the world. If classic geopolitics uses geography at all, it usually does so in a way that vilifies whole populations because of where they live. Also, classic geopolitics argues that geography is "deterministic"—meaning that a country's location in the geography of oceans and continents gives a country no choice but to act in a certain way. Usually the argument is that "geography" gives another country an unfair advantage, so the response requires more military spending and, perhaps, preemptive action.

Classic geopolitics became popular leading up to the most destructive period of geopolitics the world has ever seen—the First and Second World Wars. Hence, the resurgence of the popularity of the term should give us pause for thought. Should the geopolitical tradition of creating reasons why "we" have a need and right to fight others persist? Nineteenth-century thinking was a path toward a round of major wars, something best avoided.

The good news is that there are alternative ways of thinking about geopolitics. In this book I try to pull us away from the "us versus them" mentality. Rethinking geopolitics does not necessarily mean that world peace is likely or more attainable. But thinking in the traditional way is likely to produce the same results, and it is better to try something different—a new way of thinking about "them" that means rethinking the way we see "us."

The Geopolitics of Global Relations

It is easy to buy into the simplified and nationalist pictures of the world painted by classic geopolitics. Though based on fear and threats, their simple prescriptions are somehow comforting in their certainty. Alternatively, the effort can be made to see the world differently: namely, as a global web of economic and political relations.

A comparison of two popular board games provides a step toward understanding the complexity of geopolitics. One is Risk and the other is Axis & Allies. (I suspect that as you picked up this book you could be the type of person somewhat familiar with these games.) Risk is quite a simple game. A player gets more power and wins the game by gaining more territory.

The playing board is global. A good turn for a player allows them to march from one end of Eurasia to the other and with the luck of the dice end up in North Africa. The rules of world politics are very simple—there's no difference in roles and abilities between Australasia and northern Europe, for example. Relationships between countries are not part of the rules, though side deals of "truces" between players are often made. The geography of the world of Risk is very simple. One country simply borders another, and it's surprisingly easy to skip across the Atlantic.

On the other hand, Axis & Allies is more complicated. Players must think about their economic strength as well as their military power. In fact, you cannot build up your military without having economic strength. That's why the US usually wins in this game. Relations between countries are part of the rules of the game, with Britain's imperial relationships with India and Australia important to how the game plays out. The geography of the region is also important. Getting across the Pacific is a matter of controlling or avoiding islands. Burma becomes a pivotal location on the board.

Taking hints from Axis & Allies leads to the identification of the geopolitics of global relations. Today's geopolitics of seapower can be understood through the combination of seven building-block statements. Seven statements are much more than the simple little catchphrases used by classic geopolitics. The truth is that the world is more complex than classic geopolitics says it is. Considering a sequence of building blocks is a way to think about complexity step by step.

1. Geopolitics is about the projection of power and challenges to it

Geopolitics is about the projection of power, and the flip side is that geopolitics is also about challenging projections of power. Geopolitics is the sum of the dynamics of some countries trying to project their influence beyond their borders and across the globe to serve their "interests" and the reactions of countries trying to prevent this power projection. Some of the countries trying to challenge power projection will also be quite powerful. They are in a competition to see who will project power and in what manner. Not all countries will be successful in their goals of power projection. Other challengers will be weaker countries who see themselves as being disadvantaged by the actions of the more powerful countries. Other weaker countries may work with a more powerful country to help it project power. They may see an advantage. Or they may have little choice.

The projection of power, and resistance to power projection, call to mind Sir Isaac Newton's third law of physics: for every action there is a reaction. Admittedly, Newton says that the reaction is opposite and equal. This may not be the case with geopolitics. First, it is unlikely to be equal, as the country projecting power is likely to be stronger. Any challenge may not be as strong. Second, the challenge will not necessarily be "opposite." The word *opposite* implies something direct. If I push against a wall, the wall somehow pushes back. Geopolitics is not so simple. The challenge may be indirect. That makes sense, for why would a weaker country face a stronger one directly? In the words of Chinese military philosopher Sun Tzu, "When he is strong, avoid him. . . . Attack where he is unprepared. Emerge where he does not expect it."[21] The choice of direct or indirect challenge is often a matter of the strength of a country, which brings us to the second building block.

2. It is important to think about relations between weaker and stronger countries

To understand the world it is just as important to think about weaker countries and their relations with stronger countries as it is to think about relations between stronger countries.

Geopolitics is not simply about one-against-one battles between great powers, or even alliances of great powers. Instead, geopolitics is about a set of relations between countries.[22] Some of these relations will be with countries with a similar amount of power (strong with strong, weak with weak). Other relations will be between countries with different amounts of power (strong with weak, weak with strong). To understand the actions of one country means placing it within the web of global relations. These relations are explained later in this chapter.

A helpful starting point is the wisdom of the German actress Marlene Dietrich, who said, "The weak are more likely to make the strong weak than the strong are likely to make the weak strong." Strong countries try to use weak countries to their advantage. But involvement in the affairs of weak countries can put strong countries into situations they cannot control, either by provoking pushback from the weak country or by causing a hostile reaction by a strong country competitor.

The relations between strong and weak countries are more important in understanding geopolitics than classic geopolitics would have us think. The engine driving geopolitical change is the nature of the economic relations between weak and strong countries.

3. Economic relations between weak and strong countries are the driving force of geopolitics

We live in an unequal world, a world of persistent disparities in wealth and power between countries.[23] The relations between the stronger and weaker countries in the world constitute the main driving force of geopolitics, the engine that drives us toward periods of geopolitical change and the increased risk of war. The reason is that projection of military power is motivated by economic relations and competition.[24]

Economic relations and competition are the reason and the means of projecting military power and use of violence far beyond a country's own borders. As geopolitics is about economic relations and the projection of power, this means that businesses and countries work together to change the world. Businesses and countries both "do" geopolitics.[25] They are both players in the game, or actors on the stage. Classic geopolitics usually sees countries as the only actors on the global stage. In fact, geopolitics is about how businesses create a web of economic relations and use countries to build or protect those relations.

4. Businesses are important geopolitical actors, not just countries

Businesses and countries act together to make the geopolitical world. Economic relations and the projection of military power span the globe. Geopolitics is the combination of the pattern of economic relations between stronger and weaker countries and the way this requires the projection of power by stronger countries.[26] Economic relations are another way of talking about the trade and investment linkages between businesses in different countries. The projection of power by force and diplomacy is about establishing a military presence and political presence in countries to safeguard these economic relations that exist as a geography of trade and investment networks. Power projection can be thought of as the attempt by one country to establish a presence in the territory of another country. Economic strength helps pay for the projection of military power. And this is seen as a good investment, as military power is expected to protect existing economic relations and help make new ones.

The connections between economic relations, control of the oceans, and the use of that control to have an influence (including a military presence) on land exist within what has been called the virtuous cycle of seapower (figure 1.1).[27] The ties between economic growth and military projection within this framing of seapower are at the core of my approach to geo-

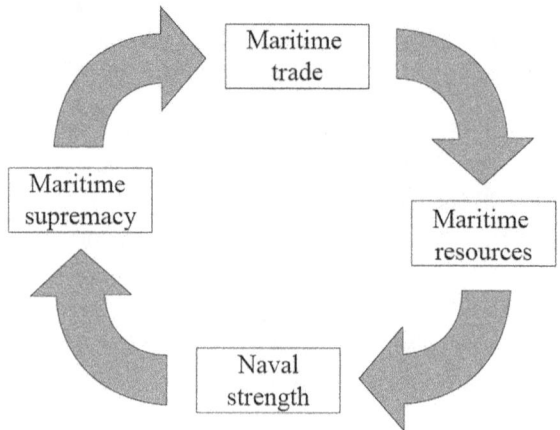

FIGURE 1.1. The virtuous cycle of seapower.

Source: Drawn by Anna Johnson, adapted from figure 1.3 (p. 17) in Geoffrey Till's *Seapower*, 3rd ed. (London: Routledge, 2013).

politics. Economic interests are created and protected by the projection of military power across the oceans, and the ability to fund a global military presence requires a thriving economy.

An important question is, virtuous for whom? Specifically, has this cycle been perceived as "virtuous" when referring to the past rise of Western seapowers, but "unvirtuous" when referring to the current rise of countries that we see as threatening to the existing global and economic and military landscape? For example, are historic Dutch, British, and US expressions of the cycle somehow "virtuous" while the broadly similar processes of the cycle occurring in the contemporary rise of China are not? The "us and them" element of geopolitics is evident in these questions. This dilemma is revisited in this book's conclusion.

Resources, trade, and naval strength are inextricably linked through the cooperation of businesses and countries. Such cooperation, not always smooth or mutually beneficial, involves the fusion of the geopolitics of territory and networks, which brings us to the next building block.

5. The geography of geopolitics involves networks and territory

Geopolitics is a combination of networks of economic relations and the political control of territory. Seapower is expressed as both the control of networks of trade across oceans, and the use of that control to further interests onshore—in other words, to protect and manage economic assets on land.

Put another way, economic interests of resource extraction, and other elements of global supply chains, are forms of territorial geopolitics. Control of the seas, especially the facilitation of unhindered trade, is required when territory is far away from the home country. Patterns of oceanic trade, and the military strength to protect them, are a form of network geopolitics.

The most powerful countries in the world have worked together to ensure free passage across the oceans. The concept of international waters has been a globally recognized legal concept since 1625. The geography of trade and the physical geography of the oceans and continents means that certain parts of the ocean are shipping "highways." These heavily trafficked routes are called *sea lines of communication* (SLOCs) (map 1.1).[28]

Just like a highway system in and through a big city that can get clogged up during rush hour, physical geography and the geography of trade patterns create *choke points*, or narrow channels that try to accommodate a lot of shipping traffic. For example, the Suez Canal was "choked" in 2021 when the container ship *Ever Given* ran aground. Some ships were stuck in the canal or at the entry points at either end of the canal, while others made the decision to sail all the way around the African continent. Choke points are a concern for countries who view them as sites of potential blockade by an enemy. Notably, China has coined the term *the Malacca Dilemma* to emphasize how its economic prosperity depends on the free flow of trade through the Malacca Straits.[29]

The ability of a country to support economic interests in faraway places across the oceans is never unchallenged. Expressions of seapower are never constant. And that brings us to geopolitical process and context.

6. The geopolitical world is always changing

Because of the back-and-forth of economic competition and military force, the geopolitical world is ever-changing.[30] Hence, geopolitics is best thought of as a process rather than a static picture. The world is always in flux. It is just that some moments of historical change are more dramatic and consequential than others. Contrary to the tendency of classic geopolitics to talk of geographies that are largely static, it is useful to think of how things change rather than how things are permanent.

Of course, thinking of geopolitics as a process does not mean that the geographic features themselves change, with distances across the Pacific Ocean shrinking and expanding, or the Himalayan mountains rising and falling. That would be absurd. Instead, the importance of different geographic features changes over time.[31] Geographic features are the

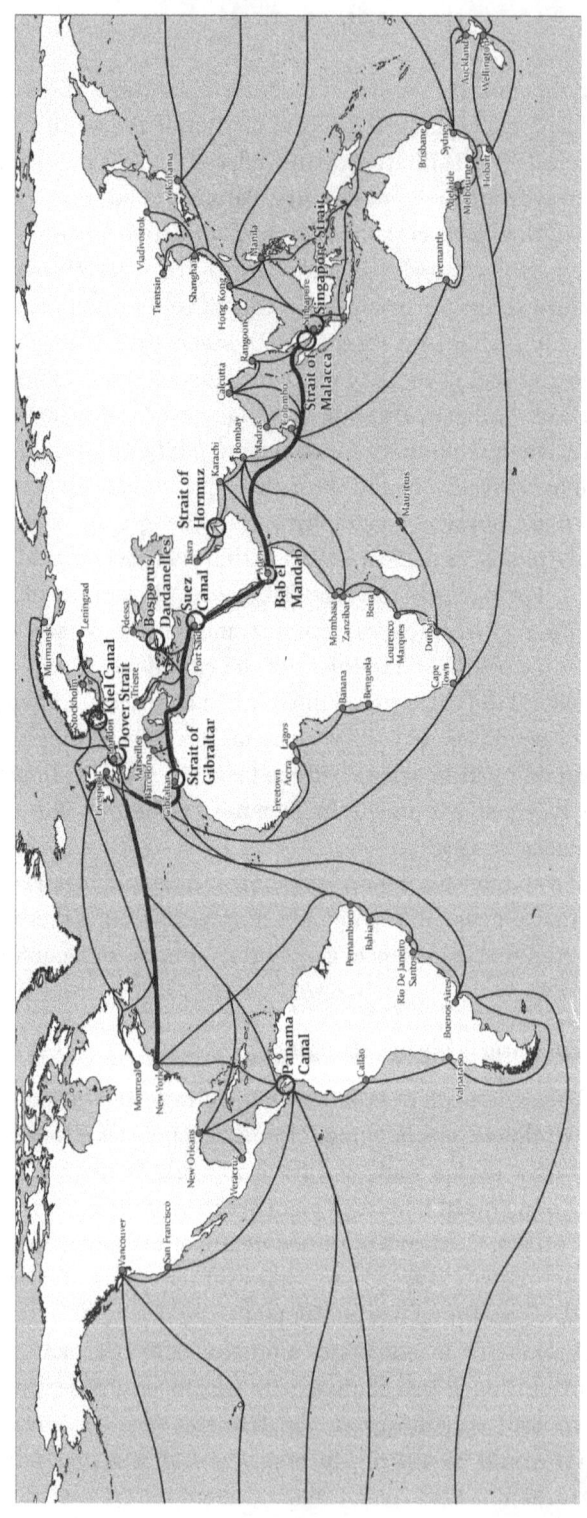

MAP 1.1. Sea lines of communication and choke points.

Source: Original work by Carson Liesik.

landscape in which economic relations are made and power is projected. Whether geographic features promote movement or present barriers to it changes with the changes in geographies of industrial production and trade, technology, and the ups and downs of relations between countries. Which country controls an area of ocean or a choke point changes, not the physical geography of the ocean or strait in question. But these physical features play a crucial role in the geographies of economic relations and power projection. They also play a crucial role in how these geographies are challenged and how they change.

7. A definition of geopolitics

Putting building blocks 1 through 6 together allows for a definition of geopolitics as the use of economic and political power to control networks, territory, and physical features, and, in turn, the use of the control of networks, territory, and physical features to increase economic and political power.[32] As you can see, there are two parts to the definition, but they are very much connected. The two parts highlight the idea of geopolitics as a process, building block 6. Economic gain and power projection are used to control parts of the world, such as countries, oceans, and islands, and the way they are connected. Being in control of these things will make you richer or stronger. Not controlling them can make you poorer and weaker.

In sum, seapower is crucial for countries to *make* global economic relations, to *grow* their own economies, to *establish* trade networks, and to *protect* these networks and relations.[33] Seapower is also necessary for a country to gain the power to challenge the established patterns. The shifts in the ability of countries to build the economic relations they desire, and to protect them through the deployment of seapower, are a key mechanism in changing the overall pattern of geopolitical relations. These patterns are geopolitical contexts.

Geopolitical Contexts

The process of geopolitics involves powerful countries creating contexts and keeping them the same to increase economic and political power, and weaker countries challenging these contexts to improve their situation. The contexts that are the stage for the actions of businesses and countries are relatively stable. The relative power of stronger and weaker countries is also fairly stable—but not completely. The power of countries, the relations they make, the challenges they face, and the opportunities they see are always changing.[34] Countries reconsider their situation regularly.[35] These reconsiderations appear as "defense reviews" of one sort or another. Geopolitical competition is about actions that make, stabilize, and challenge contexts (the geopolitics of action and reaction). But what are they?

A context is a social situation that is the setting for activity.[36] For example, we behave very differently if we are spending an evening in our house with a set of long-established friends compared to, say, having a formal dinner in a pricey restaurant with the boss. The context is not just the physical setting—our home versus a fancy restaurant—but the social setting. The social setting is made up of the sum of the social relations in play. We would choose not to dress the same in these different contexts. We would choose to say some things in one context and not the other. We would eat differently in these different contexts—depending on whether we are fighting over the nachos with our friends or wondering which fork to use in the restaurant. The context goes some way toward limiting what we can and will do. The context also goes some way toward giving us a chance to say certain things. We may want to confess emotional difficulties or health changes to our friends, and we may not do that with our boss. But in the restaurant with our boss we may go out on a limb and talk up our professional skills and ambitions. In the language of social science, we say that contexts enable and constrain; they give us chances to do some things and restrict our ability to do other things.

But how do contexts come about? Contexts don't just magically appear. They are made up of the sum of the same social relations that are occurring within them and have occurred in the past. In other words, actions make the contexts that enable and constrain us. The context of an evening with our friends is made up of all those past interactions with them: the in-jokes, the arguments that have been patched over, those arguments that are still a bit touchy, the exams we took together in college, the spring break trip with certain exploits that can't be mentioned, and so on. These are the historical relations that make up the context. The context is also made up of the relations of the particular evening. Is it shaping up to be a "good night"—one in which everyone is feeling good and interacting well? Or does it fail somehow—someone does or says something that makes the evening fall flat? It is the aggregation of these past and present set of relations that make the context.

Contexts are the sum of past and current social relations. Even as they are made by past social relations, they are the setting for what is ongoing. And they set limits on what is possible—they enable and constrain. Note that I say "constrain"—not "prevent." Contexts don't allow for anything and everything to be possible. But many things are possible. And maybe something is done that is unexpected and unusual, something that changes the context dramatically. For example, what if the evening of the group of friends is disrupted when it emerges that two members of the group are in a relationship? Maybe that relationship violates the existing relations: an affair between two members, though their spouses are also part of the group. Oh my! The context that is the sum of past and present social relations would be the setting for this revelation, and the revelation would change these relations dramatically.

The dynamics of a group of friends is just a simple and accessible example. Regarding geopolitics, activity is a matter of economic relations and the projection of power across oceans and continents. That requires consideration of three contexts: economic, strategic, and geographic.[37]

The economic context is the sum of all production, trade, and investment relations that span the globe and connect businesses within different countries. The economic context is the sum of all such relations, just as the social setting of the evening with friends is the sum of the relations between everyone. But in both cases, the entire context is something more than the sum of the parts. The same two people are likely to interact differently depending upon whether they are alone or in the group. Similarly, the opportunities and challenges facing a business are a matter of not only business-to-business connections but also the current global arrangement of possible deals and competition. Because of new economic activities such as AI and supercomputing, the economic context is in a period of flux.

The strategic context is similarly the sum of all the ways countries interact with each other militarily and diplomatically. Media stories usually focus on how two particular countries are interacting: for example, arrangements over how many US troops will be stationed in Europe and what their duties will be, or the Philippines' uneasy stance toward China, protesting the latter's claim over Whitsun Reef while also wanting to receive Chinese investment. But relations between two countries are figured out within the aggregation of all such relations. That is the strategic context, and it makes certain things possible for countries and other things impossible. It can provide opportunities for countries, but it can also pose many risks or threats. The stronger a country, the more likely it is to be able to make the strategic context favorable to its own interests. The opposite is the case for weaker countries. Currently, the relative strength of the US and China go a long way toward defining the strategic context for all other countries. The question of whether the US is on a trajectory of becoming weaker while China is gaining strength means that the strategic context is in flux.

Economic activity and strategic relations happen within the context of physical geography. In some ways, the geographic context is very stable. Again, the geography of the Pacific Ocean or the Himalayan mountains is not going to change that much, though sea-level rise is a dramatic change for many island nations. The geographic context is the setting for the geopolitics of changing economic activity and the use of seapower to project influence and violence. The geographic context, and the way it changes, is a question of who can use and control certain geographic features, rather than a physical change in those geographic features. It is not the ocean off the Horn of Africa that changes but its status as a safe water or a location of piracy that disrupts global trade. The East China Sea remains the same physically, but the change is in who is able to project power within that area—whether the area is one country's far waters or another country's near waters. As strategic contexts change, so do the meanings countries give to physical features. For example, the US and Australia are asking us to think of an Indo-Pacific region as a physical feature that requires strategic actions to counter the growing Chinese presence in that part of the world.

The geographic context is also important in understanding the changing geography of economic relations. Again, some things are going to remain quite stable, such as the Middle East as a location of oil deposits. But the economic importance of those oil deposits will change with the increasing use of alternative energy sources, the ups and downs of the global economy, and alternative oil sources, such as shale deposits. Other things change. The geography of the location of rare earth minerals in the world is stable, but their discovery and use are dynamic. The need to extract resources, the competition for access to them, where they get traded to as economic inputs, and the projection of the trade routes are in flux. The geographic context of which parts of the world are economically and strategically important, and the resulting competition between countries, is in flux.

History suggests that there are moments when the combination of decisions by countries leads to dramatic and consequential changes of the three contexts.[38] The changing contexts create more opportunities and challenges for countries, which lead them to act differently. In turn, these different actions make the contexts change even more, and the changes in the contexts lead to more changes in decision-making. This is the combination of building blocks 6 and 7, with the recognition that countries and businesses act within regional and global contexts. A period of rapid and dramatic changes in contexts and decisions is a period of consequential geopolitical change. We are living in such a moment.

Learning from History

Looking back in history to similar moments offers understanding of the current moment of flux. This is not to say that historical situations are the same as today. Changing technology, for one thing, changes the way countries interact with one another. The world has also changed in the way countries try to organize their relationships. The transformation has been from a world of European exploration and conquest of the globe, through a period of imperialism, to the current situation of a global economy or globalization.[39]

Considering the history of the Dutch, British, and US periods of global power highlights how moments of consequential geopolitical flux have come about, what they have involved, and how they have led to major war. Such a geopolitical understanding of the world asks us to step away from national identities that encourage competition and conflict. Instead, it requires us to consider the dynamics of geopolitical relations within which we live, which in turn requires seeing connections and empathizing with those in other countries to avoid war. And that is a long way from the motivations of classic geopolitics.

However, it is useful to consider what has *not* changed. Entrenched inequality between stronger and weaker countries, competition over the control of the newest and most profitable economic activities, the persistent need to secure inputs to these activities, and challenges to these conditions have all remained the same for the past four centuries.[40] Focusing on what is new, especially new technologies, draws the discussion away from the persistent inequalities between the strong and weak. In this way, such a focus is a form of bias that prevents us from bringing the persistence of inequality to the forefront of the mainstream understanding of geopolitics.

The persistent economic relations that make the world one of strong and weak countries is the topic of the next chapter.

TWO

Strong and Weak Countries and Stories of Geopolitical "Threats"

Classic geopolitics was written by people in powerful countries for powerful countries. Writers focused on relations between powerful countries—or the geopolitics of great powers.[1] Classic geopolitics presented a very limited view of how the world works.[2] A more complex, but accessible, view shows the importance of relations between stronger and weaker countries in driving geopolitical change. The next task is to go into more detail about the classification of countries as "stronger" or "weaker," and how stronger and weaker countries are connected to each other.[3] A better terminology than *strong/weak* is *primary/subsidiary*.[4]

This chapter may seem to be a detour away from the geopolitics of seapower. Classic geopolitics has tended to ignore economic issues, but global economic relations are the driving force behind cooperation and conflict between states.[5] The global nature of economic relations is closely related to seapower because of the importance of maritime trade.[6] Economics and trade are competitive. They are expressions of power. Global economic relations of trade and investment are made, protected, and challenged as part of competitive geopolitics. Seapower is the main means of making and challenging these relations.[7] To understand the geopolitics of seapower requires understanding the economic relations that are the cause and outcome of conflict between countries.[8] This chapter is not a detour from the geopolitics of seapower but the highway to seeing economic relations as a driving force behind the movement toward global war.

What Are Primary and Subsidiary Countries?

A primary country has an economy that is home to companies producing the most technically sophisticated and profitable products. The products may be manufactured goods or services.[9] The country has the military capacity to defend its territory and to project power beyond its immediate neighborhood.[10] It is able to shape its foreign policy through its own decision-making, even if that involves joining alliances or institutions that limit its behavior (such as the Paris Climate Accords or the Nuclear Non-Proliferation Treaty) or that impose commitments (such as NATO). A primary country is involved in global governance in a manner that gives it a voice in defining and policing international rules.[11] It is able to deliver a rhetorical message promoting particular norms of behavior.[12] The country is able to portray its own behaviors as moral or just, or as a "civilizing project," whether that be its promotion of ideas of "development" or its use of violence, such as drone strikes.

A subsidiary country exists within the political and economic gravitational pull of one or more primary countries. The primary-subsidiary country relationship serves, on the whole, the needs and goals of the primary country.[13] A subsidiary country has an economy that is home to companies producing the least technically sophisticated and profitable products. These include products of resource extraction, agriculture, and low-tech manufacturing. The subsidiary country has a limited military capacity that is focused upon internal order and the protection of its borders, rather than force projection. Its foreign policy is, to some degree, prescribed by the needs, interests, and demands of primary countries.[14] The subsidiary country is largely a rule-receiver within the institutions of global governance.[15] It generally accepts global rules and norms of behavior. If it does not comply, the subsidiary country becomes what primary countries label a "rogue state."[16] This label places the subsidiary country outside the international community, and its behavior is portrayed as "barbaric" if it uses violence and "irrational" if it rejects accepted economic practices. Though the world is not as simple as academic definitions, the *primary* and *subsidiary* labels help us consider broad global patterns of the virtuous cycle of seapower. We qualify the distinction between primary and subsidiary countries later in the chapter.

Geopolitical Change and Primary and Subsidiary Countries

A moment of significant geopolitical change is largely driven by the actions of a subsidiary country or a relatively weak primary country attempting to change its position within the global pattern of primary-subsidiary relations. This process involves that country attaining more of the economic, political, military, and rhetorical attributes of a primary (or more powerful primary) country. The change in the country's position may be focused on economic policy and related to its ability to influence conversations about global governance.[17] The way Gulf countries are able to use their dominance of the global oil market to participate in diplomacy is an example of this type of behavior.[18] Or the change may be focused within the area of military power projection and resistance to the foreign policy agenda and assumptions of primary countries. Russia's actions within its "near abroad," and especially its invasion of Ukraine in 2022, exemplify this type of behavior.[19]

The most dramatic moments of geopolitical change are when a country tries to become a very powerful primary country in both economic and military arenas, with a related attempt to reset the rules and norms of global governance. Today is such a moment. China is the country trying to become a powerful primary country through economic, political, military, and rhetorical change. China's increasing power is seen as a change in world politics that is deemed as "threatening" or a "security risk." Why is the process of a country trying to become a powerful primary country seen as a threat by other primary countries?

The Geopolitics of Threat and Change

Changes in the pattern of primary-subsidiary relations that are sparked by previously weak countries becoming more powerful are seen as a matter of geopolitics for their creation of what are defined as three related risks: threats to economic relations, strategic patterns, and the institutional organization of the world.

The Threat of Economic Change

Talk about economic growth, free trade, and development hides the global economics of dominance. As a group, primary countries dominate the advanced sectors of the global economy. Primary countries compete with each other to better their position as key players in the production of the most profitable goods and services.[20] To do so they look for the most beneficial access to inputs to make these things, and the most beneficial access to markets to sell them. The global economy is a competition among countries trying to create monopolistic control over inputs and markets, rather than a system of free trade between equals.[21] The more successful a primary country is in creating beneficial arrangements of input supply and market sales for companies within its borders, the greater the profitability of those companies.[22] The primary country benefits through a workforce of highly paid employees and corporate tax returns. The rise of a subsidiary country into the ranks of the primary countries, or the attempt of a primary country to become the most powerful, puts pressure on primary countries to retain the relationships that allow them to profit from cheap inputs and eager markets. The rising country may eat into both.

The economic success of primary countries requires the unequal relationships between primary and subsidiary countries.[23] These relationships ensure the flow of cheap inputs along global supply chains necessary for the manufacture of highly profitable products. Food and energy are one set of these vital inputs. Other crucial inputs are the components of finished products. Especially important are rare earth minerals necessary to produce computer chips, and also those chips as inputs for computers, robots, and AI technologies.[24]

It is not enough to make highly profitable products; they must be bought. Primary countries work to establish markets for the products made within their borders.[25] Technically sophisticated and highly profitable products are usually expensive. Hence, the largest markets are other primary countries, but not exclusively. A few countries will seek the elite-of-the-elite of these products, such as supercomputers, but many countries will want to buy airplanes, for example. Sadly, but realistically, the arms trade makes up a large fraction of the highly profitable products made in primary countries and bought by subsidiary countries.[26]

Making supply chains and maximizing markets requires investment—financial and political. Infrastructure has been a crucial focus of financial investment.[27] Infrastructure consists of the warehouses, roads, railways, ports, airports, and so on that move inputs along supply chains and move finished products to markets. Investments in infrastructure should, hopefully, provide some return on the investment, such as loan interest. The wider gain is the ease of transporting inputs and finished products. But there is a political aim in infrastructure investment as well. Financing the building of the roads, railways, and ports to help the production and trade of certain inputs will make it more likely that trading relationships will be established between the investing country and the recipient. Though never exclusive, investment often fosters an economic and political relationship that defines patterns of trade.[28] Hence, investment in transport structure often entails creating an infrastructure of financial relationships that facilitate trade.[29]

Investment within a country in research and development is intended to promote the technical ability to produce more profitable products. Such investment in the domestic economy requires investment in another country and is intended to promote the production of inputs and their movement through supply chains to build the more profitable products. Hence, investment at home and abroad are two sides of the same coin.[30]

The geography of economic activity has been a constant feature of global politics for the past few centuries. Of course, the world is much changed from the 1600s, when the Dutch were the world's greatest innovators of economic practices, to today's world of e-commerce. In between, practices of colonialism and imperialism, in various guises, were seen as necessary for capitalism. Prior to the rise of the Dutch, Spain and Portugal had become wealthy through the economics of plunder, especially silver and gold. Slavery, or various forms of forced labor, were prominent in the rise of Dutch, British, and US economic power. The issue remains pertinent today.[31] The differences between Portuguese and Spanish modes of economics, and their role in the spread of global capitalism, are much debated. Yet similarities across the past four hundred years or so remain. New products and technologies are invented, new inputs are required, and the resulting patterns of trade must be protected or constructed by force. Hence, the general pattern of the geopolitics of seapower is constant, especially the imperatives of securing near waters and projecting power into far waters.

The new period of primary-subsidiary relations and the new geopolitics of perceived threat are being driven by China's Belt and Road Initiative (BRI) and its China 2025 campaign. These are related geopolitical projects aimed at making more profitable products and securing the necessary inputs (map 2.1). They are, arguably, the most significant drivers of the contemporary moment of geopolitical flux. In combination, these two separate but related projects are designed to fuel China's economy by establishing global trade and investment relations.[32] Unsurprisingly, they have provoked a geopolitical reaction from Western countries that has focused on the BRI because of its presence in other countries where the US and its allies have established connections.[33]

The G7 meeting of the most powerful countries held in June 2021 called for an economic project to counter China's BRI. Just a day later President

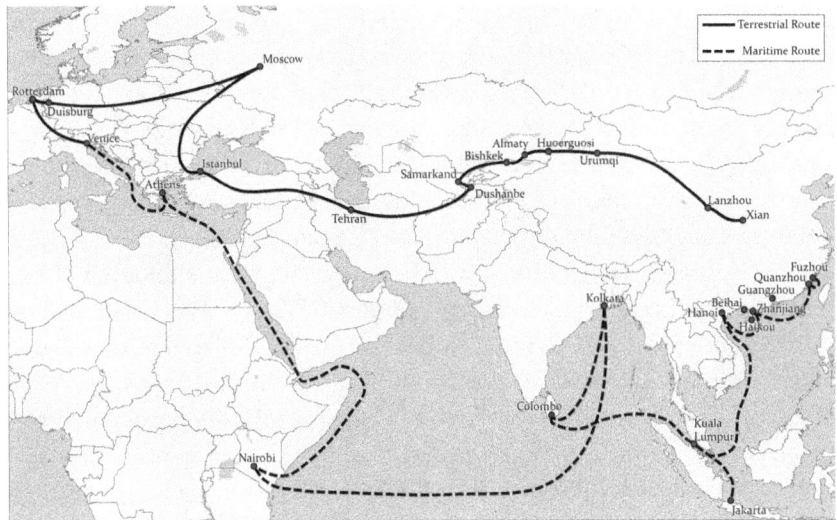

MAP 2.1. China's Belt and Road Initiative.
Source: Original work by Carson Liesik.

Joe Biden led NATO to declare China as a security threat, or a "systemic challenge."[34] This was the first time NATO had used such bold language. This was no coincidence or artifact of the diplomatic calendar. Rather, it shows how economic and security challenges are different expressions of one geopolitical process.

The Threat of Change in Strategy

In terms of military power, primary countries see rising subsidiary or other primary countries as threats because they reduce their own potential to project power. Primary countries have used their military power to create parts of the world in which they have been able to operate economically through the use, or threat, of force. Numerous historical examples exist, such as Britain's Opium Wars with China, and the US invasion of the Philippines and annexation of Hawaii. A contemporary example is China's suppression of the Uyghurs and its crackdown upon dissent in Hong Kong. The projection of force may involve physical violence, such as drone attacks or invasion. Most importantly, and consistently, it requires sending naval task forces into the near waters of other countries.

The projection of force is seen in the ability of primary countries to station their troops within other countries.[35] The current pattern of bases stems from the post–Second World War force projection of the US and the start of the Cold War. It resulted in a series of alliances: the North Atlantic Treaty Organization (NATO), the Central Treaty Organization (CENTO), and the Southeast Asia Treaty Organization (SEATO) (map 2.2). The expansion of NATO was re-energized after the collapse of the Soviet Union, with an expansion into central and eastern Europe. The Russia-Ukraine war led to Finland and Sweden joining the alliance.

The legacy of these military alliances is the current stationing of US forces in subsidiary countries, such as Djibouti. They are also stationed in primary countries, such as NATO allies, Japan, and Korea. Similar geographies of troop deployment by the Soviet Union in the past and Russia now are seen as something to fear. China's increasing military presence across the globe is seen as particularly threatening by the US and other primary countries because it intersects with the fears of economic change already mentioned.

Mostly, the geographies of the projection of military power are taken for granted.[36] The use of violence by primary countries in subsidiary countries is seen as somehow "natural," or something not to be questioned. Picture the alternative. How would you react if you saw a news story describing the establishment of a military base by, say, Djibouti, in the state of North Carolina, the British county of Kent, or the Japanese prefecture of Kyoto? It would probably be quite a surprise and would provoke a response along the lines of "What? What's going on?" And yet, a story of a US base in Germany, or a US drone strike in, say, Syria, is likely to be ignored. More than likely, it would not even be published. Certain geographies of power projection, those enacted by the established primary countries, are taken for granted. They are largely unquestioned, and so they are able to continue. Any attempt by a rising country to project violence destabilizes the existing geography of force projection and is portrayed as a threat and a possible cause for war.

Changing geographies of power projection may lead to war.[37] They certainly have in the past. To try to avoid a repetition of this history, the physics analogy of opposite reactions is useful. A country's rise in power is a force that pushes against established geographies of power and violence. Both the country trying to change the established pattern and those countries trying to maintain it have responsibilities to manage geopolitical change in a way that does not lead to war.

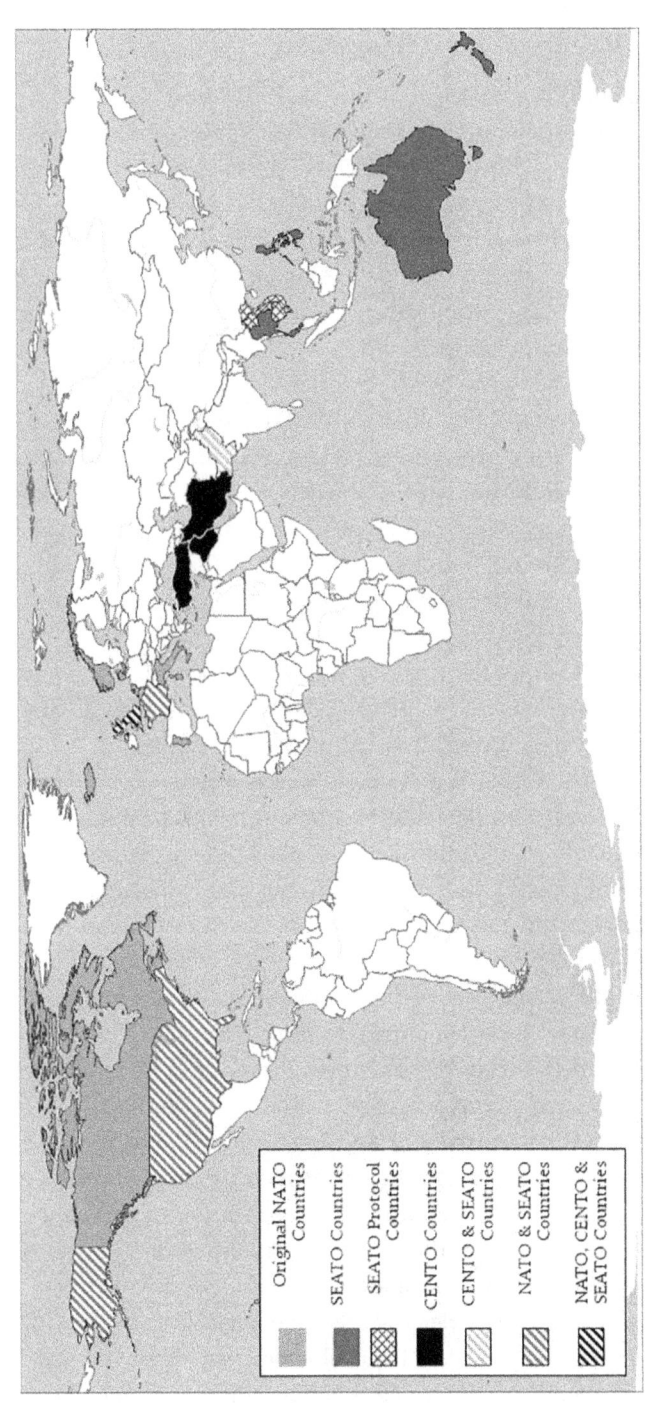

MAP 2.2. Post–Second World War US global military alliances.

Source: Original work by Carson Liesik.

The Threat to the Way the World Is Organized

There have been historical periods in which the most powerful country in the world, the hegemonic country, has been able to set, to a large but not complete degree, the rules and norms of global relations.[38] Institutions define and manage the rules and norms, most of which allow for unequal economic relations between primary and subsidiary countries and the related geographies of power projection.[39] A rising country is seen as a threat when it challenges these established rules and norms. Today is such a moment of geopolitical change.

Currently, the Black Lives Matter movement has inspired a questioning of the suitability of retaining statues and building names that display imperial power and the primary-subsidiary relationship of slavery. Imperialism was an economic relationship based on a racist vision of the world divided between the "civilized" (white) and "barbaric" (not white) peoples and geographic areas of the world. It is absurd to proclaim that primary-subsidiary economic relations today should be something like the imperialism of the nineteenth century, whatever our thoughts and connections with Black Lives Matter. And yet, at the time imperialism was seen as the only and best way to manage the world economy. Politicians took it for granted, and novelists, poets, and painters celebrated it.

Over time the United States of America rose to become the most powerful country in the world, with the largest economy and military. In the process it changed the rules and norms of primary-subsidiary country relations. Imperialism was rejected and replaced by seemingly beneficial relations organized through the global institutions of the International Monetary Fund and the World Bank.[40] The rhetoric was of development and not imperialism. Chapter 5 will discuss the practices of development that did not substantially change the unequal pattern of primary-subsidiary relations. The language of global relations is changing again in the current moment of geopolitical change. China has been critical of the primary-subsidiary relations that the US has promoted since the Second World War. It has introduced new phrases to describe how primary-subsidiary relations would be under its watch. The terms *South-South cooperation* and *mutually beneficial relations* are now part of the conversation.[41] Rhetorical weapons have always been part of the arsenal in a moment of geopolitical change. Currently there is an ongoing battle of words between China and the US.[42]

The change from imperialism to development was dramatic. Perhaps a new set of rules and norms inspired or led by China will be another dramatic change. But here is a note of caution: unequal relations between primary and subsidiary countries will probably continue. The power dynamics of the relationship will change even if the pickup line or sweet nothings whispered by the suitor are different. The imperial story of the "white man's burden," the US's promises of development, and China's claims of mutually beneficial ties are all forms of a similar siren song. In the past, unequal primary-subsidiary relations have remained, though the form and rhetoric changed.[43] There is no basis for thinking that the current moment of geopolitical change is any different.

Putting it all together, primary countries point to lots of threats to their status that come about with the rising power of a subsidiary or relatively weak primary country. These can be summarized as a set of reinforcing concerns: the concern over losing access to economic inputs and markets; the concern that the ability to project military power to maintain primary-subsidiary economic relations is being lessened; the concern that the rules in place to run the global economy may be replaced by others that are less advantageous; the concern that the global institutions put in place to make the global economy run in a certain way for the benefit of some primary countries are less relevant than they were and that new institutions are being put in place that are more advantageous to the rising country; and the concern that the rhetoric used to justify economic relations and the projection of military power is being questioned and that new ways of describing the world are gaining traction.

These are concerns about the shifts that cause moments of geopolitical change. They may be approached by primary and subsidiary countries in ways that can escalate tensions and lead to major war. But notice that none of them in and of themselves are a cause for war. None of them threaten life and limb within a primary or subsidiary country. They do not involve invasion of another country, the launch of cruise missiles or bombers, a naval blockade, or cyberwarfare. The concerns do not appear on a list of why a just war may be fought. And yet, previous moments of geopolitical change have involved these concerns, and often major war has occurred.

Caveats

Some technical matters need to be addressed. The classification of countries as primary or subsidiary is an ideal or a model that is useful to get the point across and that helps us think about the real world. But the real world is much more complicated than the models used to explain it. No country is clearly and simply either a primary or a subsidiary country. Economies display a mix of economic activities.[44] Even in the US, undoubtedly a primary country, there is a lot of agriculture and mining. There are places in the US where poverty is high. And the opposite is also true. A country classified as subsidiary, such as Nigeria, may have sophisticated banking and insurance industries.

The power of a country is also a mix of economic and military capabilities. Taiwan is an interesting example. Companies in Taiwan are the crucial producers of microprocessors. But in terms of military power Taiwan is dependent upon the security umbrella provided by the US. Taiwan can be seen as a primary country with regard to economics but as subsidiary with regard to military power. As another example, North Korea is one of the few countries in the world with nuclear weapons and the ability to launch them long distances. But its economy is in dreadful shape. Though North Korea has a key feature of a primary country, the ability to project destructive military power, with regard to other factors it is relatively weak.

The primary/subsidiary country binary helps us understand the ways in which countries are complex. To understand a particular country, think of its mix of primary and subsidiary features. But also recognize that the ability of a country to act as it wants to in the world is a matter of where it stands within the global pattern of primary-subsidiary relations.

The other way the discussion has been made simpler than the real world is by using examples of country-to-country relations (what are known as bilateral relations). But to understand geopolitics requires recognizing that no bilateral relationship exists in isolation.[45] Even the US, the most powerful of the primary countries, must negotiate with other countries to figure out its relationship with subsidiary countries. For example, the US approach to Iran over the latter's nuclear program has to be made in consultation with the foreign policy needs of European countries. Another example is the recent civil wars in Syria and Libya. In both cases primary countries were negotiating and competing with each other to try to make relations that were to their benefit. Notably, the US and Russia sought advantage through their involvement in these conflicts. The geopolitical world is a very complex amalgamation of primary-primary, primary-subsidiary, and subsidiary-subsidiary relations. To understand the relations between one country and another requires situating bilateral connections within this broader web of relations.

Time for a Recap

Let's take a breath and focus on three key points. First, economic relations are the driving force behind tensions in a moment of geopolitical change. Second, relations between primary and subsidiary countries are just as important as relations between primary countries. It is the strong country's connections to weaker countries that can lead to geopolitical downfall. To understand today's world requires more than seeing geopolitics as simply a matter of what "great powers" do. Third, the physics analogy of opposite actions and reactions is important for understanding how and why major war may occur. The reaction of primary countries to economic, political, and military changes is just as important as the actions of a rising subsidiary country.

Toward Explaining Today's Global Problems

In a moment of geopolitical change, countries with a relatively even mix of the activities described as primary and subsidiary become the focus of attention and can drive tensions with implications beyond their borders. A moment of geopolitical change is driven by countries' ability to become more primary than they have been. They do so by changing the economic activities within the country. Often the change also involves increasing the ability to project military power.

China is the country within this moment of geopolitical flux that has experienced the most change. It has moved from being predominantly rural to being predominantly urban. It has launched a plan called China 2025 to establish itself as a world leader in the most technically sophisticated economic activities, such as robotics, AI, and supercomputing. And yet much of its economy is still based on agriculture and low-tech manufacturing. It has developed its military power, including its naval forces, missile capacity, and air force. And yet it lacks the number of aircraft carriers possessed by the US or other elements of a deep-ocean naval capability. It has established new institutions, such as the Asian Infrastructure Investment Bank (AIIB), to help manage primary-subsidiary relations. And yet, the International Monetary Fund and the World Bank retain their significance. China has also introduced new rhetorical phrases to describe its relationship with subsidiary countries—such as *South-South cooperation*. And yet these phrases have still to catch on with primary countries. The rhetorical phrases of development that have been around since the Second World War are still dominant. The ongoing changes within China and the qualifying "and yets" show that the *potential* for changing established geopolitical patterns is high, but so is the *uncertainty* of whether China's intentions will be achieved. Such is the case in the midst of a moment of geopolitical change.

What's Next in the Book?

Geopolitics is a process. There is always change. But at some historical moments change is more prominent than stability. These are moments of dramatic flux, and they may culminate in war. Such is the current moment.

Moments of geopolitical change are driven by economic change that are accompanied by changes in the geography of the projection of military power. Seapower is vital in these changes. It is the type of military power projection that affects the ability to trade. The twin geopolitics of projecting seapower and resisting the projection of other countries involves controlling different physical geography features of the oceans. These features include SLOCs, choke points, islands, and near and far waters. A world in a period of geopolitical change involves competition over who controls these geographic features. Geopolitics is the competition between countries over economic relations and the projection of military power through control over the geography of near and far waters. The following two chapters explain this in more detail.

THREE

The Rise and Fall of Seapowers

The chief geopolitical concern for any country is its survival. To survive, it must be able to protect itself from invasion, face down insurgencies or separatist groups, and resist blockade. These concerns have been persistent across history, even though the form of blockade has evolved with technological change.[1] Control of near waters has been, and remains, essential for preventing invasion and resisting blockade.[2] The successful defense of near waters and territory enables a country to try to project power beyond its borders, if it wants to.

As a country becomes more powerful, it needs to consider its ability to do two things:

1) control its near waters, and not have them under the control of a primary country;

2) project power beyond its near waters to match a growing role in global trade and the ability to put political pressure on other countries.

The move from near waters to far waters is the geopolitics of power projection. It involves a process by which a country alters its foreign policy from national defense to global reach.

The emphasis in this chapter is upon how the process of power projection plays out. Countries cannot simply choose to project power and become active in far waters. Sometimes what they would like to do is not possible, as other countries and current geopolitical patterns force their hand. Often it is a country's relationships with weaker countries that are important in determining the possibility and challenges for force projection. This is the geopolitical expression of the saying that the weak are more likely to make the strong weak than the strong are likely to make the weak strong.

The existing pattern of primary and subsidiary relations has a lot to do with a primary country's need and ability to project power. Particularly, it is the primary and subsidiary relations of *other* countries that influence the need, ability, and outcome of force projection. And one other country is very important, and that is the hegemon—the most powerful country of the moment. The process of power projection is partially defined by the existing primary-subsidiary relations of the current global power.[3]

The historical cases illustrate how the process of power projection navigates, literally and figuratively, the existing pattern of primary-subsidiary relations and the security interests of the global power. In the past the process of power projection has led to military actions that were not optimal to the national security interests of the country seeking a growing presence in far waters. Wars were fought, but the general intention was to avoid them. The Netherlands projected force in a way that had to take into consideration attempts by other primary countries to establish their own primary-subsidiary relations. In the 1930s the US's calculations for its hemispheric defense were altered by the actions of the British and Britain's desires to protect its relations with India, Egypt, and China. The national defense strategy of the US was changed dramatically because of the strategic concerns of Britain and its reliance on dominance of the subsidiary countries within its empire. The US path to far waters was partially, though quite largely, created in the context of Britain's inability to defend its established subsidiary relations.

The geopolitical lessons are, first, that primary-subsidiary relations require the use of force because they are resented and resisted by subsidiary countries. Remember, the far waters of a growing power are the near waters of other countries. Second, primary countries compete with each other to form primary-subsidiary relations, and this often leads to direct and proxy wars. These geopolitical lessons from the historical cases are relevant to the current moment of geopolitical change as China projects power within its near waters and into far waters, to the chagrin of the US and of subsidiary countries such as the Philippines and Vietnam.

Force projection is a process that is both conflictual and cooperative. Understanding the process requires considering the role of weaker countries. Force projection is the outcome and expression of seapower, but the basis for growing power can be found in changes within the country, especially economic development. The rise to power is not smooth or unerring, and the path to force projection must negotiate and react to the decisions of other states and relations not directly focused upon the rising power.

The process of force projection is driven, and made possible, by a greater role in international trade, and the process is the move from trading in low-value goods to trading in high-value goods. The economic process creates the need and ability to project military force. This is the virtuous cycle of seapower with added emphasis on domestic economic change.[4] The connection between economic goals and defense actions produces a host of foreign policy decisions that play out within the arena set by the physical geography features of the sea, such as SLOCs and choke points. The discussion of primary-subsidiary relations in this chapter will lead to the next chapter's subject of the geopolitical control of near and far waters in the process of power projection.

Six Lessons from the Period of Dutch Seapower

A lot about today's world can be learned by thinking about Dutch history. Today, the Netherlands is rarely thought of as a global power. Its foreign policy is limited by membership in the European Union and NATO. But in the 1600s it was the world's dominant force. The rise of the Dutch to global power and the way they lost that power is a story of seapower and power projection. It is also a story of the use of two forms of violence. One was the subjugation of people across the globe to build plantations and monopolies over trade. The other was fighting with other major powers, with trade again the underlying cause. Also, diplomatic deals were cut to satisfy the needs of countries without resort to war.

In this book I use the term *Dutch*, though the history and geography of the country are complex. The Dutch Republic existed from 1588 to 1795, with borders similar to those of the Netherlands today. The republic was a product of war with Spain as seven northerly provinces gained independence and formalized ties between them in the Union of Utrecht (1579).[5] The southern provinces were unable to break from Spanish control and over the course of time became Belgium and Luxembourg.[6] The Dutch Republic managed to become a seapower as it managed the growing pains of a new country with tensions between the provinces and attempts to centralize control. The country is sometimes referred to as the United Provinces given its formation out of a set of separate political jurisdictions that more or less worked together because of the threat from Spain and the benefits of cooperation in driving industry, trade, and the projection of seapower.[7]

The history of the Dutch as a global power provides six lessons that run throughout the book:

1) The historic process, or arc, of gaining and losing power
2) The role of trade in achieving global power
3) The connection between trade and conflict
4) The constancy of challenges faced by a hegemonic power
5) The ability, albeit limited, of diplomacy to face challenges without resort to violence
6) The cooperation and tensions between merchants, entrepreneurs, and government within a national pursuit for global power

The Netherlands became the first modern seapower. The Spanish, Portuguese, and Chinese had sailed the oceans and exerted control beyond their borders before the Dutch. But prior to the 1500s there had been no clear center of the many markets across the globe. It was the Dutch through the 1600s who provided a focus for global trade. They did not have exclusive or uncontested control of global trade, but they were able to become the hegemonic power by dominating the most crucial trade networks and transforming their domestic economy in the process.

The Arc of Gaining and Losing Power

The history of the Dutch as a hegemonic power illustrates that the power of primary countries is best thought of as an arc, or a process, rather than a fixed or given status. Power is achieved through conflicts with other powerful countries and the growing ability to exert control over weaker countries. The other side of the arc is the loss of power through conflicts and a decline in the ability to influence subsidiary countries. In the 1500s Spain and Portugal were the most powerful countries. They gained global power through plunder of precious metals in the Western Hemisphere. The Dutch rose to power in the context of existing Spanish power and the existing geography of economic relations. The rise and reign of Dutch hegemony were neither smooth nor inevitable.

The rise and fall of the Dutch occurred from roughly 1585 to 1740, a period that has been called the long seventeenth century.[8] The arc of Dutch global power can be thought of as influenced by a combination of economics, domestic politics, and international relations. The United Provinces became the home of the world's most advanced manufacturing industry because of the growing dominance of the Dutch in the trade of high-value products. Dominance in trade further strengthened Dutch industry. The Dutch dominance in global trade was the cause and result of growing geopolitical power—the virtuous cycle of seapower and economic power.[9] However, the ability of the Dutch to gain power was partially the result of relations between other states, such as Spain and Portugal's dual monarchy of 1580–1640.[10] The Dutch rise to power was resented by other primary countries, but the competition among England, France, and the Hanseatic League prevented a united resistance to Dutch hegemony. This gave the Dutch room for maneuver.

The Role of Trade in Achieving Global Power

The Dutch rose to power by becoming the world's leading trading country.[11] Becoming a global trading power required gaining capital through trade in lower-value bulk goods in markets close to home. The capital raised through these endeavors gave the Dutch the ability to trade in more valuable and highly profitable goods across the globe. The Dutch became a power in the Atlantic, Pacific, and Indian Oceans. Illicit trade was part of this process as the Spanish imposed blockades and monopolies designed to keep the Dutch at bay. The merchants who challenged the Spanish were supported by the Dutch government and were the innovators behind the later legitimate and dominant global trade networks.

The Connection between Trade and Conflict

Merchant skills were not enough to push the Dutch to the status of a global power. Violence was also necessary. Two forms of violence were employed. One form was mainly land-based violence to establish the Dutch presence in foreign lands against the will of indigenous populations. Seapower was necessary to enable land battles and to sustain a military presence across the globe. The second form of violence was naval force, or the threat of such force, against other primary countries. The two forms of violence were the ends and means of seapower as a combination of merchant and military fleets.[12] The Dutch expansion across the globe spotlights that the purpose of seapower is to be able to operate ashore, whether to trade or fight.[13]

Constant Challenges to Hegemony

Though history tells of a century of Dutch domination and success, its hegemony should not be thought of as complete. The Dutch were not able to establish the type of trading relations they wanted in every area of the world. Though a country may be thought of as being a great power, its ability to do the things it wants to do, and have other countries act in the way it wants, is always partial. Dutch hegemony was contested in both the political and geographic sense. Sometimes the Dutch used violence to overcome challengers. It was not successful all the time. But despite challenges and setbacks the Dutch were still hegemonic in the sense that they defined rules of behavior that were largely accepted by other countries.

The Dutch rise to power was contested and negotiated. They became dominant in some economic sectors and geographic regions, while recognizing that other sectors and regions would remain the domain of other primary countries. For example, the rise of the Dutch in the East Indian spice market was a result of its exclusion from the Lisbon spice market.[14] Though the 1609 truce with Spain led to the recognition of the United Provinces, there was also concern that one outcome would be increased Portuguese influence in the spice trade and exclusion of the Dutch from the China silk trade.[15] The Dutch recognized their relative weakness in the cinnamon trade with Ceylon and their inability to break Portuguese dominance along the Malabar coast. But in the first two decades of the 1600s the Dutch pushed back in the area of the Coromandel coast, the southeastern seaboard of India. Despite the presence of Portuguese forts, the Dutch built their own, Fort Geldria, which became the main European economic base in the area.[16]

Through the second half of the seventeenth century the Dutch steadily gained dominance in world trade. The rise of the Dutch happened despite the challenges posed by Portugal, England, and France. The superiority of Dutch manufactures was the driving force behind its dominant trade position. The Dutch state played an important role by enforcing regulations that ensured the higher quality of products.[17] Most important was the 1609 intervention of Dutch jurist Hugo Grotius, who established the principle of *Mare liberum*, international waters and freedom of the seas, which is still recognized today.

Facing Challenges Without the Use of Violence

The use of violence was a necessary and important strategy in the arc of Dutch force projection. But the Dutch were also aware of the value of achieving goals through diplomacy. Recognizing reasons for conflict and using diplomacy to avoid war through compromise are valuable for both the hegemonic power and its competitors. Partial success through diplomacy is often better than the costs of war and the possibility of absolute defeat. But resort to diplomacy is a luxury afforded to primary countries. Through the nineteenth century, treaties between primary and subsidiary countries were rightly called "the unequal treaties."[18] Subsidiary countries are rarely able to resist the will of the hegemonic power by diplomacy. Futile acts of violent resistance are often the only option.

Just as conflict played a role in the rise and fall of Dutch power, so did the negotiated truces that punctuated episodes of violence. Truces were compromises that increased Dutch influence in some geographic regions and trade markets while limiting its influence in others. Geopolitical spheres of influence and regional monopolies of trade were in constant flux. The Dutch gained in power relative to the Spanish and Portuguese. They fought and won the "first global war at sea" against the Spanish, culminating in the Battle of the Downs in September 1639.[19] Later in the seventeenth century the Dutch faced growing competition from England and France. While it was sometimes possible for primary countries to come to a peaceful compromise, great power diplomacy came at the expense of subsidiary countries who had no seat at the table. Avoiding conflict between primary countries was achieved by carving up the rest of the world into a mosaic of spheres of influence. Great power conflict was limited by exporting violence and dominance to the subsidiary areas of the world. For example, the Dutch rise to power in the early 1600s was facilitated by agreement with Sweden and the Hanseatic League to weaken the power of Denmark in the Baltic.[20] And in the late 1600s, an agreement was made with France over competing trade interests in India.[21]

Cooperation between Business and Government

The phrase *the Dutch* is a useful shorthand. But it is not entirely accurate. The Dutch were not a singular collection of people. They had different interests, goals, and abilities to achieve them based upon their roles as government officials, merchants, and businessmen, and their attachment to different cities and regions of the country. Dutch success grew despite the presence of conflicts of interest between different groups and individuals within the United Provinces. The story of the rise of the Dutch to global power is about how these groups and individuals could override their conflicts of interest to unite around a common-enough purpose based on the domination of global trade and the necessary use of violence and diplomacy. The lesson is that national unity does not need to be absolute for a country to achieve global dominance.

Though the Dutch government supported Dutch merchants in their quest to dominate global trade, there were schisms between different parts of the United Provinces because of regional economic interests. Amsterdam's growth to become the world's entrepôt, with related manufacturing industry, was driven by the influx of skilled workers from other parts of the country.[22] The lure of the East Indies spice trade incited competition between rival merchants based in the cities of Amsterdam, Rotterdam, Hoorn, and Enkhuizen.[23] The competition led to oversupply and falling prices. Possible outcomes were catastrophic losses for investors and increased competition with Portugal. So the city leaders (burgomasters) led the way, initiating the formation of the United Dutch East India Company (Verenigde Oost-Indische Compagnie [VOC]) in 1602.[24] Competition between Dutch merchants would continue, of course. That is the nature of the vitality of capitalism. But the establishment of the VOC and later, in 1621, of the Dutch West India Company (West-Indische Compagnie [WIC]) meant that national success trumped business competition and drove the process of Dutch hegemony.[25]

In sum, the arc of Dutch force projection through the 1600s shows us that global power comes about through the use of a mix of economic ability and military force, avoiding and not avoiding violence, the aggregation of actions by government and business, and the reluctant acceptance that domination is never complete or uncontested. Seapower is at the center of all these themes.

The Rise and Fall of British Seapower

The six lessons from the arc of Dutch hegemony are relevant across the history of seapower projection. But the Dutch case is unique, as its decline did not lead to the immediate appearance of a new hegemonic power. Britain became a global power about a century later. Britain's rise and decline led to another unique situation when British decline went hand in hand with the rise of the US. Today's US-China tensions show many similarities to the flux of geopolitical relations in the period of transition from British to US hegemony. The six lessons of Dutch power offer a guide to this transition.

First, the period of British seapower was an arc of rise and fall, though not a smooth one. The arc began with serious challenges.[26] Between 1690 and 1715 England became the leading naval power in Europe and the world after emerging victorious in a series of Anglo-Dutch Wars from 1652 to 1674.[27] England's military prowess was funded by its innovations in public finances, especially the role of the Bank of England to provide cheap credit, as well as the profits from trade.[28] From 1739 to 1748 Britain showed its ability to fight effectively in far waters, notably the Caribbean.[29]

In 1776, the British were defeated by US revolutionaries (insurgents in today's language) in what appeared to be a signal that the idea of British Empire was a nonstarter. Soon afterward, Britain faced an ideological and military crisis on the European continent. Napoleon set out to show that there was a different way to live than under royal rule and that the new French social model could dominate all of Europe. But the game was not up. The British became a global power by using diplomacy and the threat of naval power to make sure no one country dominated Europe and therefore threatened Britain. From the early 1800s Britain was the world's dominant naval power, and it "took the leading role in exploration, trade and the assembling of knowledge about the world, including the charting of all its waters."[30]

The British learned from the American experience that formal colonial relations might not be worth the prestige. Instead, a cost-benefit balance could be struck in which different forms of control could still result in favorable trade relations. In other words, why worry about losing the US colonies when India could become the "jewel in the crown" of the British Empire? Britain built up its seapower to face Napoleon's challenge and secure trade routes. Notably, the important victories of the British hero Admiral Horatio Nelson were off the coast of Egypt to secure global connections, as well as off the coast of Spain to secure Britain's near waters.[31] After the Napoleonic Wars Britain and other European countries had to switch their attention to fighting subsidiary countries in waters further afield: the British attack on Algiers in 1816; the Anglo-French-Russian defeat of the Ottoman/Egyptian fleet at Cape Navarino off Greece in 1827; the British "action" versus Mehmet Ali of Egypt in 1839–40; the First Opium War of 1839–42; and the Russian destruction of the Ottoman fleet in the Black Sea in 1853.[32]

But global power is never complete. Britain was soon surprised and embarrassed by the nascent US Navy in the War of 1812, as Britain tried to assert its ability to act in US near waters despite the outcome of the American Revolution.[33] Even in collaboration with other primary countries piracy was a thorn in Britain's side. The British army was humiliated in Afghanistan in the late 1830s and later in the second Anglo-Afghan War of 1878–80, a campaign that was ingrained in the popular culture of the time through the PTSD suffering of Dr. Watson in the Sherlock Holmes stories.[34] And rebellion was constant, whether in southern Africa, the Sudan, or, of course, India itself. The 1857–58 "Indian Mutiny," as the British named it, was conversely called "the First War of Indian Independence" on the subcontinent.[35] Thinking of geopolitics as a process means being able to identify, admittedly in hindsight, pockets of resistance to global power as emerging patterns that led to significant challenges.

As with the second lesson from the period of Dutch seapower, trade was the driving motivation behind the British pursuit of global power. Britain became the global center of industrial innovation and needed to create a global pattern of supply to fuel its new manufacturing economy.[36] The economic geography of Britain changed with the growth of industrial cities such as Manchester, Leeds, Sheffield, Newcastle, Birmingham, and Glasgow. But the change was not complete.[37] Though Britain may well have been the "first industrial nation," it was still an economy based on the interests of the financial institutions of the City of London.[38] British investors certainly saw that money was to be made by investing in British coal mines and factories. But that financial strategy also required the making of primary-subsidiary relations.

And just with the third lesson from the rise of the Dutch, the making of primary-subsidiary relations required collaboration and a common national interest among the business community, government, and the military. Often only the notorious examples of this collaboration are remembered, such as the scheming of British traders to force the importation of opium into China in the Opium Wars of 1839–42 and 1856–58, or the cavalier behavior of British politician and mining magnate Cecil Rhodes in the pursuit of African gold that sparked the Boer/South African War at the end of the nineteenth century.[39] But more important was a prevailing commonsense understanding that trade and "the flag" were intrinsically linked.[40]

The general pattern of Britain's rise to power was an informal collaboration between merchants, government forces, and the military capacity of business interests. For example, the armed forces of the East India Company, rather than government forces, played an essential role in the conquest of India. This conquest benefited the East India Company by creating a near monopoly on the subcontinent and fueling profits. The conquest was also part of Britain's struggle with Napoleonic France. The British government was never fully in control, or fully knew, of the Company's military adventures, but it benefited from their role in the global competition with France.[41]

The Royal Navy was a military force to protect trade routes dominated by British merchants. When necessary, force was to be applied through the Royal Navy and "gunboat diplomacy." This policy was spurred by Prime Minister Lord Palmerston's use of the Royal Navy to open Chinese markets and support the British business community in Canton. It was not British policy to "abandon a large community of British subjects at the extreme end of the globe to a set of barbarians—a set of kidnapping, murdering poisoning barbarians."[42] Global economic interests required the use of violence and the ability to use force across the oceans.

Geopolitical Transition from British to US Hegemony

As Britain's power declined and as it faced challenges from Japan and Germany, it looked to another potential challenger as an ally that it thought, erroneously, could help maintain its global power. British decline as a global power was partly arrested and partly accelerated by its cooperation with the US. In turn, the rise of the US to the position of global seapower was partly helped by its ability to take advantage of Britain's needs. On the other hand, the US rise to power was partly hampered by having to do things it did not want to do because of the weaknesses of its declining ally. These trials and tribulations of transition help us consider how today's geopolitical situation is a spaghetti junction of roads, some of which lead to peaceful futures and others to warfare.

The two world wars at the beginning of the twentieth century eroded Britain's global power. They were the final and fatal challenge to British power. Managing these challenges required forming connections with the rising power. The twentieth century was to be the American century. But being a "superpower" did not mean being unchallenged. In fact, the US's arc of global power was challenged from the very beginning in what is known as the Cold War. The Soviet Union, a wartime ally, became a rival in the blink of an eye, or a mere geopolitical moment. The challenge was twofold. The US did not have an exclusive message on the best path forward for humanity: the ideal of communism challenged the US's expression of liberalism.[43] And the global reach of the US was limited by the presence of hostile governments from central Europe, across the Eurasian landmass, and into East Asia.⁴⁴ Attempts to gain influence in Southeast Asia were partially thwarted in the stalemate of the Korean War and were hammered home in the humiliating debacle of the Vietnam War.

Yet there are also many similarities with the arcs of Dutch and British global power. The period of US power began with victory in a global war and the ability to set the agenda of the postwar world. It built global institutions in the name of common benefits to humanity that also advanced its own political and economic agenda. The United Nations was a way to end European empires and colonialism, and the World Bank and International Monetary Fund promoted global free trade.⁴⁵

Trade again was an essential factor. As the US became home to the new dominant global businesses, it needed a supply of inputs and access to markets for the finished products. The Dutch and the British had tackled these economic problems by making a common national enterprise connecting economic, government, and military interests. The US did something similar by establishing a trans-Pacific and trans-Atlantic military and diplomatic presence, thereby creating an environment for US businesses to become multinational.⁴⁶ The US rise to a global economic power was enabled by an active state department and the persuasive techniques of the CIA.⁴⁷

The US is often thought of as a continental power that became, some say reluctantly, a global maritime power.⁴⁸ But there is another interpretation. From the early days of US independence, the country has always looked toward expanding its geopolitical reach.⁴⁹ In other words, the US has acted more like an empire than the rhetoric of national exceptionalism would like us to believe. But rather than throwing the word *empire* around as an insult, we might more usefully see the growth of US power as the ability to control a continent and then become a seapower. However, it had to become a seapower with an eye to the existing seapower, Britain, its own challenger in Japan, and the way Britain was trying to cope with the twin challenges of Germany and Japan.

The US established its Department of the Navy in 1798, soon after its successful bid to cut colonial ties with Britain.⁵⁰ In the War of 1812 the US achieved a number of successes against the assumed might of the British navy.⁵¹ The new US Navy was effective in countering piracy in the far waters of the Barbary coast and joining Britain against France in the "Quasi-War" of 1798–1800.⁵² But in terms of global reach, the nineteenth century was the era of British seapower. The US established itself as a continental power through its wars against the indigenous peoples of North America. Part of this process was the securing of rivers that led into near waters to the south and west of the continent: the Mississippi River basin through the Louisiana Purchase (1803) and the Columbia network through the Lewis and Clark expedition (1804-6). Territorial expansion led to the ability to control the coastline of the continent and made it possible for the US to look over the horizon to far waters.

In 1853 American commodore Matthew Perry made a statement of intent by leading four warships into Tokyo Bay, resulting in Japan opening to trade with the Western world. In the 1860s and 1870s, the US attempted to establish coaling stations in the Pacific, with very limited success. It had more success through the 1890s, following the advocacy of Alfred Thayer Mahan. Mutual suspicion between Britain and the US over the establishment of coaling stations and other logistical bases developed through the early 1900s.[53] The purchase of Alaska (1867) and the annexation of Hawaii (1898) secured the Pacific near waters. The Spanish-American War (1898) removed a potential challenger from the Caribbean. In 1899 the US promoted its "Open Door policy" toward China advocating for equal privileges and port access for countries trading with China. This policy was partially a recognition of the weaker US presence in China compared to European countries and Japan. Force projection followed through the control of the Philippines, and the statement of global intent in President Theodore Roosevelt's "White Fleet" promenade around the world from December 1907 to February 1909.[54]

The US rose to become a seapower through a series of uncertain stutters rather than a planned or preordained process. The rhetoric of isolationism may have been loud, or the dominant story we hear today, but it belied many US military expeditions, including Honduras (1911), Nicaragua (1912), Haiti (1915), and the Dominican Republic (1916).[55] The tone changed with entry into the Second World War in December 1941. But the attack on Pearl Harbor was not the utter surprise it was portrayed as. This portrayal was useful rhetoric to generate the necessary public outrage to push open the political door to joining the war. But tensions between the US and Japan had been growing for a while as the US eyed access to oil and rubber in the East Indies and was concerned about Japan's imperial ambitions.[56] Following the pattern of previous global powers, the US was becoming a global economic player as New York developed into a global financial center and as US manufacturers sought global markets.

China was also an arena of US-Japanese competition. The US took a paternalistic stance toward China driven by a mission of Christian proselytization. But there were also material calculations, as the US had been concerned for a while that European powers and Japan were carving up China into spheres of influence from which the US might be excluded, or at least be dealt the weakest hand.[57]

Through the course of the Second World War the weaknesses of Britain and its historic vision of empire became entangled with the growing strength of the US and its vision of global capitalism free from the fetters of imperial territorial blocs.[58] The US envisioned a new world based on free trade, broadly understood, that would benefit the efficiency and prowess of its growing industrial base. The US was wary of Britain's hopes to remain a global power through the maintenance of empire. But the US also saw Britain as a necessary ally in the fight against German and Japanese visions of economic regions to which the US would struggle for access.[59] The US and Britain had to dance together, but they preferred different music and had different hopes for what would happen when the dance was over.

Despite these tensions, the US adapted its national security strategy in recognition of the threat to Britain from Germany. Especially, the US recognized that the Atlantic would become a vulnerable flank if Germany were to be victorious in Europe.[60] The vulnerability would be even greater if Germany were to invade and defeat Britain. As shown in the following chapter, Britain's near waters were vulnerable to the German onslaught. And these near waters of an ally had to become far waters central to US national security. Securing its near waters was no longer sufficient for the US. The near waters of others were also a security concern.

The odd thing was that Britain's near waters were not solely a defensive concern. The near waters of the North Sea and the English Channel led to the Mediterranean Sea, a maritime geopolitical arena that was important for its role as a set of channels: the British channel to Egypt and the Suez that was the highway to India and beyond; the Italian channel to imperial ambitions in Africa; and the German channel accessing Balkan and Middle Eastern oilfields. Germany also knew that wresting control of these channels from the British would strangle the flows of imperial trade that were the foundation of British power.[61]

While this was clear to the British, the picture was murkier for the US. The strategic vision of security of Atlantic near waters required a degree of force projection into far waters, and that meant becoming embroiled in Britain's attempts to defend its empire.[62] Near-water security could also mean empowering an ally in a way that hindered the long-term vision of US seapower: free trade through open far waters. In the end, the free trade vision of the US won, and the US became the world's leading economy and seapower.

But that project was incomplete, given the challenge of communism.[63] The global reach of the US was limited, and a country that had been seen as a vital arena for the global economic project since the last half of the nineteenth century became one from which US business was excluded. That country was, of course, China.[64] It was also an ideological thorn in the side of US attempts to promote liberalism, and a military foe in the region. But China was to rise just as the US had. Intriguingly, the US was to play a key role in its growing economic and military power. Just as Britain and the US had conducted an uneasy dance, the US and China were to become the eye-catching pair on the dance floor.

China's Rise in Historical Perspective

The same six lessons that have helped us understand the arcs of Dutch, British, and US power help us understand the rise of China. In a similar fashion, China has a history of increasing economic and political power that includes a growing presence across the globe. The decline and fall of the Celestial Empire, China's last dynasty, lasted from 1840 through 1919.[65] This was the time of imperial competition among primary countries, and China was one arena for that competition. China did not have full sovereignty over its own land, as European countries, Japan, and Russia were establishing concessions in eastern cities and carving out territorial control in parts of Manchuria (map 3.1). China was preoccupied with how the

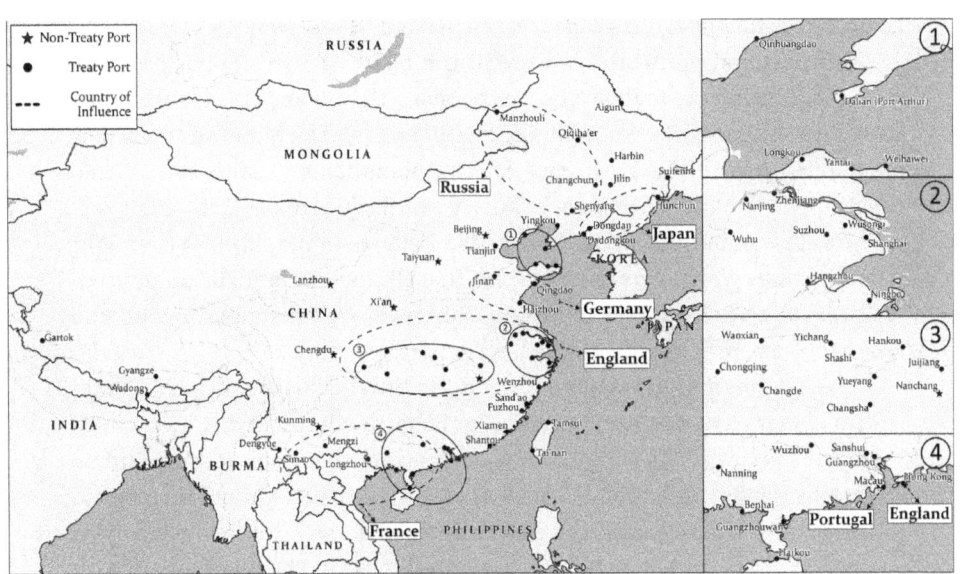

MAP 3.1. Imperial concessions in China.

Source: Adapted by Carson Liesik from Chinasage, "Foreign Treaty Ports and Enclaves in China," last updated December 7, 2016, https://www.chinasage.info/foreign-enclaves.htm.

foreign policy of other countries was focused on its own territory. Hence, China was having to adopt a defensive stance, and a weak one at that, rather than being outward looking.

One egregious example was the sequence of Opium Wars in which China had to submit to the whims of foreign powers, led by the British. The result was the creation of Chinese cities as markets for imported narcotics. Another event was defeat in the Sino-Japanese War of 1894–95, leading to the loss of control of Taiwan and a further weakening of China.[66] On land, a secret treaty with Russia in 1896 allowed the Russian railway system to nudge toward the northeast of China.[67] Internally, dynastic control was under attack from nationalist and liberal forces looking to Western countries as models of government. One set of these models was the various notions of socialism and communism that held sway at the time.

But even with these wars and defeats, China established peaceful political relations that would contribute to its rise to power, including for a moment relations with the US during its own rise to hegemony. The opportunity for political change within China was heightened across the period of the two world wars that marked the decline of the European imperial system and the rise of the postwar US-led era.[68] China was on the side of the eventual winners in both world wars. Chinese were employed as sappers digging trenches on the western front in the First World War.[69] Chinese forces fought against Japan in the Second World War.[70]

Cultural and political ties were at the heart of a strong but problematic relationship throughout the war between the US and President Chiang Kai-shek, leader of the Kuomintang (Nationalists). The hope was for a new relationship with the West once Japan's plans for an Asian empire had been thwarted and European influence similarly reduced.[71] In 1949, victory of the communist forces, led by Mao Zedong, in the Chinese Civil War that began as global war ended meant that China was to focus on internal reform for a while. It was to be the Chinese nationalists in Taiwan who soon took the pathway to establish an export economy.

The communist government on the mainland looked to continental allies rather than maritime trade. The People's Republic of China (PRC) adopted a policy of "leaning to one side" to establish economic and political ties with the Soviet Union.[72] The goal was to provide a united ideological and military front against the power of the US and its allies, while also using the alliance to launch industrial development. The relationship with the Soviet Union always had some level of tension. Chairman Mao sensed an element of disrespect from Moscow, an assumption of China being the junior partner.⁷³ The massive internal disruption of the Cultural Revolution (between August 1966 and August 1977) and the millions who died in the Great Famine (1959–61) were brutal manifestations of the changes China was making to its economy—changes that would ultimately allow it to look outward through global trade.⁷⁴

Even within this period of turmoil and transition China was able to exercise some power in the world. China was an aid donor to subsidiary countries and coined the rhetoric of acting within "the principle of equality and mutual benefit" with "respect for the sovereignty of aid recipient countries." The stated goal was to help countries along a "path of self-reliance and independent economic development."⁷⁵ This language was a rehearsal for the current time, in which China has reached the economic and political position of a global power, as discussed in chapter 7.

China has risen to the status of a global power by restructuring its economy to become the world's leading exporter. This is like the arcs of the Dutch, the British, and the US. And as before, this process has involved conflict. Chinese foreign policy went through a crucial change of orientation between 1979 and 2009.⁷⁶ During this period, which was commonly known as the era of globalization, China continued moving from an agricultural to an industrial economy with a focus upon exports. But more specifically this was also the period in which primary-subsidiary relations were changing through the creation of "outsourcing," "global supply chains," and "just-in-time" manufacturing.⁷⁷ Certain subsidiary countries were able to change dramatically as they became the locations of new manufacturing roles in intense networks of production and trade. After the 1972 recognition of the PRC by the US, China was able to take on the role of potential friend rather than being the Soviet-Chinese ideological pariah. In hindsight, always valuable, it is evident that this phase of Chinese foreign policy was the one that kick-started its rise to a global role.⁷⁸

However, in this phase of China's arc to power its economic relations were reactive. China took advantage of the moves being made by the more powerful primary countries, especially the choices of Western firms to locate manufacturing plants in areas of cheaper labor. This meant that China began to have a global economic presence through the export of low-value goods. At the same time, China rebooted its relations with Russia through the Shanghai Cooperation Organization, ostensibly a defensive move with an eye to the threat of Islamic fundamentalism.⁷⁹ More importantly, it was an alliance that would hopefully provide for a secure continental flank while establishing Russia as a supplier of energy to drive further Chinese economic growth. China was changing its global orientation, making sure its land borders were secure, while venturing into the economics of global trade.

China's rise to power has required taking on challenges from other countries. As a reminder, the path to global power is not smooth. The wars China has fought since the Second World War have been matters of border security and, in the eyes of the Chinese, matters of creating internal peace, though "internal" is a matter of perspective. The 1950 annexation of Tibet and subsequent acts of suppression have resulted in its current status as an autonomous region of China. Controlling Tibet was followed by a busy 1960s. Border wars with India and the Soviet Union were fought to define the geography of China's territory and to prevent internal and external challenges to the government. Also, border skirmishes with Burma around 1960 pushed the remnants of the Kuomintang out of that country and prevented a challenge to the ruling Communist Party. From about the same time there have been various forms of control and suppression to ensure control over Xinjiang Province. The 1962 war with India over the geography of the border has been recently renewed. The 1969 Sino-Soviet border conflict included skirmishes in Xianjiang Province and, more notably, conflict in the eastern section of the border defined by the Argun, Amur, and Ussuri Rivers. Armed conflict over control of Zhenbao/Damansky Island in 1969 showed the world that China not only was separate from Soviet influence but was a country with military clout. This changed the US attitude to China and set up the later recognition of the PRC by the US.

China not only had to think about defining its border and suppressing challenges to PRC rule but also had to contend with the presence of the hegemonic power in its own backyard. In addition to providing support for the Nationalists in Taiwan, the US waged war in two of China's neighboring regions, the Korean peninsula and Vietnam.[80] The imperative of limiting US influence in what China considered its own backyard also meant a Chinese presence and involvement in conflict in Cambodia. Though China could not directly challenge the military might of the US, it did what it could to reduce US presence in the region, leading to the creation of North Korea and continued ties between the two countries, as well as the satisfaction of seeing the US be forced to leave Vietnam.

Historic lessons point to the need for a global power to increase its military capacity and, as in the case of the US's relationship with Britain, to have some sort of cooperation with the current hegemonic power. These two lessons came together with China's pursuit of nuclear weapons. Surprisingly, it was the US that encouraged and enabled China's nuclear weapons program. The main reason for the Nixon administration's recognition of the PRC was to weaken the military position of the Soviet Union. During President Ford's administration (August 1974 to January 1977) the US facilitated the military supply of equipment and know-how to China, including powerful computers that were valuable in the development of nuclear warheads and ballistic missiles.[81] The US also sent China its "Air-Land Battle" manual designed to counter a Soviet invasion of Europe. But it was China's *lack* of nuclear capacity that the US was most concerned about, especially its poor early-warning technology.

In 1979, the Sino-US "Chestnut" program helped build early-warning systems in Xianjiang Province, and Chinese military officers were trained at a SIGINT training center near San Francisco.[82] The flow of military equipment helped China modernize its nuclear capacity. In 1984 the Defense Intelligence Agency argued: "There is evidence that the Chinese have been successful in assimilating into their nuclear program United States technology in areas such as high explosive, radiochemistry, metallurgy, welding, super computers, numerical modeling, high speed photonics, and underground drilling. . . . Increased access to this technology and continued Chinese efforts will in the 1980s and early 1990s show up as qualitative warhead improvements."[83] The development of China's nuclear weapons program was a result of overt and covert flows of information and technology from the US.[84] Through the realist wisdom of Secretary of State Henry Kissinger, the US taxpayer helped modernize China's nuclear weapons program.

The strategic context is always dynamic. In the Cold War context there was some logic in the US helping China launch its nuclear weapons program. At the time, the decision helped the US in its actions toward the Soviet Union, the main challenger to its hegemony. But now the calculations of the US are different. It is wary of China's growing military role across the globe. As China has increased its global economic reach, it has begun to flex its growing military muscle beyond its neighbors. China signed on to the War on Terror. It saw the change in global geopolitics as an opportunity for further suppression of the Uyghur Muslims in Xinjiang amid fears of jihadism among its Central Asian neighbors.[85]

In alliance with many countries, including NATO members, India, and Australia, China also participated in Operation Ocean Shield against Somali pirates disrupting maritime traffic in the Indian Ocean (map 3.2).[86] Though this operation showed a recognition by all the trading countries of the world that a key SLOC crossing the High Seas was under threat, it marked the emergence of China as an important policeman in the task of

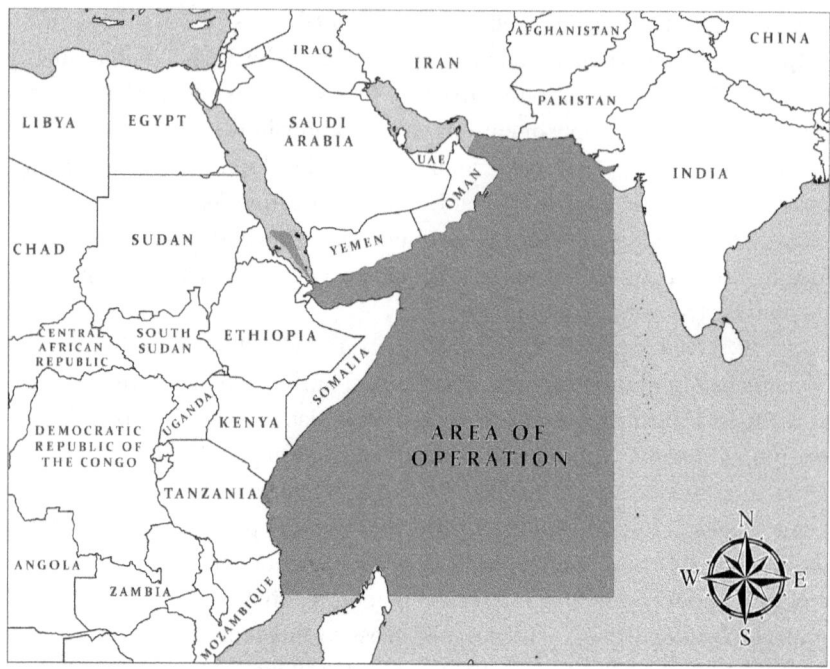

MAP 3.2. Operation Ocean Shield.

Source: Adapted by Carson Liesik from NATO-OTAN, "Operation Ocean Shield," accessed December 5, 2023, https://mc.nato.int/missions/operation-ocean-shield.

maintaining oceanic trade. Operation Ocean Shield came at a time when the African continent was playing an increasing role in China's economy.[87] In 2017 China opened a naval base in Djibouti, strategically located in the Horn of Africa in relation to the SLOCs of the Red Sea and the Suez Canal and into the Indian Ocean. The strategic value of this location is evident, seeing as China's base has neighbors just down the coast—bases for the US, French, and Japanese navies.

The Chinese prefer to call the Djibouti facility a "support base" rather than a military base. In the words of Chinese foreign minister Wang Yi in March 2016:

> Like any growing powers, China's interests are constantly expanding overseas. At present, there are 30,000 Chinese enterprises all over the world.... An urgent task for China's diplomacy is to maintain the growing overseas interests. How to maintain? I would like to tell you clearly that China will never go through the expansion path of the traditional

powers, nor will China pursue hegemony. We want to explore a path with Chinese characteristics that both follows the trend of the times and is welcomed by all parties.[88]

To put it another way, China's export footprint requires a military footprint, and China certainly sees Djibouti as an important economic partner.[89] The geography of "national interests" is following the logic and patterns seen before in the arcs of Dutch, British, and US hegemony.

Since 2009, China has become more assertive in world politics. With the travails of primary countries that became evident in the financial and debt crises of 2008–12, China saw new opportunities and reasons for investing abroad. It needed to ensure domestic economic growth to satisfy its population and ensure political peace. The dramatic urbanization of China was regionally imbalanced. The eastern coastal cities were booming, threatening to leave interior cities and agricultural areas behind.[90] The development plan to try to create some sort of internal regional economic balance was coupled with a new policy, the "Going Out" strategy announced in 2017. This policy recognized that China's economic growth could not be sustained by domestic consumption. It required an export strategy. The seeds for this idea had been sown in 2006 with the Overseas Investment Industrial Guiding Policy, which prioritized accessing raw materials and resources not readily available in China, facilitating Chinese export of products, technology, and labor, and making investments that would be "able to clearly enhance China's technology research and development capacity, including an ability to use international leading technology and advanced management experience and professional talent."[91] The focus of China's overseas investment is to gain access to markets and inputs, including natural resources, that will allow it "to progress faster and make bigger leaps in shifting its economy to its far from achieved new model."[92] In other words, big changes are afoot but success is far from guaranteed.

The focus of China's policy has been the Belt and Road Initiative (BRI). Announced by President Xi Jinping in 2013, the BRI consists of two related parts:[93] a land-based set of roads and railways across Eurasia, originally called the Silk Road Economic Belt, and a sea-based route through the South China Sea and into the Indian Ocean and beyond, known as the Maritime Silk Road Initiative. The BRI extends across Eurasia into western Europe and across the Indian Ocean to the east coast of Africa, where it hooks into Chinese-made roads and railways spreading through the continent. The land and sea elements of the BRI are linked to produce an expansive network of ports, warehouses, airports, and storage sites that are a system of arteries for Chinese trade and investment. Though many segments of the BRI project have stalled, the scope is so large that even substantial failures would not prevent it from transforming the economic geography of the world.

The BRI is the foreign policy initiative that drives Western fears about the rise of China. It is the concrete manifestation of China's arc from subsidiary to primary country. Western fears are not just about the economic shifts that the BRI may cause. Rather, the BRI is a manifestation of China's switch from a recent historical concern with continental geopolitics to the goal of becoming a seapower.

The history of China's rise can be understood through the six lessons from the Dutch period of global power. Today's geopolitical tensions are informed by the history of the rise and fall of seapowers. The rising arc of China's power is driven by a change in its economy and global trade connections. It is a result of the mutual interest between government and business, though mutual interest does not necessarily make for smooth relations. The tension between entrepreneurial freedom and authoritarian control may well be the barrier to China's becoming a hegemonic power. China's rise has also required growing military strength, and this produces tensions with existing seapowers, especially the US.

To date, China's arc of power mirrors the path of the US. Both were subsidiary countries that had to fight to free themselves from the shackles of control imposed by primary countries. They transformed their economies from agriculture to industry and became primary countries. In the process they established influence within subsidiary countries to their own benefit. And their rise came through a tense mixture of cooperation and conflict with the current global power. This arc of power required the growth of seapower to establish control within near waters and to launch the subsequent reach into far waters. That is the topic of the next chapter.

FOUR

The Geopolitics of Near Waters and Far Waters

The geopolitics of global trade and power projection discussed in the previous chapter have been, and remain, largely dependent on seapower. The oceans are means of passage for trade through sea lines of communications (SLOCs), which are defined through UNCLOS as the "High Seas" with the right of the freedom of navigation. Also, the oceans are means of power projection that allow countries to land and station forces, or threaten to do so. In this chapter the focus is upon the physical geography of the sea and the dynamics of geopolitical power.

Two physical geography features are near waters and far waters. Introducing these physical geography features requires us to see geography as something that changes with changing politics, rather than something permanent. And it requires us to think about the way the actions of other countries, including those that do not seem directly relevant, are necessary to understanding how a country develops its security strategy.

Defining a piece of the ocean as either a near or a far water is, of course, relative with regard to a particular country. For example, the Caribbean Sea is near the US, and the Mediterranean Sea is far away. This is a simple, and unchanging, geographic fact. However, the geopolitical significance of these waters is dynamic because near and far waters are physical geographic arenas of the shifting pattern of global geopolitical relations.

The significance of the Caribbean Sea for the US, and how the US was able to act within that region, changed as its relationship with Britain changed. Britain's presence in the Caribbean as a far water was a manifestation of its ability to project its power across the globe. This meant that a US near water was a geographic arena in which its geopolitical opportunities were limited. As Britain's power declined, it lost its ability to project power in the Caribbean, and the US was able to assert control over this near water. The geographic meaning and geopolitical function of the Caribbean Sea changed for the US and Britain as their relationship with each other, and the rest of the world, changed. This dynamic relationship, and the way geopolitical control of the Caribbean Sea was exchanged peacefully, can be understood only in the wider pattern of global geopolitical shifts.

Simply, a country (Country A in figure 4.1) gains the power to be present in/encroach upon the near waters of another country (Country B). Over time a country can effect control over its near waters by being able to prevent encroachment by another country or to drive out any country that has encroached. Subsequently, that country may build up its seapower and encroach on the near waters of another country. In figure 4.1, the starting point is a moment when Countries A and B have control of their respective near waters. Over time, Country A retains control of its near waters and encroaches on the near waters of Country B. Country B is not able to encroach upon Country A's near waters. Hence, Country B's near waters become Country A's far waters, but the relationship is not reciprocated.

This simple pattern introduces the role of near and far waters in geopolitics through two separate but related dynamics:

a) The current global power's presence in far waters becomes contested by a rising primary country who identifies them as its own near waters. Schematically, Country A's encroachment in the near waters of Country B is contested by Country B. Country A can no longer be sure it can retain its presence in its far waters that are Country B's near waters.

b) The current global power's near waters become a rising primary country's far waters. A country that has become accustomed to having control of its near waters while assuming a secure presence in far waters (encroachment in the near waters of other countries) finds that another country is encroaching in its near waters.

The two statements clarify the contemporary geopolitics of China's growing power. Especially, they help us think about the importance of the South China Sea as a geopolitical arena, and the Belt and Road Initiative (BRI) as a form of global power projection.[1] Geopolitical tensions in the western Pacific and the South China Sea are a conflict over China's near

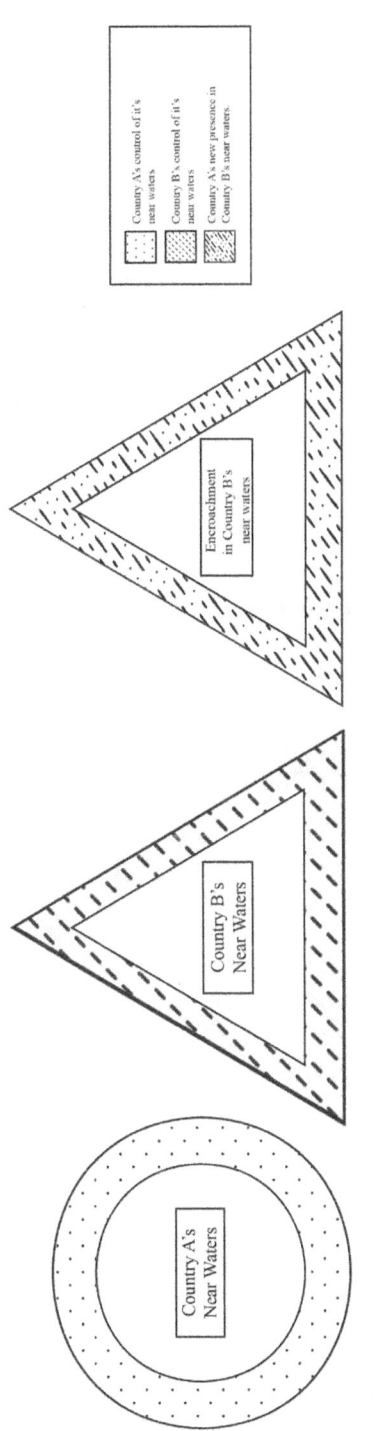

FIGURE 4.1. The process of force projection in near and far waters.

Source: Drawn by Anna Johnson.

waters and US far waters. In turn, the ability of China through the geopolitical projects of the BRI to project power across the globe is evidence of its increasing ability to act within far waters that are the near waters of other countries. This is the geopolitical appearance of action and reaction. And it plays out in subsidiary countries, the weak that can make the strong weak.

Today's geopolitical tensions can be understood by looking at the role of near and far waters in the eras of Dutch, British, and US seapower. The shared interests and disagreements between Britain and the US in the transition of hegemony from one to the other especially inform today's geopolitical tensions.

The Dutch Move from Near to Far Waters

The process of power projection is driven by a country's expansion from trading in near waters to cornering markets in far waters. This geographic process occurs in tandem with an economic shift from trading in relatively low-value goods to dominating trade in high-value goods. Initially, the Dutch traded in their near waters of the Baltic. In the sixteenth century they shipped bulk goods: tar, pitch, hemp, flax, timber, grain, wool, copper, and iron (map 4.1).[2] These goods may not hold the romance of global trade, but they provided the foundation for what was to come. Through the course of the seventeenth century the Dutch expanded into the global trade of high-value products, such a spices, precious metals, and silk. This trade was accompanied by the innovation in banking and insurance necessary for new forms of global trade.

The Dutch became more influential in the Baltic by expanding their trade from some bulk goods to more profitable "southern goods," namely pepper, sugar, figs, raisins, almonds, currants, olive oil, and spices.[3] Success breeds success. The shift to "southern goods" led to increased Dutch trade in the Mediterranean Sea and then "the Guinea trade" of gold, ivory, and gum.[4] Next, the Dutch established trade in the Caribbean.[5] The arc of Dutch seapower reached its peak with trade in the East Indies, especially in spices. The dominance of the Dutch was made clear in 1640 when it became the only European country permitted to trade with Japan.[6] The Dutch were able to gain control, though not monopoly, over key material imports, such as Spanish wool, Turkish yarn, Swedish iron and copper, and Spanish-American dyestuffs.[7] Controlling trade in key raw materials and high-value goods through trade in far waters meant that they were able to survive a relative decline in their role in bulk trade in the near waters of

MAP 4.1. Dutch near waters.

Source: Drawn by Carson Liesik, based on and adapted from figure 2.1 (p. 19) in Jonathan Israel's *Dutch Primacy in World Trade, 1585–1740* (Oxford: Clarendon Press, 1989).

the Baltic.[8] Increased seapower in far waters helped the Dutch cope with economic fluctuations closer to home.

The Dutch dominance of the oceans became possible with changes in the geopolitical situation on the European continent. Conflict with Spain and the changing balance of power led to the coming together of the United Provinces as a country. This allowed the Dutch the chance to build a unique set of economic and political arrangements, and the breathing space of security to concentrate on building up their trade. The Spanish siege of Antwerp in 1584–85 was the catalyst for a change in the center of gravity of economic activity to the north Netherlands.[9] Soon after, territorial victories against the Spanish and the lifting of the Spanish embargo on Dutch shipping allowed the Dutch to negate the privateer threat from Dunkirk. These victories enabled the Dutch to replace the English as the dominant trader with Russia and establish their trade dominance in the Baltic.[10] As trade expanded, the government provided the trading fleets with armed escorts.[11]

Expansion into global trade also resulted in conflicts. For example, the East Indian trade led to conflict with the Portuguese, who, along with the English, created their own zones of influence.[12] In 1618 there was a short and limited Anglo-Dutch War over control of trade with Java and Banda Islands.[13] Throughout the 1600s conflict between the Dutch and a combination of the Spanish, Portuguese, and English flared over trade competition, especially for high-value Asian goods. Such conflict between primary countries was largely conducted at sea. Denmark and Sweden challenged the Dutch presence in the Baltic Sea, as discussed in chapter 8. Even the near waters of the Dutch were contested.

Seapower was also necessary for another key element of global force projection: namely, seizing the control of subsidiary areas from other primary countries and, relatedly, subjugating indigenous peoples. As the Dutch were able to create trade relations across the globe they conquered islands and territories and established a global network of forts, such as those in the "spice islands" of Amboina, Tidore, and Ternate taken from Portugal.[14] By 1617 the Dutch had about twenty garrisons stretching from Pulicat to the Moluccas and a dedicated fleet of forty fighting ships.[15] The purpose of these forts and ships was not only to subjugate the locals but to protect a zone of influence from English, Portuguese, and Spanish incursion.[16] Such competition led to control of territory and islands from southern India through Ceylon and the Moluccas to the Philippines (map 4.2).[17]

The other form of violence that occurred was primary-versus-primary conflict but in the territory of subsidiary countries. For example, the Spanish reacted against the Dutch push into the Caribbean and northern South America by trying to depopulate the cattle-ranching area of northwestern Española to nullify Dutch trade. In 1606 the Spanish attacked the Dutch traders in the area of Venezuela and Española, seizing ships and killing Dutch seamen.[18] It's also important to note that a global war of this era, the Thirty Years War of 1618–48, was played out in the subsidiary areas of Brazil, Ceylon, the Philippines, and the Caribbean.[19] Global war is usually seen in terms of primary-versus-primary or "great power" struggles,

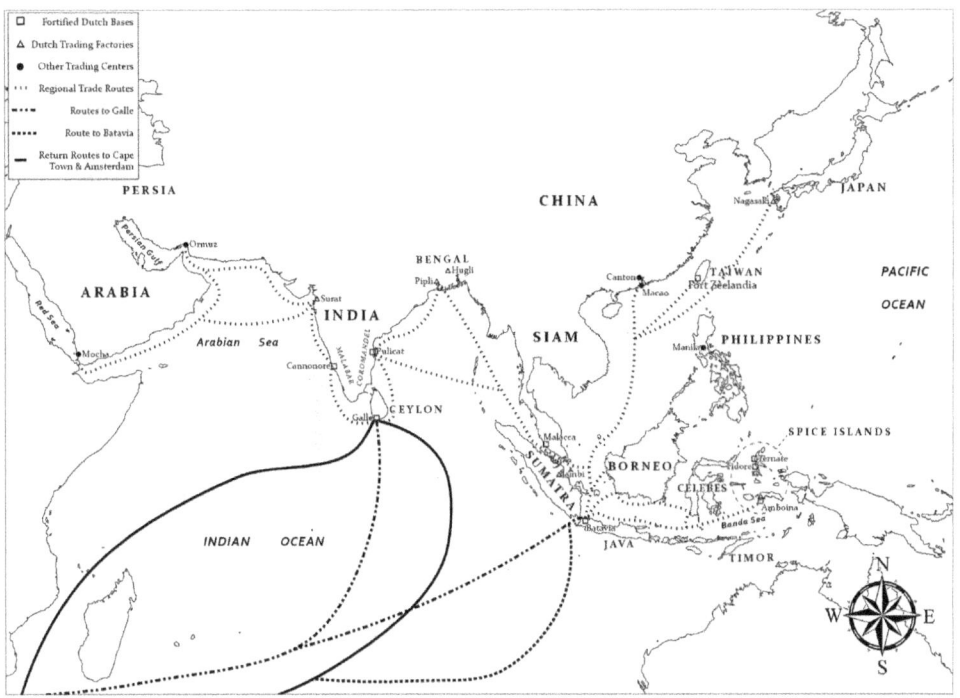

MAP 4.2. Dutch far waters.

Source: Drawn by Carson Liesik, based on and adapted from figure 5.4 (pp. 182–83) in Jonathan Israel's *Dutch Primacy in World Trade, 1585–1740* (Oxford: Clarendon Press, 1989).

but throughout history they have been motivated by control of subsidiary states, and those states have been key arenas in deciding the global struggle.

The projection of Dutch seapower to subjugate indigenous populations and be able to fight other great powers, directly or indirectly, on foreign shores is an example of the value of navies. They allow you to do what you want to do on shore.[20] Trade is often portrayed as a peaceful, progressive, universally beneficial, and purely economic relationship. But it is also geographic and political. The Dutch case shows that becoming a global trade power is a matter of geographic diffusion from near waters to far waters. And that process of diffusion requires force.

Certain lessons can be learned from the history of Dutch seapower. But the Dutch established their presence in far waters without having to force or encourage an existing power to leave. The relationship between Britain and the US as the former lost its ability to defend its near and far waters brings attention to other lessons.

The British and US Exchange of Near and Far Waters

The role of the oceans in the rise of the US as a global power was the focus of Alfred Thayer Mahan's writing at the turn of the nineteenth century. He advocated for the protection of near waters to allow for projection into far waters. The first naval priority was the defense of the coastline because, "though distant, our shores can be reached; being defenceless, they can detain but a short time a force sent against them."[21] Mahan's hypothetical "force" referred to European countries. Once near waters had been secured, Mahan saw the imperative of building the US economy through commerce and power projection in far waters: "The interesting and significant feature of this changing attitude is the turning of the eyes outward, instead of inward only, to seek the welfare of the country. To affirm the importance of distant markets, and the relation to them of our own immense powers of production, implies logically the recognition of the link that joins the products and the markets,—that is, the carrying trade."[22]

The process of US expansion into far waters was energized by Mahan's writing, and early steps can be seen in the annexation of Hawaii and the construction of the Panama Canal. Mahan wrote about both. The Central American Isthmus was identified as the "natural centre, towards which, if not thwarted by adverse influences the current of intercourse between East and West inevitably must tend. Here the direction of least resistance was indicated clearly by nature."[23] Using the language of geographic determinism, Mahan stressed the "inevitability" of the geopolitical importance of the isthmus and the threat of losing it for the US because of "indolent drifting, in wilful blindness to the approaching moment when action must be taken."[24] A classic geopolitician was encouraging the US government to adopt a policy that secured near waters to launch expansion into far waters.

It did so. The Pacific Ocean was the arena for the earliest successes in the process of US expansion into far waters. To become the dominant seapower required more time as it entailed expanding into the Atlantic Ocean without provoking the wrath of Great Britain. The Second World War, with the two allies' cooperation and tensions, was the turning point in which the US became a trans-Pacific and trans-Atlantic seapower.

In September 2021, television audiences in Britain were informed and entertained by a documentary about the D-Day landings of June 1944. The Second World War was still seen as worthy of evening time viewing, seventy-seven years after the event. Apparently it's not just that the war is still relevant within national identity and politics. It's also interesting to note what aspects of the war are promoted. A documentary on the D-Day landings shows the *offensive* aspect of the war as Britain's near waters of the English Channel were crossed. The assault not only ensured the safety of the British homeland but was a vital step for the US projection of force across the Atlantic into new far waters and establishment of a military presence in western Europe.

And yet, despite the focus on D-Day, the Second World War was primarily a *defensive* war for Britain. The defense of Britain's far waters was as important as the defense of near waters. The war was a crisis for Britain because near and far waters were threatened at the same time. It was not just the homeland but threats to Britain's presence in far waters that caused strategic headaches for Prime Minister Winston Churchill and his chiefs of staff. It was this inability to project seapower that provided clear evidence of Britain's hegemonic decline.

After the shock of retreat and the frantic evacuation of the British Expeditionary Forces from Dunkirk in May and June of 1940, the British military was largely on a defensive footing until 1942.[25] About half of the British Army was deployed in far-water theaters trying to defend British colonial possessions in Asia from Japan, as well as maintaining a large force in the Middle East. The Middle East was not just a crucial source of oil but the communications crossroads connecting the homeland with India and far-water interests further east.[26]

The Mediterranean Sea became a key theater of war and the first combined US and British military operation of the war: Operation Torch, the Allied landings in North Africa. But the attitudes of the British and the US were different. Though a general level of agreement was achieved between the two allies, the difference of opinion was partly a result of different visions of the war. The US saw its presence in the Mediterranean theater as a set of defensive actions to encircle Germany and enable a larger and decisive attack in Northwest Europe as quickly as possible. Hence the US favored landings in the western part of the Mediterranean.[27] In contrast, Britain saw the landings as an offensive opportunity to bring Germany to a decisive battle. They also needed to ensure that the Mediterranean remained a channel to Asian far waters. Hence, the British wanted landings as easterly as possible.

The stances of the two countries depended on their understanding of the role of the Mediterranean as a near water or a far water. But despite these different visions it became the first theater of the war in which the rising and declining hegemonic countries fought together. They did so because of the interplay of the near and far waters of the two countries.

The US had agreed that it was to become involved in far waters to prosecute the war against Germany. The question was which far waters. The US was concerned that the Mediterranean was a far water that would take military resources away from the shores of Northwest Europe, which they saw as the location for the decisive battle. Though committed to war in Europe, the US was concerned that the British wanted to focus upon the Mediterranean because it was the SLOC that was the conduit to Britain's imperial far waters, rather than an arena that would lead to the quickest defeat of Germany. The different evaluations of the Mediterranean showed the diplomatic tension between allies when it came to the strategy of war and how the same maritime theater was regarded, depending on whether it was a near water or a far water. But more importantly the Mediterranean strategy illustrates the level of agreement between Britain in decline and the US on the rise. The two countries were able to fight together in the same oceans. It didn't matter whether the Mediterranean was a near or far water, or the strategy offensive or defensive. Mutual benefit meant that the declining hegemon cooperated with the rising hegemon.

Whether they were being entangled in surreptitious British plans to prolong the security of their imperial far waters or not, the US knew that the Second World War was the moment that it would be projecting force into far waters in both the Eastern and Western Hemispheres.[28] The pernickety details of squabbles between US and British military planners should not distract us from the bigger picture. Britain was in a process of being excluded from its far waters and accepting that it would need the military might of another country to secure its near waters. The US was in a process of extending its reach into far waters, even though it had to do this by negotiating the needs and legacies of a wily ally that was trying to maintain its own agenda.

But for the US, part and parcel of this change was securing its own near waters. US national security was dependent upon gaining and keeping control of three sets of near waters: the Atlantic and Pacific seaboards and the Caribbean Sea.[29] The near waters of the Pacific had been secured through two bold geographic moves. First was the annexation of Hawaii in 1898 and the creation of the Pearl Harbor naval base in 1908. Second was the purchase of Alaska from Russia in 1867 and the consequent control of the Aleutian Islands. The eastern flank of the Pacific Rim was under US control.

Securing the near waters of the Atlantic flank and the Caribbean was more complicated. The reason was that they were the far waters of Great Britain, the existing hegemonic power. Alfred Thayer Mahan's vision for US seapower was concerned about the potential reaction of the British.[30]

The easiest pathway to US seapower was through the avoidance of war with the British over the oceans that were both British far waters and US near waters.

The US success in controlling their Caribbean and Atlantic near waters was made possible because of the threat to British near and far waters. Britain was struggling against Germany and wary of the likelihood of war with Japan. The British retreat from the European continent meant that the "home waters" of the English Channel and the North Seas were under threat. The very homeland was under attack. The Battle of the Atlantic (which lasted from 1939 to 1945) was a grave concern. The British recognized that their ability to continue the fight against Germany could require a relocation of their armaments industry across the Atlantic into Canada and the US.[31] Churchill's doggedness to pursue the war against Germany from the Dominions if Britain was invaded showed how the loss of control of its near waters meant that invasion was a strong possibility.[32]

As German U-boats savaged the convoys providing food and industrial material to a vulnerable Britain a bargain was struck that would have made Mahan smile.[33] The Destroyers for Bases deal was negotiated in 1940 and finally settled in March 1941. It saddled Britain with fifty US destroyers to help patrol the Atlantic. The Town class destroyers dated from the First World War and were essentially useless. The superstructures were too weak to withstand Atlantic storms. The location of their guns meant that the ships were unstable and had a limited field of fire. And the torpedoes were ineffective at high speed and in choppy seas, common Battle of Atlantic conditions.[34] In return for these shoddy goods the US gained the leases of ports and waters of the British colonies of Trinidad, St. Lucia, and Bermuda, and the port of Halifax in Nova Scotia (map 4.3).[35]

Out-of-date warships for control of bases that secured the Caribbean and Atlantic near waters of the US: there's no doubt who got the better deal. The US Navy now had control of the bases, the islands, and US near waters to the extent of three hundred miles out to sea from the Newfoundland Bank to the West Indies islands.[36] Yet the geography of near and far waters is not precise but fuzzy. The extent of US control was written into the treaty. What it actually meant was less clear. For Secretary of State Cordell Hull, the arrangement was "flexible" and was the foundation for the US to "patrol out to sea whatever distance as might be necessary to protect our shoreline and territorial waters."[37] In other words, the Destroyers for Bases deal gave the US control of its near waters that not only provided immediate security but was the launching pad for projection into far waters.

But which far waters? And why? And in what way was the US in control

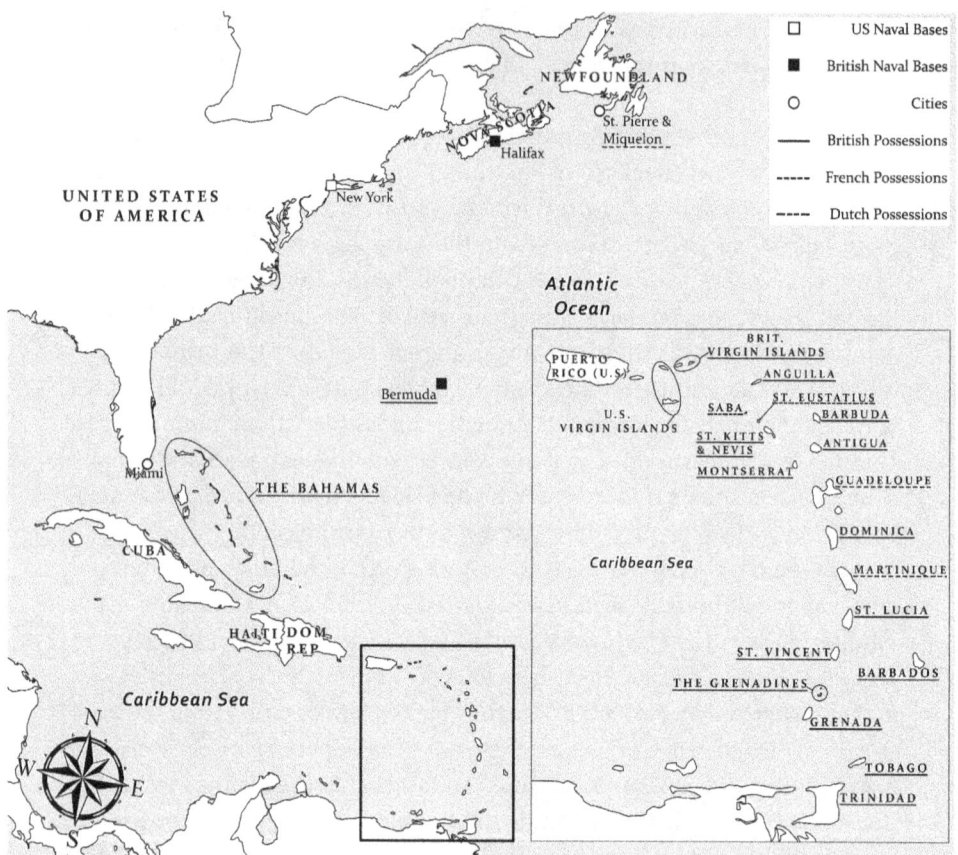

MAP 4.3. Destroyers for Bases and US near waters.

Source: Adapted by Carson Liesik from Maps of World, "What Was the Destroyers for Bases Agreement?," June 22, 2017, https://www.mapsofworld.com/answers/defence/destroyer-bases-agreement/#.

of this process or dependent, to some degree, on the needs and circumstances of the declining power Britain, and the challenges of Germany and Japan? Control of its near waters gave the US a secure foundation to project its power into far waters. The geography of one strategy of force projection is somewhat obvious. Controlling its Atlantic near waters allowed for projection of power into Atlantic far waters. But there's more. Projection of power into Atlantic far waters was part of a national security strategy that allowed for projection of power into Pacific far waters as well.[38]

Once the US entered the Second World War it knew it would be fighting on two flanks, in a Euro-Atlantic theater and an Asian-Pacific theater. What is surprising is that it made a commitment to aid Britain in the European theater before focusing upon Japan. The US knew that its Atlantic near waters would be threatened if Germany was to defeat Britain and control the western portion of the North Atlantic. Soon after the Destroyers for Bases deal, the US stationed troops in Iceland and Northern Ireland. The Brazilian coast and the West African port of Dakar were also identified as strategic points. These points were simultaneously defensive in that they countered German control of the Atlantic and a route to US territory, and a step toward force projection that resulted in military deployments in the Mediterranean, North Africa, and Europe.

Deploying troops to Iceland and Northern Ireland, and securing Brazil and the west coast of Africa, were done with an eye upon naval calculations, namely how to counter German force in the Atlantic.[39] The next step was to prepare for an invasion of the European continent itself, specifically Northwest Europe, to liberate France and march toward Berlin. Operation Bolero was put into effect, with the first convoy sailing from the US in April 1942.[40] This massive transfer of military personnel and armaments made Britain a military warehouse for US forces. The British Isles were a staging post for invasion and the subsequent US military presence in western and southern Europe.

But force projection toward Europe was done with an eye to US force projection in the Pacific. And this plan was hatched by considering the inability of the British to control both their near and far waters. The new American-British Conversation (ABC) Plans of March 1941 made clear that US force projection was a matter of British force projection. The security of the US depended upon preventing German control of the European continent. The US's "paramount territorial interest was in the Western Hemisphere."[41] But the ability of the British to exert control on the Continent required the support of the British Commonwealth and, specifically, its far waters in the Far East. If Britain could maintain control in those far waters, this would "assure the cohesion and security of the British Commonwealth; and the security of sea communications."[42] But once Japan's victories in Indochina exposed Britain's inability to secure those far waters, concern grew that Britain would not have the resources to defend its position in Europe and the homeland.

Britain's inability to control the Continent could result in German control of the French fleet, Britain being unable to control the eastern Atlantic, and an emerging threat to US Atlantic near waters. As stated by the Joint Planning Committee on December 21, 1940: "Our interests in the Far East are very important. It would, however, be incorrect to consider that they are as important to us as is the integrity of the Western Hemisphere, or as important as preventing the defeat of the British Commonwealth. *The issues in the Orient will largely be determined in Europe.*"[43]

The framework of near and far waters allows us to see the bigger picture. Only once the continent of Europe was secured could the US homeland be defended. The security of the Atlantic Ocean would then follow. The security of Atlantic near and far waters would then allow for power projection in the Pacific. And the insecurity of the Continent arose because Britain could not maintain its imperial assets in its Pacific far waters.

The US was reluctant to enter a war over control of the European continent. It took the initial step to enter the war for two reasons. First, it wanted to secure its Atlantic near waters. Second, it wanted to improve its position in Asian far waters. Fittingly, the political and military leaders of the US and Britain met on warships off Argentia, Newfoundland. The British made it clear that national security was a matter of access to far waters by securing the Middle East and the Mediterranean Sea.[44] Hence, the seeds of the future US commitment to fighting in North Africa were sown. The mutual concern over securing the Atlantic was also on the agenda. The primary concern was to neutralize the French Fleet before it could be used by the Germans in the Battle of the Atlantic. The failed British attempt to seize the West African port of Dakar in September 1940 had heightened this concern. There was also worry that Germany could control North and West Africa. German control of the African coast would secure the Mediterranean Sea for them and provide a launchpad to interdict Atlantic shipping and potentially attack the Americas.[45] German control of the African French Empire would give them control of ports from the North Cape to the Gulf of Guinea.[46]

In December 1941, the conversation between Britain and the US continued through meetings in Washington, D.C. The context had changed with the Japanese attack on Pearl Harbor. Yet while the US knew that an offensive campaign against Japan had to occur at some time, the Atlantic and Europe remained a focus. The split focus can be seen in US priorities for the deployment of the army: 1) "establishment of an air force based in Australia; 2) strengthening of other positions in the Pacific, especially Hawaii; 3) reinforcement of British troops in the Middle East; 4) 'acquisition' of positions in the South Atlantic—in northeastern Brazil, the Cape Verde Islands, or on the northwestern coast of Africa; and 5) relief of British garrisons in Northern Ireland and Iceland."[47]

The strategic puzzle that the US was now faced with was a mixture of two separate but related sets of near and far waters, their own and those of Great Britain. A September 1941 memo of the Joint Board of the Army and Navy had summarized the web of commitments:

Prevention of Axis Penetration into Northwest Africa and the Atlantic Islands is very important, not only as a contribution to the defense of the Western Hemisphere but also as security to British sea communications and as a potential base for a future land offensive. In French North and West Africa, French troops exist which are potential enemies of Germany, provided they are re-equipped and satisfactory political conditions are established by the United States. . . . It seems clear that a large proportion of the troops of the Associated Powers employed in this region necessarily must be United States troops.[48]

The memo showed awareness of a threat to US near waters from across the Atlantic; it also showed awareness that the defense of these near waters depended on British strength, which, in turn, depended on Britain's continued access to its subsidiary countries in its far waters. Security of US near waters required force projection in the form of troop deployments across the Atlantic and the Pacific and the making of "satisfactory political conditions."

In May 1941, President Franklin D. Roosevelt had painted a picture of threat to near waters through a radio broadcast to the American public by emphasizing that Dakar was just seven hours flying time from Brazil. He claimed that "the war is approaching the brink of the Western Hemisphere."[49] The previous month the secretary of the navy, the Honorable Frank Knox, had set the stage for the president in a speech with its own scary imagery: "Too few of us realize, and still fewer acknowledge the disaster to American hemispheric safety if Germany, already the conqueror of France, should establish herself in Dakar. From there, with her surface ships, submarines and long-range bombers, a victorious Germany could substantially cut us off from all commerce with South America, and make the Monroe Doctrine a scrap of paper."[50]

Prior to entry into the war American military planners had recognized that security of their near waters required preventing hostile forces controlling air and naval bases on the Atlantic African coast as far south as Dakar.[51] The success of Operation Torch in North Africa meant that Dakar could be secured through negotiation. With Dakar under their control, the Allies "could thus exercise undivided control of sea communications from the United Kingdom to the Cape of Good Hope."[52]

The US had taken the massive logistical undertaking of Operation Torch to alleviate the problem of near-water security that had concerned the US since before Pearl Harbor. By doing so it had crossed the national Rubicon of military commitment to ensure friendly control of the European continent. US near waters were suddenly more secure, but this had involved projection into far waters of the Mediterranean and the eastern Atlantic.

Yet other countries' far waters also had to be considered. Germany's invasion of Russia had given Japan the strategic room to advance into southern Indochina. An attack on the British subsidiary countries of Malaya and Singapore was in the offing. The US had to consider increasing the size of its military base in the Philippines.[53] The inability of Britain to defend its far waters meant that the US had to plan for a transfer of military capacity in the Pacific Ocean and make a declining hegemon's far waters its own.

Prior to the US entry into the Second World War, the spread of US political influence had begun through military missions within the Lend-Lease Agreement.[54] Lend-Lease was an extension of the Destroyers for Bases deal. It allowed President Roosevelt to support Britain, and later Russia, by sending war supplies across the Atlantic without formally joining the war. Notably, the first such mission was the American Military Mission to China (AMMISCA), created in August 1941 under the command of Brigadier General John A. Magruder to ensure the movement of material to China.[55] There were defensive and offensive components to the US commitment to Lend-Lease. It enabled control of near waters while also building the foundation for the projection of power into far waters, both Atlantic/Mediterranean and Pacific.

As the war developed, the US strategy of force projection included the transfer of subsidiary countries from prewar European colonial control to renewed stewardship within the new US-led world order. In November 1943 President Roosevelt emphasized to his military staff that the US should not make any commitments about returning colonies to France. These places included Indochina, New Caledonia, the Marquesas Islands, and Dakar. The president regarded Dakar as a continental outpost of the Americas.[56] The burden of force projection would be shared by junior allies. For example, the responsibility of keeping Dakar and its ports, airfields, and armaments under United Nations control was to fall to Brazil.[57] The mental map of US strategists blurred the importance of near and far waters as the US assumed Britain's prewar strategic dilemma of simultaneously securing near and far waters.

For Britain the geopolitical transition meant the loss of their dominance in once taken-for-granted far waters in the desperate exchange of Atlantic and Caribbean bases for dodgy destroyers and a retreat from Asia. It also meant British acceptance of the US as the defender of its near waters through the stationing of bases in the UK and the subjugation of British defense policy within NATO. The course of the First and Second World Wars changed global geopolitics. The shift in the geopolitical landscape can be marked as beginning with the Battle of the Somme as the mark of failure of Britain's attempt to pacify Europe and allow for dominance of trade and the oceans, and ending with the US taking on the role of the architect of a new "Congress of Europe" and establishing itself in the far waters of the western Pacific.

The US securing control of islands in the Atlantic enabled the islands of the Pacific to be seen as the next stepping-stones in US force projection through seapower (see chapter 8). It was a geopolitical transition in which Britain and the US cooperated. But what if the rising hegemonic power and the existing one are combative rather than cooperative? That question drives the contemporary relevance of the history of China's near and far waters.

China's Testing of Near and Far Waters

In June 2018, I was attending a conference held at Wuhan University. During a break I was invited, along with fellow geographer James D. Sidaway, to see the new Institute of Boundary and Ocean Studies. The foyer of the building was dominated by a metallic globe. The region of the South China Sea was facing the doorway, and a nine-dash line was the clearest feature on the artwork. The nine-dash line is China's statement of, in its view, the rightful claim to its self-defined near waters. We were invited to have our pictures taken next to the globe—two political geographers prominent in Western academia framing the representation of China's claim over the South China Sea. Tactfully, we declined.

Though I did not want to be caught in a picture that could be used to claim a tacit, at the least, endorsement of China's maritime claims, I am also uncomfortable with the way that the dispute is framed in most Western literature. Two major arguments concern me. One is that China is a new maritime power, with the implicit argument that it should leave the pursuit of seapower to the established Western powers. Of course, this is never said in such an explicit or crass way, but it is implied. The second argument is that the geography of maritime security in the Western Pacific, the South China Sea, and the Indian Ocean established since the Second World War is a peaceful one.[58] China is seen as the "assertive" country that must be "contained" to maintain a "balance." There needs to be more reflection on how and why China is "contained" and the way the status quo and the need to "balance" to protect it are the expression of dominance and power. The historic process of the geopolitics of near and far waters helps us understand China's current position and goals.

The Western Pacific and the South China Sea are a maritime region that became, through war and postwar militarization, the far waters of the US. They are also seen by China as its near waters, or important SLOCs that it needs to control to prevent interference in its near waters. And they are the parts of the ocean that China needs to control to prevent other seapowers from barring its access to far waters. In other words, the current moment is one in which the present global power's presence in far waters is being contested by a rising primary power, just as the US "asserted" control of its near waters from Spain and Britain in a previous era of "rebalancing."

The current discussion of China in the West raises a specter of growing Chinese "influence" across the Pacific and Indian Oceans. This type of rhetoric rests on an implicit message, or writing of history, that China has never been a maritime power. This is simply not true. Admittedly it has been a long time since China was a seapower, but in the 1400s it possessed oceangoing vessels five times the length of European ships, such as Christopher Columbus's *Santa Maria*.[59] And China was at the forefront of exploration, with Admiral Zheng He famously making seven trips to the Persian Gulf and the coast of East Africa between 1403 and 1433 (map 4.4).[60] I say "famously," but that needs to be qualified: recently and in China. Admiral Zheng He's feats have become part of China's representations of its history of friendly economic ties across the world that are being used in an attempt to nullify concerns about the BRI.

It is certainly true that China's age of maritime exploration was not only a long time ago but also short-lived. By the late 1400s the imperial navy was in decline, partly because of court politics as well as a changing economic situation. In sum, oceanic trade was less profitable and was part of a political minefield.[61] Chinese far-water ambitions were thwarted just when European countries were finding their oceangoing sea legs.

From the early 1500s China's maritime geopolitical concern became focused upon its near waters. China made attempts to exclude Western countries from establishing trade. This came as quite a shock to the Europeans, self-assured of their own superiority. Rebuffs from the Imperial Court evolved from being a puzzle and a nuisance to an economic crisis. In the mid-1800s the East India Company suffered a balance-of-payments crisis, as it was exporting tea, silks, and porcelain from China to Europe, but the Chinese had no desire to buy European manufactured goods. Importing opium from India was designed to solve this economic problem. The result was that Chinese near waters became the far waters for European countries and the US. China became the arena for primary country rivalries in the search for new markets.

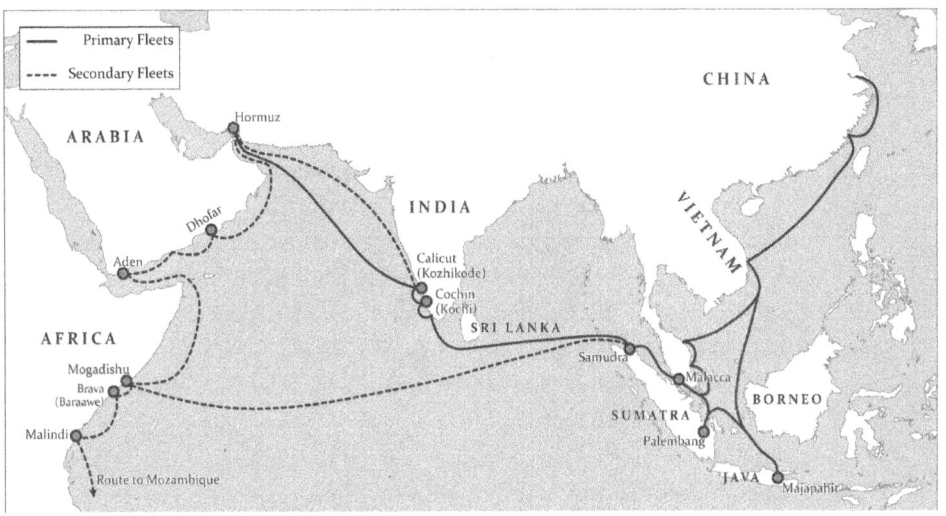

MAP 4.4. The voyages of Admiral Zheng He.

Source: Adapted by Carson Liesik from Brittanica, "Zheng He Timeline," accessed December 5, 2023, https://www.britannica.com/summary/Zheng-He-Timeline.

As easily as Chinese maritime power has been airbrushed out of history, so has its role as a member of the "united nations" alliance of the Second World War fighting Japan and Germany. China, along with Japan, also fought on the side of Britain, France, and the US in the First World War[62] (though the word *fought* has to be used generously, as the racism of the time relegated the role of the Chinese to sappers digging the trenches for white-skinned troops). Chinese people suffered casualties in the name of the cause nonetheless. China, simply but importantly, is the "forgotten ally."[63] Why importantly? Because the attempts and successes of the US to cultivate ties with China were a particular geographic strategy in their goal of extending reach into far waters. The US wanted to have, at the least, "influence" in China and Asia—that very same word that is used today to paint a picture of insidious Chinese goals in the very same region of the world.

The US goal of "influence" was so prized that the blame game of who was responsible for "losing" China, as if the country was akin to a set of keys, was a political wedge in the US partisan battles of the early Cold War. Politicians, government officials, and academics came under the scrutiny of Cold War zealots such as Senator Joseph McCarthy at the culmination of his campaign in 1954.[64] The geopolitical backdrop for these unsavory and damaging actions was the frustration of the US. Its arrogance had hidden the likelihood that China could resist the projection of US power and limit the extent of its influence. The 1949 victory of Mao's Chinese Communist Party in the civil war that was already brewing before the Second World War ended meant that US ideological and territorial ambitions were going to be limited to some degree. Ideologically, there was an alternative to US ideas of development, or the global adoption of a postimperial capitalism. Communist ideology and practice had their Soviet and Chinese variations, differences that were later to be exploited by the US. But immediately after the Second World War the US response was to identify communism as a monolithic and singular form of challenge. Territorially, Mao's victory in the Chinese Civil War meant that all the hopes for postwar trade and business ties with the US were halted.

And yet Mao's victory and US defeat were both partial. The Chinese Nationalists retreated to the island of Taiwan. The US played a role in the political machinations that ended the Chinese Civil War. In the words of Secretary of State Dean Acheson, there was a "wish to separate the island from mainland control."[65] The US hope was for rule by military commanders who were "liberal and efficient."[66] The Nationalists took control of Taiwan Island, and other offshore islands, but the government was close to bankruptcy and collapse. The Nationalist presence on Taiwan was initially bankrolled by US support.[67] In hindsight this support can be seen as a step in establishing a strong US presence in Chinese near waters. But the pathway was tentative and piecemeal. On January 5, 1950, President Harry S. Truman said the US would not get involved in this "civil conflict" and would not provide military aid. The British recognized the People's Republic of China on the same day.[68] It seemed that the "forgotten ally" had been abandoned and that battles over control of China's near waters were to be left to the Chinese.

But with the PRC's invasion of Hainan Island and the outbreak of the Korean War in 1950, Taiwan became part of Cold War calculations. The relationship with Taiwan was far from perfect or satisfactory, but President Truman promoted economic aid, military training, and intelligence cooperation with the Nationalist government.[69] A frustrated PRC had to go along with the arrangement. It had neither the military or political clout to change the situation until 1971, when Secretary of State Henry Kissinger and President Richard Nixon saw a way out of the quagmire in Vietnam and a way to split the Sino-Soviet relationship by recognizing the PRC. The Taipei delegation to the United Nations was ousted, and the PRC took its place on the Security Council. Part of the deal was a US military withdrawal from Taiwan.

In some ways, Taiwan was sold down the river. It lost its status as a member of the United Nations, but it also knew it had political support from the US and the promise of military protection. On the other hand, China labeled the island as a "breakaway province." The strong economic ties between China and Taiwan have not been enough for President Xi Jinping and an increasingly raucous set of nationalist devotees. As China's political, economic, and military strength have grown, so has its ambition to, in its view, "unite" China. It retook control of Hong Kong in 1997, not through war but by waiting for a postimperial agreement to expire. Since then Taiwan has become the focus of geopolitical tensions in Chinese near waters/US far waters

Through the lens of near and far waters, China became an independent country after the Second World War, free of the shackles of imperial competition. But its near waters were not its own. The US presence in the Western Pacific, gained through the bloody struggle with Japan, included US support for Taiwan. Though the US military presence was reduced after the recognition of the PRC, it was not long before the US started to sell arms to Taiwan and commit to defending the island if China were to invade. Until recently, without the necessary naval power China had little ability to police its own near waters. The situation is akin to the US's concern over the presence of Spain and Britain in the Caribbean through the 1800s. For the latter half of the twentieth century this was not too much of a problem for China. It was not an export-oriented economy, nor did it have the wealth to build a strong navy. Its wars were with its territorial neighbors. The US presence in, for them, the far waters of the western Pacific was largely uncontested.

China's attitude toward its near waters has changed as its economy has grown and come to rely on maritime trade. The view from the shores of China is one in which a foreign power is on the horizon.[70] China wants control of its near waters, those areas of the ocean that have been US far waters since the end of the Second World War. The projection of US power through its Pacific navy and its bases in Japan, Guam, and the Philippines is no longer an uncontested or reluctantly accepted geopolitical circumstance. Instead, US force projection into far waters is facing a counterpolicy of "area denial"—a very geographic term describing the military strategy of employing defensive devices to prevent forces from traveling through or occupying an area.[71] The US military recognizes that its aircraft carrier task forces would be in extreme danger from missile attack if conflict were to break out in these dual near waters/far waters, depending on the national perspective.

One part of such calculations is debate about the military ability and political will of the US to defend Taiwan if China were to invade. Military maneuverings are matched by a rhetorical battle. The US presence in China's near waters is seen as defense of a "rules-based" global order.[72] This rhetoric is similar to language seen throughout history, in which the dominant maritime power and its allies advocate for an environment of freedom of navigation to support the patterns of global trade they benefit from. But freedom of navigation for some is presence in near waters for others.

China's desire to eject the US and its allies from Chinese near waters is not necessarily a threat to a global norm of maritime trade.[73] Why would China want to challenge that system? It needs to export its products, and it needs to import the necessary inputs. An economy based upon supply chains is not going to oppose maritime trade. Another way to look at this is to recognize China's concern that lack of control of its near waters could easily lead to economic strangulation, the old geopolitical weapon of blockade—a concern for the global Dutch, a key part of Britain's strategy against Napoleon, and the way that Germany nearly brought Britain to its knees.

Global, regional, and local calculations lie behind China's drive for seapower.[74] This project starts with China's desire to secure its near waters and prevent them from being US far waters. But China's economic strategy is also one that harks back to the dynastic days of China as the Middle Kingdom. In modern-day language China wants to be the dominant economy in the region of Southeast Asia. It also wants to claim sovereignty over fishing and oil and gas resources in the region. Plus, it needs the South China Sea to be free from the threat of blockade so that its global trade cannot be impeded. Hence, it has created the idea of the nine-dash line that it so proudly displays (map 4.5). Legitimizing this claim to mastery of a key maritime region would be a geopolitical success for China. That's why it would like smiling Western academics to be photographed next to one such representation, the one on the globe at Wuhan University.

But it's not all just representation. A legal route to claiming the South China Sea as near waters was rebuffed in July 2016 when the Permanent Court of Arbitration at The Hague rejected China's argument that it had sovereign rights because of a history of control. Since then, the matter has become increasingly military, with the US frequently sailing through oceans claimed as EEZs by China in what it calls "freedom of navigation" operations to uphold the "rule of law."[75] Since the legal rebuff China has been busy creating a military navy.

China's regional and global ambitions require building a blue-water navy that can reach into far waters. The process is underway, but the pace

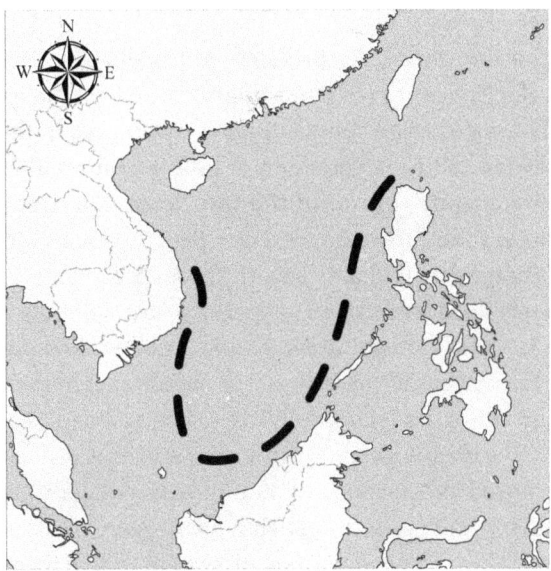

MAP 4.5. CHINA'S NINE-DASH LINE.

Source: Original work by Carson Liesik, using multiple sources freely available on the internet.

and intended scope are unclear.[76] The current means of global projection of seapower are aircraft carrier task forces and landing units. Such military hardware is designed not just to secure far waters but to use that ability to achieve goals *on land*. At the moment, China is a long way from that sort of capability. And yet, the potential for China to build the naval capacity to have a presence in far waters, accompanied with the vague yet apparently threatening potential for "influence," has been enough to ratchet up a Western response.

In a relatively short period of time, policy has moved from President Obama's "pivot to Asia," to academic debates about the making of a new geopolitical region (the Indo-Pacific), to the formation of the AUKUS alliance and the Quad.[77] Area denial in China's near waters may be largely accomplished, or at least a game changer. China's challenge to other countries' presence in the near/far waters of the Western Pacific indicates that a new geopolitical moment has emerged. The assumed far-water presence of the US is no longer a given. The focus is now on the potential conflict between China and the US in those parts of the ocean that are far waters for both countries,[78] especially the western part of the Indian Ocean and the SLOCs connecting the Middle East to the rest of the world.

The presence of the Dutch, the British, and the US in far waters was intended to develop trade ties with subsidiary countries. The end result was not a strengthening of weak countries but a weakening of the strong. The primary countries had to juggle many military commitments across the globe, and subsequently this taxed the very economic strength that they had used to build their far-water presence. Seapower may well be a virtuous circle of increasing national wealth through the projection of naval power on the upside of a country's geopolitical arc.[79] But the downslope is one in which the commitment to far waters is costly. And one reason it is costly is that the actions of the country in far waters are met by reactions from subsidiary countries who would like to control their near waters.

In contrast to a classic geopolitical view that these rising military tensions can be viewed as "great power" conflicts, the underlying cause is the need of primary countries to establish advantageous economic ties with subsidiary countries. The geopolitics of seapower is driven by the economic imperatives of trade. And that geopolitics of trade is the topic of the next chapter.

FIVE

The Geopolitics of Primary-Subsidiary Trade

The strong will not make the weak strong. This maxim applies to global trade relations that generally benefit the richer countries. And because of the inequity of the relationship, the required use of force should be expected; that's one purpose of seapower. Yet it is also likely that the weak will make the strong weak. As this chapter shows, hegemonic countries have felt the need to project power into far waters to maintain unequal trade relations, and over time that projection has led to security concerns that have challenged their power and required the use or threat of violence. These security concerns related to subsidiary countries in far waters have been the chief driving force behind hegemonic decline. They have also been a driving force in processes that increase the likelihood of global war.

Securing passage across the sea is necessary for trade. The ocean as a means of passage for commerce has been a constant focus of geopolitics.[1] The extreme acts of blockade, and the sinking and seizing of ships, are at one end of a continuum of the geopolitics of trade. Cooperation to ensure passage through choke points and shared rules of navigation lie at the other end. The most powerful countries in the world have promoted freedom of navigation as a commonsense policy.[2] The ability of some countries to dominate global trade across the oceans is presented as something to be taken for granted. It is not seen as political, or an act of geopolitics, just as common sense. On the other hand, actual and potential challenges to freedom of navigation are seen as acts of geopolitical bravado. Outside periods of declared war, established primary powers advocate for, and manage, freedom of navigation.[3] Countries attempting to challenge the geopolitical status quo may resort to challenging established patterns of ocean trade.[4] In a moment of geopolitical transition, the established practices and patterns are no longer to be taken for granted, and gunboat diplomacy comes to the fore. We are in such a moment.

Patterns of ocean trade are a matter of the geography of production and how it changes over time. The geopolitics of production and trade rest on a global relationship in which some countries can capture within their territories the new and highly profitable production of new things. Other countries must settle for making and trading less profitable products.[5]

The relations between these two forms of production drive maritime trade in two ways. One is the need to sell the finished product by exporting to markets beyond one's border. The other is the need for inputs to make the highly profitable products. These relationships are unequal.[6] The inequality is the main driver of the geopolitics between primary and subsidiary countries. It has also been, throughout history, a source of antagonism and conflict between primary countries. It is at the center of the tensions of the current state of geopolitics.

Production in primary and subsidiary countries is connected by what have been called commodity chains or global production networks. These connections have certainly become more complex in the recent age of "globalization" and just-in-time manufacturing.[7] However, the fundamental relationship of lower-value and less profitable products being shipped across the globe to be assembled in another country to become a more expensive and more profitable product has been, in one form or another, a long-standing feature of the world.

The products that make up the inputs have been called "the generative sector" because they generate the wealth of the primary countries.[8] Any country wishing to climb to the top of the economic ladder needs to gain secure access to the generative sector. The problem for them is that established primary countries have gotten there first and are reluctant to give up control of their source of wealth. For example, Japan's attempts to modernize required greater access to oil and rubber in Southeast Asia. This ambition led to Japan's Second World War ambitions to oust European imperial powers amid the US's own ambitions to strengthen its economic presence in Asia.

The generative sector consists of two separate segments. One is the already-existing combination of required inputs and their geographies. For example, oil has been an essential input since the beginning of the twentieth century and, despite moves toward other energy sources, will remain important. The Middle East has been the focus of the geopolitics of the oil industry.[9] The other segment is the newly essential inputs for new highly profitable products. For example, rare earth minerals have come to the fore as essential in the production of computing technologies and renewable energy production. China has dominated the production of rare earth minerals, though this is now being challenged by concerned primary countries.[10] Underlying the two segments of the generative sector is the need for food imports as countries trying to industrialize become more urban.

To put it simply, unequal economic relations with subsidiary countries are necessary for the success of primary countries. The creation and enforcement of these relations have required violence, or the projection of power to places across the globe. Seapower is the way force has been projected and trading relations protected. As Admiral Corbett noted in 1911, seapower is a matter of being able to achieve things on land.[11] Those things are usually matters of establishing economic relations favorable to primary countries rather than great land battles of history. The former is the everyday way in which the world works. The latter are notable moments of military history. The geopolitics of seapower works to allow the former to seem mundane and to avoid the latter.[12]

This chapter explores the interconnected geopolitics of production, trade, and the projection of force. Historical lessons from the periods of Dutch, British, and US hegemony help us understand the contemporary geopolitics of China's Belt and Road Initiative (BRI) as a means to establish new generative sector relations. The story of the Dutch shows how domestic economic growth is based on relations with subsidiary countries in far waters. The transition from British to US hegemony shows how the rise to power occurs within, and because of, existing primary-subsidiary relations. The geopolitical stage is set, to some degree. The period of US hegemony shows how primary countries create "interests" in subsidiary countries. Finally, the chapter focuses on the extent to which China's new connections with subsidiary countries suggest that they are following a historical pathway similar to that of previous hegemons. The historical comparisons are of concern, as such geopolitical transitions have in the past led to global conflict.

The term *interests* is used by politicians and commentators to refer to economic activity by companies with a national affiliation that may warrant intervention by the government if that activity is threatened. It is a clever geopolitical representation because it implies that the economic activity of a company is for the benefit of all citizens of a country rather than just the shareholders. Using the word *national* justifies the use of a country's military to ensure a company's profit margin, though the general public does also benefit from trade in, say, oil or bananas. I use *"interests,"* with quotation marks, when rhetoric is used to justify a country's military action, and I use *interests* without the quotation marks when I am simply pointing out economic activity in another country. The key point is that interests are protected through the projection of force that seapower allows.

The Dutch Innovation of the Active Entrepôt

The greatest Dutch innovation was the entrepôt: a port city where goods were held for import and export. It may seem odd that a variation of warehousing would prove to be a means and outcome of geopolitical success. But the ability to control when goods were shipped from place to place allowed for the manipulation of their price. Storing things ashore meant that ships could be just ships, freeing them up to carry more goods more frequently from place to place. And storing things meant that they could be put on the market at a time and in a quantity that maximized profit.[13] Amsterdam became what Jonathan Israel has termed an "active entrepôt," or one that was at the center of a global network of trade, rather than relying on a more geographically immediate pattern of trade.[14] The idea of the "active entrepôt" points us in the direction of the geopolitics of near and far waters. Building Amsterdam into an entrepôt in the latter decades of the sixteenth century and into the next century makes sense only in connection to other parts of the world, the ones from which commodities were brought and the places where finished products were sold. Looking at Amsterdam alone, despite its majesty as the most dynamic and modern city in the world at the time, gives us an incomplete picture.

The success and wealth of Amsterdam were built by what the Dutch were doing in other parts of the world: business and military actions that ensured the flow of products into the warehouses of Amsterdam. The active entrepôt is at one end of a global trade network. At the other end are places that are being dominated and maneuvered to act as sources of commodities that are fed into the manufacturing economies of primary countries. In other words, at one end is the generative sector of extraction.[15] Dominance in global trade connects regions of extraction to the active entrepôt. Or the activity of the entrepôt is to build the geography of the generative sector. And the entrepôt is the beating heart of new industries that are selling new products for great profit.[16]

Amsterdam made the switch from just any old location of warehouses to an active entrepôt through dominance of a regional trade system, the near waters of the Baltic.[17] The growing wealth of Amsterdam stemmed from the Dutch dominance in the Baltic trade in the 1500s. This trade required relations with other places, such as Gdansk to establish the grain trade. The flow of whale oil, potash, leather, and caviar from Archangel in the White Sea, or the unromantic commodities of tar and pitch from Viborg, meant that Dutch merchants could build up a pool of savings and invest in bigger and better trade networks.[18] The money from the bulk trades in the Baltic was the means to make Amsterdam an active entrepôt. The method was to make new global trade networks connecting to other places. Curaçao in the Caribbean was captured in 1634, and Fort Maurits in Brazil was first controlled three years later. Both were key starting points of the Atlantic trade (map 5.1).[19]

And success bred success. Around 1670 the Dutch presence in Asia was at its height, with forts on the eastern and western coasts of India, and forts and ports stretching from Fort Zeelandia in Taiwan to Manila in the

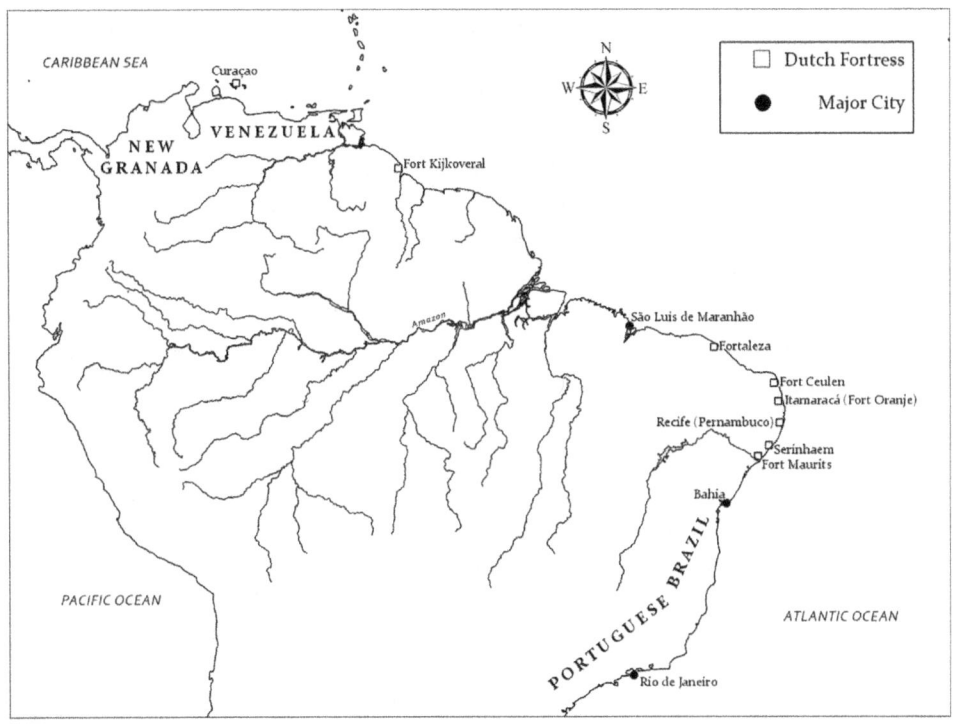

MAP 5.1. DUTCH BRAZIL.

Source: Drawn by Carson Liesik, based on and adapted from figure 5.3 (p. 166) in Jonathan Israel's *Dutch Primacy in World Trade, 1585–1740* (Oxford: Clarendon Press, 1989).

Philippines, and through the East Indies to Jambi in Sumatra and Malacca in what is now Malaysia.[20] Amsterdam, the city at the heart of the national rise of the Dutch, was an economic success because of its trade ties with other places. Those ties were bound up with the geopolitics of coercion and influence through seapower and the making of far waters.

Amsterdam was at the center of another web of geopolitical relations, and that was competition between primary countries to host the world's most important entrepôt. The period of Amsterdam's dominance was bookended by the eclipse of Antwerp around 1580 and by the emergence of ports in England as the new center of global trade beginning in the 1720s.[21] The eclipse of Antwerp as the dominant entrepôt was partly a result of war with Spain, which laid siege to the city and was able to approach the Scheldt, the waterway that connected Antwerp to the ocean.[22]

Similarly, the decline of Amsterdam fed, and was fed by, competition between primary countries. Especially, the growing presence of Britain in India and in the Caribbean and trans-Atlantic trade was coupled with the loss of the ability of the Dutch to trade directly with China. In the mid-1700s the world began to drift to war between primary countries, with tensions between France and Britain, and with the American Revolutionary War. Despite these rivalries and conflicts, the world's trading countries looked to Britain to be the major shipping power and set the rules of oceanic trade.[23] In tandem, Amsterdam ceased to be an active entrepôt and resorted back to its former role as simply a point for storage rather than storage as part of a manufacturing economy that was able to make a lot of money.[24]

Unsurprisingly, active entrepôts are the key locations of wealth generation in the world. Primary countries vie for their cities to play that role and contribute to the national economy. Such competition requires, at times, the threat or use of force, whether in near waters or far waters. In a geopolitical transition where there is a clear declining and rising hegemonic power, there is potential for a transfer of control of economic interests and near waters without conflict between them, though such a process involves conflict with other primary countries and though the fading and emerging hegemonic countries are not always on the same page. The transition from British to US hegemony is a case in point.

The Twin Trends of British Decline and US Rise

Surprisingly, immediately after the First World War Britain's strategic position seemed quite rosy. This is because it was still thinking in terms of global seapower and far waters, rather than a continental battle and threats to its near waters and homeland. The British strategy depended on maintaining control over subsidiary countries through the institutions of empire (map 5.2). It also required a global network of naval bases.[25] But in the period of British decline this control began to require considering rising primary countries: Japan, Germany, and the United States. Despite the continued focus in British culture on the fight with Germany in the Second World War, it was the questions of primary-subsidiary relations that were central to Britain's predicament and the transition from British to US hegemony.

When Neville Chamberlain became prime minister in 1937 a new strategy was adopted in which attempts to use a British show of force on the Continent as a form of deterrence was replaced by a defensive stance. The call was to build fighter planes rather than bombers, and the Army Field Force to be deployed in Belgium and France was "pared down into insignificance."[26] Neville Chamberlain and Foreign Secretary Lord Halifax showed sympathy for the German leader Adolf Hitler's plans to move eastward across the continent to gain *lebensraum* (living space) for the German people.[27] After a meeting with Lord Halifax and Sir Nevile Henderson, British ambassador to Germany, Hitler thought he had a green light for his military campaign to the east. He was encouraged by Britain's refusal to make any form of agreement with the Soviet Union.

Britain seemed to have no interest in getting embroiled in a territorial conflict in central and eastern Europe.[28] In early 1939, Britain thought the threat of a European war had declined, and it planned to take advantage

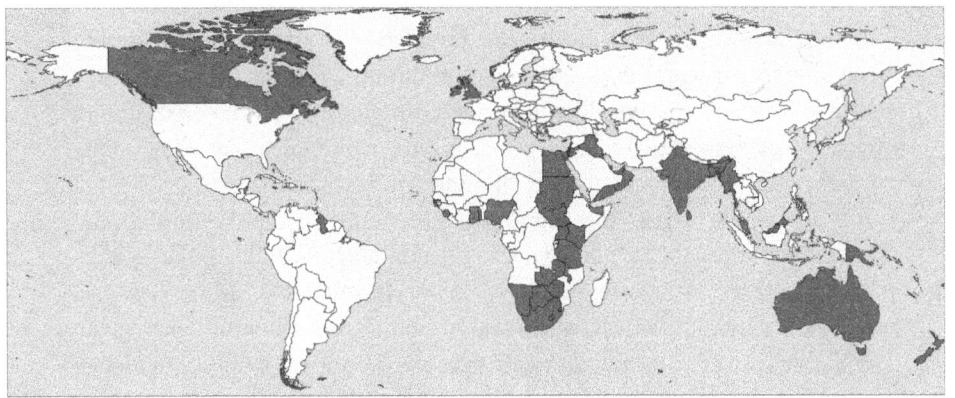

MAP 5.2. The British Empire.

Source: Original work by Carson Liesik, using multiple sources freely available on the internet.

of a perceived weak German economy by working on a commercial treaty with what was soon to become its archenemy.[29] For Britain, the near waters and the neighboring continent were not the area of concern.

Instead of Germany and Hitler, the strategic troubles for Britain stemmed from problems with subsidiary countries in far waters. In terms of trade and economics Britain had benefited from a global and decentralized system. But this very same system came to be a problem once its hegemony was challenged. Economic success had meant that a controlled wartime economy was an unnecessary burden.[30] A lot of faith was put in the international system and its institutions to maintain global peace, mainly because Britain had created the system.[31] But strategically the system that allowed for economic success was a doorway to military vulnerability.

The flip side to global economic reach with minimal political control to reduce costs was a loosely connected set of allies and interests. Britain's ability to coordinate and mobilize resources was surprisingly limited.[32] And it was the past benefits of global seapower that now became a strategic weakness. British hegemony was based on a "marine archipelago"—or a set of islands and territories that were the means and ends of global force projection into far waters.[33] Its resources were spread thin and hard to coordinate. Naval power that had helped Britain become a global power was not easy to reorganize when the balance of power shifted and challenges appeared in far waters first, and then near waters.

It was Japan in far waters rather than Germany in near waters that first concerned Britain after the First World War. Britain's global reach included interests in China. The Opium Wars of the 1840s and 1850s had cemented China as an important arena in the circuit of global trade. In the 1930s, Britain still wanted to keep its trade interests in China. It worried that opposing the Japanese invasion of Manchuria in 1931 would bolster the Chinese nationalist movement, especially the Kuomintang.[34] If Japan's presence in China was to be challenged, would Britain's presence be the next foreign power to face resistance? Hence, Britain did not challenge the imperialism of one country to protect its own far-waters imperialism (map 5.3).

What can be seen as the opening gambit of the Second World War, the Japanese invasion of Manchuria, was not challenged by Britain because of the importance of its own primary-subsidiary relations. Britain was also worried about how its fleet would fare in a confrontation with Japan, given the latter's surprising success against Russia in 1905.[35] Britain's tendency toward appeasement arising from self-interest and worries about relative military prowess was first seen in Asian far waters and not European near waters.

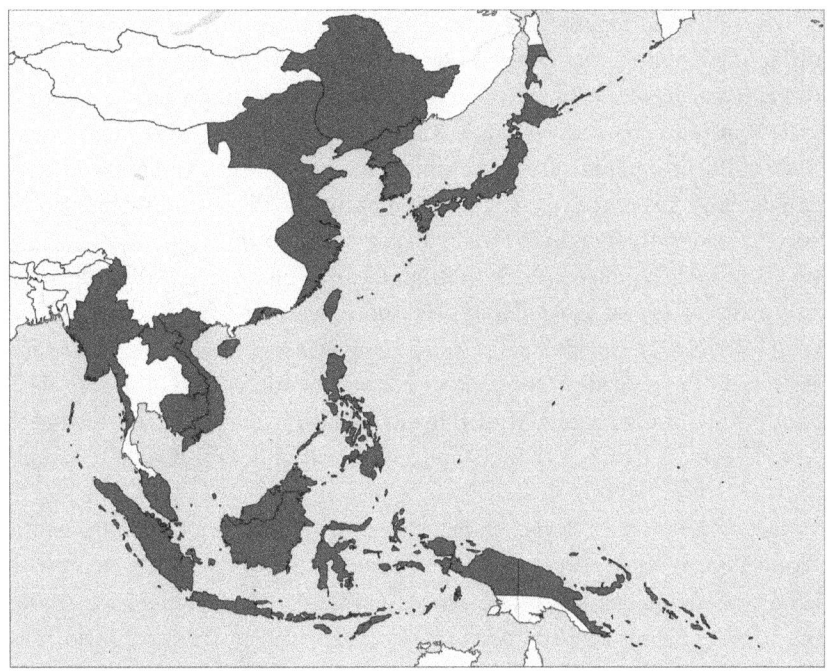

MAP 5.3. The Japanese Empire.
Source: Original work by Carson Liesik, using multiple sources freely available on the internet.

It was the oceanic connections of Britain's "marine archipelago" that concerned its admirals.[36] The oceans were the conduit of Britain's primary-subsidiary relations, the framework of its global power. But Japan had been building naval strength from its northern borderland with Russia (the Kuril Islands), through the western Pacific (Taiwan), and into the Central and South Pacific.[37] Japan's continental ambitions were also a threat to British subsidiary interests in Burma, Singapore, and Southeast Asia. The Dutch still retained their own subsidiary interests in Southeast Asia but could offer limited military help.[38]

What had been assets for British seapower quickly became vulnerabilities. The SLOCs connecting the Pacific Ocean to the Indian Ocean were under threat. The once-loyal Dominions that had been a source of manpower in the First World War were now restless and seeking British resources for their defense. The strategic and economic balance had flipped. If British possessions in the Pacific and Indian Ocean were lost, then Australia and New Zealand were also threatened, and next would be the east coast of Africa.[39]

The situation had certainly been building over time, reminding us to think of geopolitics as a process. Before the First World War, British imperial defense was based on two likely challenges. The first was a European-wide war, and the second was a Russian invasion of India.[40] The Royal Navy believed it could defend the sinews of empire because there would be one decisive sea battle, a concentration of forces, that Britain expected to win.[41] Any relatively minor threats to remote parts of the empire could, it was assumed, be taken care of through local defense forces.[42] But the 1899 war in South Africa showed that local forces were insufficient. In the First World War Britain needed help from its overseas territories to defend itself, especially the crucial crossroads of communications in the Middle East and the Mediterranean.[43] After the war Britain came to recognize that it would have great difficulty in defending its near and far waters at the same time.

New friends had to be made. And given knowledge of the Second World War, it may be surprising to recognize that it was with Japan that Britain made its first twentieth-century alliance. This happened in 1902, three years before the infamous secret deal with France tying Britain to the defense of France and Belgium that led to slaughter in the battles of the Somme and Passchendaele. The British trained and equipped the Japanese fleet.[44] The deal with Japan paid dividends as the Imperial Japanese Navy helped secure British imperial trade routes in the Pacific and Indian Oceans and the Mediterranean Sea in the First World.[45] In other words, Asian far waters led Britain away from its established policy of "splendid isolation" and was the motivation for British rearmament.[46] Concern for near waters followed.

The situation changed after the First World War in three ways. First, the heavy losses of life had changed public opinion in the Dominions. If they were to fight for Britain's survival again, they would demand a stronger say in strategic decisions. And this opinion was not helped by a sense that the British fleet would not always be willing and able to appear on the horizon when needed.[47] Second, Japan now appeared to be a threat rather than an ally, but the likely point of conflict was between Japan and the United States. The latter had become Britain's key ally. So Britain had to balance its relations with two potential adversaries while thinking of its own interests.[48] But such balance was increasingly difficult to maintain because of the third change, the growing influence of the United States.

The US had become a global power through its military intervention in the First World War and its diplomatic and financial management of the postwar peace. It now used that power to establish the balance of global seapower. The Washington Conference of November 1921 led to the three Washington Agreements of 1922.[49] They were

a) A naval limitations agreement that established a 5:5:3 ratio of capital ships between, respectively, the United States, Great Britain, and Japan. Not surprisingly, the British and the Japanese had their own reasons for being upset with this arrangement.

b) A broader agreement that respected the sovereignty and territorial integrity of China—more accurately a way for the United States to protect and expand its influence in China.

c) An agreement between the United States, Great Britain, Japan, and France not to build new fortifications and bases in the "Pacific region," which conveniently for the US excluded Hawaii and, for Britain, excluded Singapore but not Hong Kong.

These three agreements were the building blocks for the emergent US global seapower. They were also all about the far waters of great powers and not their near waters. The naval limitations agreement was a step toward putting US seapower on a par with Britain. The agreement on China was the US attempt to make sure it could develop its economic interests across the Pacific and make primary-subsidiary relations to its benefit while trying to limit similar opportunities for others, especially Japan. And the third agreement was an attempt to "demilitarize" the Pacific, which was advantageous to the US as a growing, rather than established, power. The changing balance of power between primary countries was being driven by geopolitics in the far waters of two countries and the near waters of another. The driving concerns were building and keeping primary-subsidiary relations.

The British were wrestling with a security dilemma that stretched them between near and far waters. They were trying to show a credible response to Japan's threat to Britain's imperial Asian interests. But it was certain that they could not defend those interests if a war in Europe occurred at the same time. The very idea of being able to respond to Japanese aggression anyway was undermined by building a naval base in Singapore of an inadequate capacity to house a fleet large enough to protect Britain's Asian far waters. "Despite that, by 1930 it was the only British empire grand strategy for any war against Japan."[50] Britain had no strategy to defend its Asian far waters. It was going to need help from the United States. The way Britain and the US cooperated resulted in British far waters becoming US far waters.

The strategic dilemma was that if the East was neglected the empire might fall. But if the West was exposed, Britain itself might be invaded. Britain's near waters and far waters were at risk. The two oceanic areas were connected. There was no such thing as a British domestic economy or national defense. Britain's economy was global, and its defense required protection of interests in subsidiary countries, including its Dominions, and its homeland. Losing control of the subsidiary interests in far waters, or the trade connections between them and the "home" economy, would mean even less funding for homeland defense. Japanese military strength had made this clear. One way out for Britain was to make friends with an emerging power that also had interests in the Far East: in other words, a common area of far waters.

Britain and the US Begin to Share a Concern about Japan

In fact, the much-vaunted "special relationship" between Britain and the US was founded on a need to work side by side in the Far East.[51] Without formalizing a security arrangement, Britain and the United States made a "parallel but not joint policy" for the Far East.[52] The policy recognized that though Japan's main adversary was the Soviet Union, any conflict between the two countries would likely be fought in China. And if Britain became involved it would have to face its biggest naval rival—Japan.[53] But Britain and the US were wary of developing a formal alliance. The British thought that an alliance would provoke a Japanese attack. And the US was concerned that public opinion would oppose a foreign policy seemingly supporting British imperial interests.[54]

But of course the Japanese did attack and the US joined the Second World War to support Britain. The Japanese had gained the confidence to attack British possessions in the Far East after Operation Barbarossa, the German attack on the Soviet Union. Soviet troops moved to the European front, and with China under Japan's thumb, and the French out of the war, this seemed like Japan's opportunity.[55] The reason for Japan's attack on Pearl Harbor (December 7, 1941) was a concern that the US would act to support Britain in Asia.[56] Japan wanted to expand into the common far waters of Britain and the US. Though there was an opportunity to do this, attacking the far waters of the declining hegemonic power and the near waters of the emerging hegemonic power was always going to be a huge, if not impossible, task.

Japan's strategy of modernization and economic growth began as a continental strategy. The maritime focus was on near waters. The steps toward military involvement in East and South Asia were a peripheral or attritional strategy aimed at US and British interests in Asia to get them to cut off aid to China.[57] Subsequently, the peripheral strategy became the "southern strategy" as oil resources in the Dutch East Indies were eyed in light of the US embargo and the awareness of a need to expand the scope of the struggle in the Pacific. Japan's movement away from the near waters necessary for its continental ambitions was made with some reluctance and with a recognition that it was unlikely to result in victory.[58]

The movement away from Japan's near waters into conflict in the eastern Pacific, or US near waters, would have seemed surprising just a couple of decades earlier. Japan depended on imports of US iron and steel scrap, gasoline, and oil.[59] Japan's main concern was growing Soviet influence in Siberia and its Pacific near waters.[60] Trade between the US and Japan was high—a cautionary tale when considering today's web of economic connections between China and the US. In fact, the US interest in Pacific far waters was rather muted until the combination of German and Japanese military expansion changed the equation.

The US had been promoting a "balance of power" strategy in the region that mirrored the "level playing field" hopes of its Open Door policy, making China something of an equal-opportunity generative sector for primary countries. The hope was for a multilateral approach to restrict Japan's ambitions.[61] The Washington and London peace conferences of the 1920s had limited US ability to project naval power into the western Pacific. Increasingly, frustrations with these restrictions meant that the US presence in the region was to be achieved through cooperation with Britain. The western Pacific was to be both US and British far waters. As the US and British were both restricted from building military installations east of Singapore, the future ability of US naval force projection was to be made in collaboration with British needs and strengths,[62] though such perceived strengths were to prove very disappointing.

Japan's military presence in China that turned into full-scale war shattered US attempts to maintain peace and open trade policies. The US tone became tougher. Secretary of State Henry L. Stimson had tried to draw a line against Japanese expansion. But in 1932 he had to admit that his diplomatic weapons were merely "spears of straw and swords of ice."[63] The changing global context gave room for a new policy favorable to naval projection of force when navy veteran Franklin D. Roosevelt became president. "The Roosevelt navy was a growth enterprise."[64] Naval expansion into far waters was now on the agenda. It was connected to the goal of expanding global trade in Roosevelt's 1937 "quarantine speech": "The overwhelming majority of the peoples and nations of the world today want to live in peace. They seek the removal of barriers against trade. They want to exert themselves in industry, in agriculture and in business, that they may increase their wealth through the production of wealth-producing goods rather than striving to produce military planes and bombs and machine guns and cannon for the destruction of human lives and useful property."[65] In other words, the expansion of global trade was going to require US presence in far waters.

The irony was that the US was going to have to expand into the far waters of the Pacific because these were also the far waters of European allies, whose empires President Roosevelt wanted to throw in the dustbin of history. But Japan's own growing military arrogance and expressions of Pan-Asianism were set to disrupt the established geography of imperial access to a generative sector. US growth would not be possible if that generative sector region was firmly within a Japanese Co-Prosperity Sphere (in reality, a bounded Japanese empire). In conjunction with weakened European allies, the US realized that establishing Pacific far waters would have to go hand in hand with its postimperial visions of global free trade. A further irony was that the ability to project power into the Pacific required that the imperial powers stay standing in the face of German aggression, and that meant presence in another set of far waters—the Atlantic and the Mediterranean.

The US and Britain became entwined in their shared far waters in Asia. It was a simultaneously competitive and cooperative relationship, and one that, surprisingly, meant that the US became committed to the defense of British near waters. The weak had made Britain weaker, but in the process the US became stronger. That strength was built on seapower that forged new primary-subsidiary relations and a postwar geography of US "interests" in subsidiary countries. As in the past, those interests had to be defended.

The Defense of US "Interests" in Subsidiary Countries

Interests in the western Pacific led to US presence in the far waters of the eastern Atlantic and the Mediterranean. But global economic interests require not just seapower to protect oceans, or SLOCs, but also the ability to reach across oceans to be present in other countries. This is the ugly and brutal side of power projection in the name of protecting unequal economic relations.

The ideals of the hegemonic power may well be earnest, especially among the general population. But in a competitive world in which the supply of resources is relatively fixed within certain time frames and those resources are often located in other countries, the practice of accessing those resources is a grubby affair that violates ideals. The rise of the US to the position of global power was, like that of the Dutch and British before them, built upon the control of near and far waters and coastal territories and an accompanying mission to "defend ideals of freedom."[66] Also similar to the patterns of Dutch and British power, the process of becoming a global power begins with the belief that naval power is sufficient and ends in bloody, murky, likely immoral, and often illegal entanglements with unsavory local leaders. The CIA has been the major institution in defining and controlling such "interests."

Of course, the process began long before the creation of the CIA after the Second World War. Securing near waters was a key goal of the 1898 war with Spain and the "liberation" of Cuba. What was an imperial war, in that it involved the US to gain influence or even control of foreign territories, was portrayed as an anti-imperial crusade. This contradiction was not seen as one at the time. In the words of Congressman John B. Corliss, "What greater liberty, freedom, and independence can be obtained than that enjoyed under the protection of our flag?"[67] The defeat of Spain required a compliant Cuba if near waters were to be secure. The 1901 Platt Amendment ensured that goal by curtailing national independence. It established a US naval base at Guantanamo Bay and reserved the right of the US to intervene within the country to ensure the "maintenance of a government adequate for the protection of life, property and individual liberty."[68]

But "interests" were not only to be located in US near waters. The war with Spain involved the US military conquest of the Philippines in a deployment of troops that has since become familiar. In the words of historian David J. Sibley, it was a war that combined the US projects of frontier and imperial geographic expansion.[69] President William McKinley supported the Philippine-American War, which lasted from February 1899 to July 1902. Partially, his calculation addressed a concern that the Philippines would be colonized by France or Germany.[70] President McKinley and members of his administration, especially his assistant secretary of the navy Theodore Roosevelt, were very clear that pushing Spain out of the Philippines would lead to control of an archipelago that would give the US a strategic foothold for further projection of power into East Asia.[71]

While the Philippines were a stepping-stone into Asian far waters, there was still work to be done in near waters. The machinations that split Panama from Colombia to allow for the construction of the Panama Canal allowed for Atlantic, Caribbean, and Pacific near waters to be connected. But that was not enough, and the "right" to intervention in the "backyard" of the US was exercised in the form of military interventions in Honduras, Mexico, Nicaragua, Haiti, and the Dominican Republic between 1911 and 1916.[72] Though often portrayed today as a globalist and an idealist, President Woodrow Wilson declared, "I am going to teach the South American republics to elect good men."[73] The ugly nature of these military interventions, especially atrocities in the Philippines, laid bare Admiral Mahan's false assumption that a strong navy was enough to secure a presence in far waters—an assumption that was betrayed throughout the twentieth century and to the very present.

In the wake of the Second World War the ideological rallying cry of "freedom" was amped up and given a foil in the form of the Soviet Union's expression of communism and the ideology of global Bolshevism. But it was economic "interests" that became the underlying engine of an intensified US presence in more far waters. Of course, near waters had still to be secured. Cuba became a focus of concern after the Castro-led revolution. The failure, or farce, of the Bay of Pigs invasion in 1961 did not prevent the landing of twenty-three thousand US troops in the Dominican Republic in 1965. This action echoed President Wilson's earlier concerns about the people of Latin America supporting governments that were not to the taste of the US.[74] Policing was recognized to be cheaper than military action. Simply, "Latin American military establishments were restructured in accordance with American views."[75] This understatement should not finesse the horrors of gross human rights violations sponsored by the US in Guatemala, Nicaragua, and El Salvador. And since the Second World War the US has been present in far waters in all the world's major oceans and seas.

The US became a global seapower through a relationship with Britain and its connections to imperial far waters. Through this process the US established control of the late twentieth-century generative sector. It required a foreign policy driven by a four-pronged strategy of thwarting a primary country competitor, securing near waters, maintaining the general set of unequal primary-subsidiary relations, and ensuring access to generative sectors in far waters. Historical circumstances and national characteristics gave this strategy its particular character and geography of conflict.

A similar strategy is likely to be the course, by choice or by reaction, of any emerging hegemonic country. Is China taking on this strategy? Or does it believe its national history makes it different from prior and Western hegemons? And even if that is the case, will the actions and ideas of the people in subsidiary countries have a large say in writing the historic narrative, as they have done in Afghanistan, Iran, the Korean peninsula, the Sahel region, and so on?

China's Ambitions and Historical Precedents

China is now active in the areas of the world where the CIA and the US military worked hand in hand to secure US economic interests. These are also areas where the heavy yoke of Great Britain's imperialism was also once present. Currently, China's presence is weak relative to the heights of British imperialism and the wide range of US Cold War–era support of governments or, as deemed necessary, opposition movements. Also, this is a moment when China's presence is primarily economic. Indeed, China is eager to contrast its economic relations with the military "bullying" of US hegemony.[76] However, the visions and actions of the Dutch, Britain, and the US were initially based on an optimistic notion that "money talks," or that economic ties would be enough to secure interests. The revolt of Portuguese Catholics in Dutch Brazil,[77] Britain's need for numerous military "expeditions" across the extent of its empire, and the persistence of US military interventions and engagements since the Second World War should act as a cautionary tale for Chinese foreign policymakers and those affected by their decisions. The promises of peaceful economic connections and the claim all ships will rise on the same tide of investment and trade have, in the past, resulted in costly military engagements that appear as shipwrecks in the history of national foreign policy.

Without a doubt, China has become present in new far waters. Beginning with a focus on its western and southeastern neighbors, it has developed a mantra and practice of "Going Out" to build a global network of trade and investment.[78] The Belt and Road Initiative is as ambitious as previous British visions of an empire upon which the sun never sets or the US vision of a Pax Americana, a world of free trade between democratic countries free of colonialism.[79] The BRI is vague and amorphous, yet simultaneously specific and defined.[80] In some ways, maps of the BRI represent the classic topological representation of the London Underground system. But that similarity is deceptive, for the Underground map offers a clear guide to where different lines begin, end, and intersect with each other and identifies each stop on the way. Maps of the BRI, on the other hand, are a broad-brush representation of the *desire* for China to be at the center of a global network. If you want to see the actual routes being built, it is better to focus on the set of "corridors," though some are more established than others (map 5.4).[81]

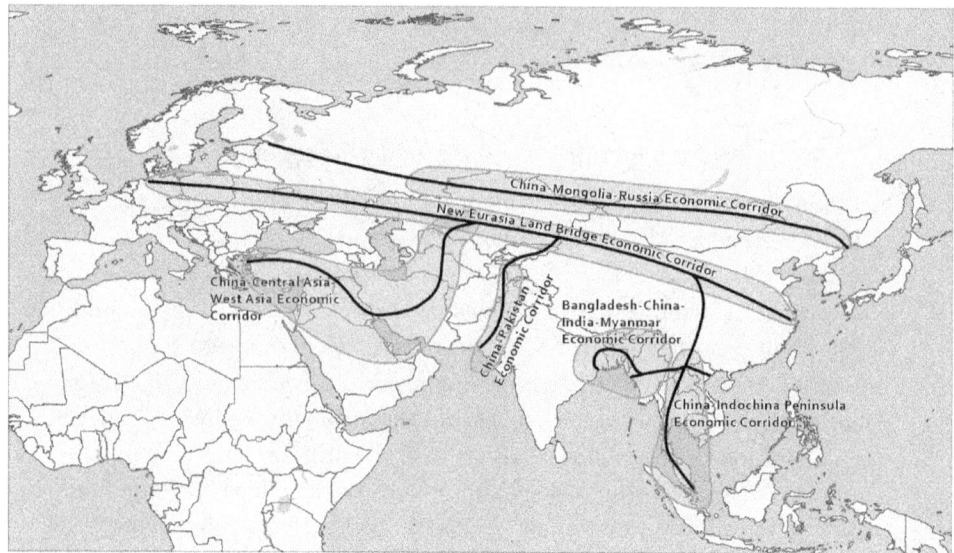

MAP 5.4. The corridors of the Belt and Road Initiative.
Source: Original work by Carson Liesik using multiple sources freely available on the internet.

The term *corridor* is helpful to identify the purpose of the BRI, which is to link one part of a structure with another. The corridor itself is the concrete set of means of connectivity: roads, railways, pipelines, airports, broadband networks, and (last but not least) SLOCs in the High Seas. Just as in a house, some corridors are more attractive or spectacular than others, but their essence is utilitarian; they are necessary to get you from one room to another. The rooms themselves are what matter, and each room has a different purpose. The same is true of the corridors of the BRI: they are designed to connect different parts of the world, with each part having a particular function. The BRI is connecting the domestic space of China with parts of the world that are sources of raw materials, or inputs to a manufacturing process completed in China. The BRI also connects China to markets for Chinese-produced goods. The crucial corridors to far waters have been built to establish China's access to existing and new generative sectors. The existing sector is the Middle East with its oil and gas fields. The new sectors are those that give China access to minerals necessary for the new technologies of supercomputing and the quest for ever more powerful artificial intelligence capacity.

An important corridor within the BRI is the China-Pakistan Economic Corridor (CPEC), formally agreed upon through a Memorandum of Understanding in 2015. Its economic feasibility is a matter of debate. The ambitious and breathtaking Karakoram Highway through Himalayan passes connects inland China to the port of Gwadar in Pakistan. The main reason for the CPEC is energy security. Though the geography of China's energy supply is a complicated mixture of domestic production, supply from Russia, and (perhaps surprisingly) supply from the US, SLOCs are at the heart of China's calculations. China imports about 83 percent of its oil needs, and just over three-quarters of that runs through the choke point of the Strait of Malacca.[82] Consisting of railways, roads, and pipelines, CPEC would reduce the distance of sea travel for Chinese imports and exports from the Persian Gulf from twelve thousand to two thousand kilometers.[83] The main imports to China would be oil from Saudi Arabia, Kuwait, and Oman, and cars and car parts from Germany.[84] Going the other way, the exports from China would be computers and communications technology, going mainly to Germany and Saudi Arabia. The ties to the Middle East through the CPEC include China's ties with Iran, which has been increasingly isolated from the rest of the world by the diplomatic efforts led by the US.[85]

The CPEC has the potential to be more than an economic corridor. It could also become the passageway allowing for political, and even "security," ties between China and Middle Eastern countries. Ironically, as the US has made China its national security priority, Middle Eastern countries feel that they have become ignored. To put it bluntly: "There is a feeling in the region that the United States is actively on the way out, and that's an opportunity for China."[86] China has begun to fill that gap by providing infrastructure investment, telecommunications know-how, and military technology. It helps that China and its Middle Eastern friends are more than happy to ignore each other's human rights records. The stated economic goal of the Pakistan port of Gwadar may be a new entrepôt, a stepping-stone to ports such as Chabahar in Iran, Duqm in Oman, and Abu Dhabi.[87] It is possible that Gwadar may be an economic flop; and perhaps it will be nothing more than an oil terminal with the added benefit of being a support base for the Chinese navy.

Whether individual ports such as Gwadar are a success remains to be seen. It does seem evident that China is seeking a new generative sector by establishing ties with African countries.[88] The slogan may be clumsy in the English translation, but the meaning speaks for itself: Uphold the Tradition of Always Standing Together and Jointly Build a China-Africa Community with a Shared Future in the New Era.[89] The Forum on China-Africa cooperation (FOCAC) established in 2000 aims to promote friendship and cooperation between the continent and China, in a spirit of equality and respect. This is just one example of China's efforts to woo African countries and establish economic relations. But China-Africa relations include some of the same paternalistic attitudes seen in the behavior of previous hegemons with subsidiary countries. For example, President Xi Jinping's speech to FOCAC began with the immediate concern of helping African countries tackle the COVID pandemic.

The speech soon went on to the central theme of plans to "open up new prospects for China-Africa cooperation, expand trade and investment, [and] share experience on poverty reduction." This was not advanced as a narrow national agenda. Rather, the hopes were framed within the proposed UN Global Development Initiative, connected to the African Union's Agenda 2063 and the UN's 2030 Agenda for Sustainable Development. In other words, yet again Africa was to be the focus of global development hopes and plans, but this time China would be the driving force.[90]

And yet, perhaps ominously, the ninth and final theme was "the peace and security program." President Xi promised to "undertake 10 peace and security projects for Africa, continue to deliver military assistance to the AU [African Union], support African countries' efforts to independently maintain regional security and fight terrorism, and conduct joint exercises and on-site training between Chinese and African peacekeeping troops and cooperation on small arms and light weapons control."[91] The promise is a potential pathway to military commitments that have historical echoes in previous Dutch, British, and US military interventions. And while Chinese voices would certainly protest my point of view, it should be noted that none of the previous global powers wanted the costs and burdens of a global military presence. These nevertheless became necessary as a global network of "interests" was created, though not to the liking of some local inhabitants and to the concern of other primary countries.

Throughout history, seapower has not been just about the sea: it allows for access to land. Seapower has been the means to build primary-subsidiary relations, especially by hegemonic countries. These relations have led to the establishment of "interests" abroad, in far waters, that have driven economic growth back home. But these "interests" have had to be defended. The action of making interests has led to the reaction of challenging them. Though the technology may change, the geopolitics of primary-subsidiary relations has remained essentially the same over time. Today, the military and security commitments to Africa promised by President Xi require connections across the globe to provide logistical support. Airlifts, drones, and satellites are all necessary for a modern military mission; but the amount of equipment needed to sustain an operation still requires naval power.

Economic interests connecting near and far waters, ambitions for peaceful integration, and the quicksand of security commitments are a matter of history. Are there any reasons to believe that history will not repeat one more time?

SIX

The Geopolitics of Innovation

The naval power of the hegemon rests upon its economic strength. It gains strength by establishing a generative sector. The purpose of the generative sector is to fuel the domestic economy by becoming the country that can capture, to a large extent, the most profitable and advanced economic activities. Waves of innovations spark competition between countries to capture the business activities that promise to be the most profitable. The action of national economic growth leads to responses, or reactions, from other countries. Perhaps seapower is a virtuous circle of naval power, economic wealth, more naval power, and more wealth.[1] But looked at another way, the geopolitics of far waters is about building a national economy that is competitive rather than virtuous. Geopolitics is a matter of the inseparable connection between economic and military competition, and that is very clear in the actions and words of US and Chinese politicians today.

Businesses make the innovations that can lead to national economic success. But they do so with a lot of help from governments. In the past there have been periods when countries have been particularly anxious to support industries. These moments occur when innovations appear that are potentially transformative. The result is competition between countries to make sure that the companies making these new products are located within their borders. This competition has involved industrial espionage, government subsidies, protectionism, appeals against the protectionism of others, and the use of universities and the military to kick-start innovation. The goals of economic success are wrapped up in concerns about national security. In the past, a country that has been most successful in capturing these innovations has become the hegemonic power.

But it is not enough to make the fancy, expensive, and profitable new products. They also must be sold. This requires markets outside of the country's own borders. A country wants the world to buy the products made by its companies. The hegemonic power is the home of businesses making the newest and most attractive stuff, and it has an incentive to reduce barriers preventing people from buying it. The hegemonic country also wants to reduce the costs of the inputs in the highly profitable products received from subsidiary countries. Free trade is the imperative, and it is a geopolitical project.[2]

The previous chapter discussed how the geopolitics of the generative sector requires the management of subsidiary countries to ensure they continue to provide the necessary goods and do so cheaply.[3] This entails the creation of spheres of interest that once appeared as colonialism and imperialism. Though a primary country may be able to establish a sphere of interest for a while, it is never guaranteed. In the past, spheres of interest in far waters have had a limited shelf life. One reason for the historic patterns of near-/far-waters geopolitics is that economic strength changes. Economic growth, or lack of it, can disrupt a country's virtuous cycle. Hence, national economic policy is part and parcel of the geopolitics of seapower. And this part of geopolitics is starting to intensify today.

The Dutch Make Modern Manufacturing

Making Amsterdam into an active entrepôt helped the country become the world leader in innovative manufacturing. It was not simply the dominance of trade that led to Dutch power but the processing of the high-value goods obtained. For example, the Dutch led the way in making dyes and glass, blending tobacco, finishing diamonds, refining sugar, refining whale oil to make soap and lighting fuel, and grinding lenses.[4] Innovation in manufacturing, and the development of a global entrepôt, demanded and resulted in new forms of banking and financing.[5] It was the emergence of the textile industry in the province of Holland that spurred on the increasing presence of Dutch merchants in markets across the globe.[6] However, the merchants in Amsterdam and manufacturers in other parts of the country were not always on the same page.[7] Instead, the rise of the Dutch to a global power was the result of a creative tension, or continual give-and-take, between different economic interests in different parts of the country.

Competing interests around a common goal led to the establishment of a new form of economic enterprise, the Verenigde Oost-Indische Compagnie (United East India Company or VOC, established in January 1602). The VOC was a combined political and military enterprise that was built upon pooled investment from merchants based in cities across the country.[8] In this way it gained capital, financial security, resilience, national buy-in, and no lack of military capability. The Dutch story reminds us that national projects for economic superiority have included new forms of corporate organization.

In another development that resonates with current geopolitics, the growth of Dutch industry provoked jealousy and concern in other countries. Protectionist policies emerged, such as the Dutch refusal to import dyed cloth from England.[9] Even the country that held the economic advantage had to close its borders to certain products to distort the market in its favor. Despite innovations in sack and canvas manufacturing, paper, linen, and gin in the latter half of the 1600s, other countries eventually caught up with the Dutch with regard to economic innovations. In the 1720s and 1730s a new type of industrial mercantilism took over the European continent and the Dutch industrial base was no longer cutting-edge.[10] The dominance of the Dutch in the trade of high-value goods soon withered. What had once been the world's most advanced economy lost its position as the site of the world's most advanced manufacturing. The loss of the VOC's status as the world's dominant economic and military force was soon to follow.[11]

The Dutch model was groundbreaking. Their industrial, financial, commercial, and political innovations led to the ability and need to be present in far waters. The basic ingredient of their success was a competitive but collaborative relationship between business and government. Both business and the government need to establish global seapower for their mutual benefit. The Dutch model is not suitable for today's world, but the basic ingredients have been, and remain, the fundamental drivers of global power.

Groundbreaking models are still fragile. The constant competition between countries has produced a history in which no country has remained the strongest national economy and greatest seapower without challenge and decline. The story of Britain shows how economic rise requires creating global linkages, and how a period of economic decline is a result of other countries taking the lead in new economic activities. The periods of rise and fall are both periods of competition in far waters.

Britain: The Up and Down of the Virtuous Cycle

Was Britain "a nation of shopkeepers" (in Napoleon's alleged pithy insult) or the first industrial nation? It could be both. Being the most powerful industrial nation in the world generates wealth, and with wealth people can buy things. But to be the country that produces things and has a high standard of living is not simply a national project. It is a global project that requires networks of imports and exports. For Britain, the project of empire was to create those connections. London, Bristol, Liverpool, Manchester, Leeds, Glasgow, and Newcastle, the manufacturing and trade hubs of industrial Britain, were imperial cities. At the other end of the network were the cities of Calcutta, Bombay, Singapore, Mombasa, and many more.

Through much of the nineteenth century Britain was the dominant manufacturing economy. The "dark Satanic mills," in English poet William Blake's famous words, that were built in the late 1700s and early 1800s became the dominant form of production. This industrial development coincided with the defeat of Napoleon on the European continent in the early 1800s. The diplomacy of the Congress of Europe allowed Britain to dominate the global economy, face limited naval competition, and nullify any threat from the European continent. Global trade fueled national economic growth, and vice versa. British cities grew accordingly.[12] Britain's urban population grew from just under nine million in 1801 to just over twenty-five million in 1901.[13] Along with London, the growth largely occurred in major industrial centers such as Birmingham, Liverpool, Manchester, Leeds, Newcastle, and Sheffield.[14]

Imperial Britain was a "vast commercial republic."[15] Much as with the growth of Dutch trade and cities, merchants were the driving force. Government was the enabler of the last resort. British exports grew in value from GBP38 million in 1830 to GBP60 million in 1845 and GBP122 million in 1857. Unsurprisingly, maritime trade through British ports grew as a result, a fourfold increase from 1834 to 1860.[16] The geography of Britain's trade became more expansive. From the established trade in the Atlantic, Britain expanded its trade with Asia and the Near East, plus Africa and Australia. The Indian and Pacific Oceans and the South Atlantic became important new far waters.

Britain's economic strength was a result of its entrepôt functions as much as its manufacturing strength. The two economic activities went hand in hand, just as they had for the Dutch. British ports served as entrepôts for two of the world's key economic networks. One was the connection between Europe and the US, with its rapidly growing economy. The other was between Europe and Asia, especially before the opening of the Suez Canal in November 1869.[17] Britain had established a dominant presence in Brazil during the early nineteenth-century wars with France. And the old ways of doing business through chartered monopolies opened up possibilities in the Near East, India, and China. Unsurprisingly, the growth of British trade led to its growth as the center of global finance, but it was manufacturing prowess that allowed for global economic domination. British cotton manufactures, the most important commodity of the mid-nineteenth century, could be sold up to two hundred times cheaper than locally produced goods in many parts of the world.[18]

Britain's economic expansion was given further impetus by the move toward an open economy and free trade that was more or less complete by 1851. British ports were now the world's most important entrepôts, the ports through which "the world's goods could be carried without commercial restriction."[19] Manufacturing and commercial success meant that Britain had money to invest. The City of London became the world's financial center, and much of this investment was in infrastructure that would allow for more global trade and at a reduced cost. "Railway mania" began, resulting in not just an empire of trade but "an empire of overseas property."[20] For Britain, building a global infrastructure of trade was a geopolitical project that was an investment strategy in and of itself, but one with benefits for trade and the projection of military power.

To be British was to be imperial and imperious. As Charles Dickens put it in his 1848 novel *Dombey and Son*: "The earth was made for Dombey and Son to trade in, the sun and the moon were made to give them light. Rivers and seas were formed to float their ships; rainbows to give them the promise of fair weather; winds blew for or against their enterprises; stars and planets circled in their orbits, to preserve inviolate a system of which they were the centre."[21]

Britain may have seemed inviolate and robust in 1848. But the vitality of British cities as manufacturing, entrepôt, and financial centers was dependent upon ties across the world. And they were vulnerable to challenge. The lifestyle of the British middle class, fictionalized as Dombey, required that British merchants had access to cities in India, West Africa, and China. It also meant that the far waters of the Mediterranean Sea, the western Pacific, and the eastern part of the South Atlantic were free of threats to maritime traders. In other words, thriving British cities required a military presence in far waters. British culture was largely silent about the violence behind the trading patterns of empire.[22]

National economic dominance is not permanent. Just as the circumstances that led to Dutch dominance changed and allowed Amsterdam's role as the commercial center of the world to be eclipsed, Britain was to lose its competitive edge. Perhaps surprisingly, the thoughts of the communist philosopher Karl Marx help us explain this change. The cities of Britain were the dominant commercial and manufacturing centers of the world because investors had sunk a lot of money into building factories, ports, housing, and so on. In other words, Britain had built the infrastructure necessary for production and trade. Profit on these investments required that they remain "sunk" for a while, or that places stay the same and continue the economic activity that the investment was based upon to get a return on the initial investment. Cities and their economic purpose have some sort of shelf life because of the time span of economic investment. But economics is driven by innovation and change, and sometimes the shelf life of a city's industrial role is out of sync with the latest innovations.[23]

Toward the end of the nineteenth century Britain's cities were facing competition from economic growth in Germany, Japan, and the US. New products had been designed, new ways of making them had been dreamed up, and new profits were about to be made. US car manufacturer Henry Ford became the new type of entrepreneur. The time of the imperious English nineteenth-century engineer Isambard Kingdom Brunel was over. Aviation, chemicals, automobiles, and optics were the new industrial growth industries.[24] Britain's economic prowess meant that it had the know-how to be part of this change, but only a part. Industrial growth in Detroit, Los Angeles, Dusseldorf, and Tokyo, for example, was at least competitive with British industry, and in many cases more advanced.[25]

The emergence of new industries, and of cities as new centers of industries, was seen as both an economic opportunity and a security threat. Britain's economy was still one of the world's most innovative and strongest, even in the wake of the First World War. In fact, the new economies were seen as potential trade partners. Adolf Hitler's Germany was identified as one such partner.

Amid Prime Minister Neville Chamberlain's much-maligned strategy of appeasement toward Adolf Hitler's aggression in Europe, his government was actively seeking trading relations with Nazi Germany.[26] New industries meant new investment opportunities. The political context was one in which Britain had little appetite for another conflict, as the memories of the First World War were still raw.[27] Economic growth was the imperative, and the ugly side of a country's domestic and international politics could be brushed under the carpet. The economic benefits of trade with Nazi Germany were advanced. The military calculations were not too scary, as

Hitler's goals seemed to be in central and eastern Europe, and not Britain's near and far waters.[28]

Sir Basil Liddell Hart, the country's leading military thinker, was advocating a "British way of war" that was intended to avoid another bloody commitment on the European continent.[29] Naval power was to be the bastion of British security, blending protection of near waters to prevent invasion with force projection in far waters to protect colonial possessions. In this context, trade with Nazi Germany seemed to offer more benefits than costs. The realization that Germany's expansion eastwards threatened the Balkans, and hence control of the Mediterranean Sea and SLOC linkages to imperial far waters, was to come later.

There was a sense that Britain's economic situation could be managed. Yes, the economies of Germany, the US, and France were growing. Yes, accommodations had to be made. But Britain would still be a strong economy, and its scientists would ensure that innovations would find a home in the economy as long as the global nature of Britain's economy remained intact: in other words, as long as Britain could retain its presence in subsidiary countries through a naval presence in far waters.[30]

Hence, Japan's industrial rise and its search for access to raw materials was the bigger disruption. Japan was the more significant geopolitical spanner in the virtuous cycle of British seapower[31]—not just because of its industrialization, but because its economic growth required the country to establish its own connections with subsidiary countries. The problem was that these subsidiary countries were ones that the European countries assumed were "theirs": colonial possessions in Asia. The industrialization of Japan, on the wave of economic innovations, was not simply a competition between primary countries. To compete, Japan had to upset established primary-subsidiary relations. This meant competition with Britain and the US in their Asian far waters.

Japan's military victory over Russia in 1905 shook the Western world out of the complacency of its assumptions of racial superiority. Japan's expansion was given a green light by President Theodore Roosevelt, who brokered the postwar agreement that sanctioned Japan's control of Korea, an act of diplomacy for which Roosevelt was awarded the Nobel Peace Prize. The necessary geographic expansion for Japanese economic growth was given all the encouragement it needed.

Japan's economy faced the headwinds of global economic depressions between the wars. The general picture was one of industrial transformation through an industrial policy that was generally protectionist to nurture Japanese industry.[32] Japan's industrial growth was promoted by national policies such as a railway network to connect the four main islands and the Tokaido line connecting the Tokyo/Yokohama and Osaka/Kobe conurbations. This railway line was also known as the "ocean line," recognizing the link between land and sea. The geographic growth of these conurbations went along with industrial agglomeration through the growth of the *zaibatsu* (financial cliques) that became industrial combines powered by a national project of electrification.[33] Such economic growth required maritime connections. The ports of Yokohama, Tsuruga, and Nagasaki provided links east, west, and south, respectively, and became key entrepôts.[34]

Japan's ambitions grew and culminated in its June 1941 proposal for a Greater East Asia Co-Prosperity Sphere. The name was a rhetorical trick to claim that a generative sector spanning Malaya, the Philippines, Indochina, and the Dutch East Indies was a beneficial Pan-Asian project.[35] In reality, the goal was to replace European empires with a Japanese empire and to ensure access to iron ore, oil, and rubber to fuel Japanese industry.[36] The other countries of the Sphere were to be the recipients of the high-value goods made in Japan. The plan was a reframing of the persistent global pattern of primary-subsidiary relations.

Japan was seeking its own access to commodities to fuel its growth. The problem was that Japan's near waters were also the far waters of the world's imperial powers, and of interest to the rising US. In hindsight, the argument can be made that Japan's plan to fuel economic growth through replacing European empires in Asia with its own was unlikely to succeed. Instead, its postwar economic growth came about through willingly tying itself to its conqueror, the US. The US victory in the Second World War led to its global economic dominance, the feature of a hegemonic power,[37] though it wasn't long before Japan was able to achieve economic success because of its cooperation with the US.

Understanding the geopolitics of seapower requires a focus on the period in which innovations are catalyzing economic competition between countries and resetting established patterns of primary-subsidiary relations. The beginning of the twentieth century was one such period. Britain thought it could deal with a growing Continental economic and military power, Germany. The lack of perceived threat to British near and far waters, and the likely economic benefits, meant that cooperation through trade agreements rather than military confrontation—that is, appeasement—seemed a viable path. When the German threat to British near waters became clear, it appeared in tandem with a threat to British "interests" in Asian far waters.

The "maritime trade" part of the virtuous cycle of seapower is the connection between primary and subsidiary countries to establish a generative sector, and connections between primary countries to trade in high-value goods. Trade is just part of the equation that provides the wealth to build the seapower that sustains economic growth. Economic growth is given a spurt when innovations and new products emerge, and that is likely to catalyze the need for new economic kids on the block to foster their own primary-subsidiary relations. That is the situation today. And, of course, the new kid on the block is China.

China as the New Economic Power

Why is this a period of military and political tension between the US and China? The underlying reasons are economic. The two countries are in the midst of a competition to be the most powerful economy in the world. Being powerful rests on two separate but related trends. The first is about being the country that manages to be home to the newest and most profitable economic activities in the global economy. The second is about being the dominant trading country in the world. These dual goals require the construction and control of ports, at home and in far waters, to ensure trade flows that drive the domestic economy. The current period is changing the global geography of port cities as China is building a system of domestic entrepôts in its near waters, regional hubs to facilitate imports and exports, and ports in far waters to ensure access to generative sectors.[38] Though these dynamics have their own particular contemporary flavor, the general pattern and purpose are the same as practiced in the historical eras of Dutch, British, and US power.[39]

Starting with the domestic economy, there is a battle over the geography of new economic activities—those innovations that will constitute the new highly profitable and transformative sector of the world-economy.[40] Artificial intelligence, 5G telecommunications technology, supercomputing, biotechnology, and renewable energy are the interconnected set of innovations that make up this new sector.[41] China recognizes that its growth as an economy relies on being the dominant player in this new sector. The US recognizes that retaining its position as the hegemonic country means it must resist China's surge of economic innovation and renew its economy. The challenge for China is to encourage such economic growth without catalyzing social change that will challenge its political system. The challenge for the US is to modernize when there is inertia built into the economic geography of existing industries and the related political power. Can China create an entrepreneurial class and a consumer culture that are willing to accept authoritarian control? And can the US break free from coal and oil interests in the states of Texas, Wyoming, and West Virginia?

The competition to have a domestic economy driven by innovations leads to a lot of government involvement. Both the US and China have government initiatives to promote new technology, and they are not shy in identifying the potential of the other country as a motivation for action.[42] It is not an arms race but a technological race.[43] In the past, arms races have followed or been part and parcel of these technological races, and much of the interest in these technologies is related to their use in future war-making.[44]

Ironically, this state-versus-state competition involves trade and investment connections, including those between the competing countries. For example, US banking and finance firms are eager to be players in the Chinese market. Their presence would increase company profits while also giving China ways to participate in global investment transactions. The dilemma of maximizing economic goals while recognizing political tensions is clear when looking at the presence of Western companies in Hong Kong. Such companies, many historically based in the territory when it was a British colony, are balancing the economic advantages of staying with the political and everyday difficulties posed by an increasingly interventionist and repressive Chinese government.

China has made its intentions for the future clear through its China 2025 program. This government-led program is aiming to change China's economy by promoting new and highly profitable industries. As identified by the US Congressional Research Service: "The 10 sectors identified in the State Council's 2015 plan are (1) next-generation information technology, (2) high-end numerical control machinery and robotics, (3) aerospace and aviation equipment, (4) maritime engineering equipment and high-tech maritime vessel manufacturing, (5) advanced rail equipment, (6) energy-saving and new energy vehicles, (7) electrical equipment, (8) agricultural machinery and equipment, (9) new materials, and (10) biopharmaceuticals and high-performance medical devices."[45]

China 2025 is a geopolitical project. It is state sponsored. Politicians and commentators in the US have pointed to the role of the Chinese government in this project to identify China's economic growth as a threat. For example, "China's incomplete transition to a free market economy stands out as one of the biggest sources of trade friction with the United States. Recent proposals by the Chinese government, such as its 'Made in China 2025' initiative, appear to signal an expanded role by the government in the economy, which many fear could distort global markets and negatively affect U.S. firms."[46] Unsurprisingly, the US rhetorical reaction chooses to ignore the role of the US government in its own economic history.

Though China has transformed itself from a poor country with an agricultural economy to a manufacturing powerhouse, its success goes against US ideas of how development should work and, instead of being celebrated, has been seen as a threat. The abandonment of the rhetoric of development that justified US political and economic involvement in other countries after the Second World War is evident in numerous commentaries that portray China's economic development as something to be feared. For example, and without any shame over how developmentalist language has been used in the past to justify US political actions, *New York Times* opinion columnist Farhad Manjoo claims he is "so impressed with the aggressive and creative way the Biden administration has gone about curtailing China's alarming, decades-long effort to build a domestic semiconductor industry."[47]

In 2022, US politicians in the House passed a bill to prime the pump of scientific research, especially regarding semiconductor production. The target of the bill was China or, in the words of then Speaker of the House Nancy Pelosi, to help US manufacturing "outcompete any nation." Of course, there was partisan disagreement. The minority leader of the House, Representative Kevin McCarthy, criticized the amount of government expenditure. Notably, he said that the wording of the legislation "includes no measures to make China pay for the chaos they created."[48] From this vantage point, China's economic transformation, the new patterns of global trade and investment it has catalyzed, and its ability to mold patterns of supply and demand to its advantage are seen not as the normal dynamics of capitalism but as a form of geopolitical "chaos."

Though identified as matters of national security and competition, the political interests and the economic consequences of the geopolitics of technological competition are local. The factories and offices in which new technologies are made and in which the processes are managed and financed are sited within particular cities. China's centralized political system makes it easier to implement a national plan. In the federal system of the US, politicians representing the fifty states lobby for policies that favor investment for the voters in their states or congressional districts. For example, in 2021 the then state of Utah representative Blake Moore called for "reshoring" manufacturing activities, with the understandable hope that new firms would choose to locate in Utah. His language was unabashedly geopolitical with echoes of Cold War rhetoric: "Surrendering critical manufacturing capabilities and losing our position as the world's No. 1 innovator would erode our ability to hold the CCP accountable and defend our free system. Our partners in the Indo-Pacific and across the world are willing to join forces."[49]

Representative Moore would like Utah cities and towns to thrive and sees competition with China as both a threat and an opportunity. Interestingly, his statement coincides with the construction of an "inland port" outside Salt Lake City—with the goal of making a land-locked urban area an entrepôt connected to the west coast of the US and the Pacific region. Utah's politicians have recognized the local opportunities within the current moment of geopolitical change. They would like to have a piece of the pie that comes from establishing trade relations. Such politics highlights the connection of local and national economies in the virtuous cycle of seapower.[50] Some cities are more important than others, though. Throughout history, those cities are port cities and entrepôts.

The Geopolitics of Port Power

Port cities are necessary for the import of goods from the generative sector and the export of high-value goods to global markets. Hence, they are essential for economic ambitions and, in turn, connect near waters and new far waters.[51] A port is a key site in the virtuous cycle of seapower that connects economic activities at home and abroad.[52] Ports are an economic beachhead to domestic industry. They are the conduit to markets for goods and inputs from the generative sector. Ports are also necessary for projecting naval power. They support a navy with global reach by providing places to repair and restock warships. They also allow for a constant military presence in SLOCs far away from near waters.[53] And, in the continuing tradition of Admiral Corbett, they provide a military beachhead to ensure that economic interests may be protected and political influence wielded—with a troop presence if necessary.[54]

The Dutch, the British, and the US built their networks of ports to secure near waters, SLOCs, and far waters. For the British and the Dutch, forts were an imperial presence. A patch of territory was carved out in foreign lands, sovereignty was established over a piece of land, and the national flag was flown. Imperial forts may have covered a relatively small acreage, yet their goal was to provide access to a hinterland where inputs were harvested or mined to be shipped home and where finished goods from back home were sold. At one end of the connection were mines or plantations. At the other were entrepôts such as Amsterdam or London in which incoming goods were stored and repurposed.

Though they may be small in area, ports in far waters are the gateway to much larger economic regions that operate to the benefit of the primary country. For example, in the 1880s and 1890s Britain's ports on the West African coast were the beachheads of imperial control in a "meta-economic" vision for a long-term commercial future on the continent rather than specific and immediate profit.[55] British interests in "the Coast"—the stretch of near waters running from Sierra Leone to the Congo—provided access to the "Oil Rivers" and the export of palm oil.[56] Similar issues were occurring in East Africa, part of a trans-Indian Ocean system of interconnected far waters. British entrepreneurs recognized that the opening of the Suez Canal provided an opportunity to develop the long-existing Indo-Arab trading networks to the British advantage. New areas of far waters could be developed with inland connections to the African Great Lakes region.[57]

In imperial times, primary countries reinforced the military forces of empire necessary to build such "meta-economic" regions by befriending a particular ethnic group to ensure loyalty and compliance to imperial edicts. Today, the principle is the same, but the means are different. In subsidiary countries receiving Chinese development projects, the Chinese investment is often funneled into the hometowns and provinces of the ruling elite.[58] Port power has always involved the greasing of palms, in one form or another, to make sure that some in the subsidiary country benefit from the inherently unequal primary-subsidiary relationship.

Internal agreements between African leaders and British entrepreneurs (with ties to the government) were made to create a British-dominated West and East Africa so that one set of far waters linked to other far waters and to the domestic economy. The problem was that these geographic regions, and the economic opportunities they provided, were appealing to other powers. West and Equatorial Africa was coveted by the French, and East Africa by the Germans. Islands were a key strategic focus, the topic of chapter 8. In the 1890s Zanzibar acted as a regional entrepôt on the East African coast and could easily be targeted by Germany (map 6.1).[59]

The post–Second World War hegemony of the US was based on the importance of ports on the Pacific and Atlantic coasts, as well as connections to Central and South America through Miami and Houston. US port power was a mixture of commercial and neocolonial politics. The defeat of Japan allowed for the permanent siting of military bases in Japan, especially the collection of bases in Okinawa to police the near waters of China and Southeast Asia. The US also took over the military ports of imperial Britain, such as Diego Garcia in the Indian Ocean.[60] A network of military bases and naval ports was established as a geography of presence in far

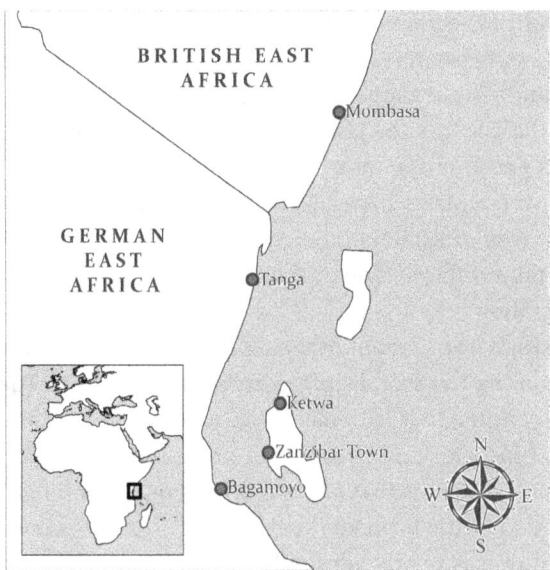

MAP 6.1. The Heligoland-Zanzibar Treaty.
Source: Adapted by Carson Liesik from History@Kingston, "The Anglo-German Relationship and Heligoland," July 12, 2017, https://historyatkingston.wordpress.com/2017/07/12/the-anglo-german-relationship-and-heligoland/.

waters to police economic "interests" and the SLOCs necessary for global trade.

Contrary to the imperial geographies of the Dutch and the British, US commercial activity required a port presence without carving out formal imperial control within countries. Instead, the context of the Cold War fueled connections between the US and economies in far waters. During the Vietnam War the South Korean economy was fueled by the US military's offshore procurement program. The growth of Korean industrial *chaebol* (industrial agglomerates) such as Hyundai was catalyzed by American funding that armed the US presence in far waters.[61] Japan's postwar growth was also accelerated through its connections to the US. The need for allies in Pacific far waters meant the US was willing to assist Japan by providing investment, buying Japanese-made products, and being tolerant of protectionist policies.[62] In addition, the Marshall Plan jump-started the war-torn economies of western Europe to ensure a postwar global economic boom that drove profit-making for US companies.

The post–Second World War US economy grew because of these connections—a political-economic mixture of business, diplomacy, and a military presence—between foreign economies and economic operations based in the homeland. These connections required physical connections across oceans, and the US was the postwar port power. But things change. The nature of port power is dynamic, and so is its geography. Today, China and Middle Eastern countries have become the dominant port powers.[63] And the dominant way of establishing a presence in ports across the globe is commercial, not military—though that does not mean that a military presence will not follow.

Unsurprisingly for a country trying to project power into far waters, China is becoming the world's preeminent port power.[64] The global port power is the country that is home to the world's busiest ports while also being the lead investor and manager of ports across the globe. Being the world's port power means that a country has control of a network of ports connecting its domestic economy to the international economy. Currently, China's port power is overwhelmingly focused upon commercial activity, though the potential for developing dual or sole military capacity within ports outside of near waters must be considered.

Seven of the world's top ten ports, in terms of volume of trade, are Chinese: Shanghai, Ningbo-Zhousan, Shenzen, Guangzhou, Hong Kong, Qingdao, and Tianjin (map 6.2). China is also investing in ports across the globe. Three Chinese port companies (Cosco Shipping, HPH, and CM Ports China) are among the world's top ten port operating companies. US companies are barely present in the list of the world's biggest port operators. China's emergence as the global port power shows up even more clearly in figures on national investment in global ports.[65] China dominates global investment in ports, with long-term investments in ports in Asia, Africa, the Americas, and Europe.[66] Notably, this investment includes US ports such as Long Beach, California. China is a major investor, and often the controlling investor, in all the world's top fifteen ports ranked by container volume.[67] This one statistic drives home the extent of China's role in the world's trading ports: at least two-thirds of the world's top fifty container ports are owned by the Chinese or supported by Chinese investments.[68]

To establish a presence beyond its near waters, China has invested in more than one hundred ports in sixty-three countries.[69] It is the world leader in developing and controlling ports. China's commercial development of ports overlays the geography of the set of international corridors it has developed to link markets and sources of commodities and industrial inputs across the globe.[70] The geopolitical strategy of the BRI requires becoming a port power. It is one element of the pursuit of an economic plan to

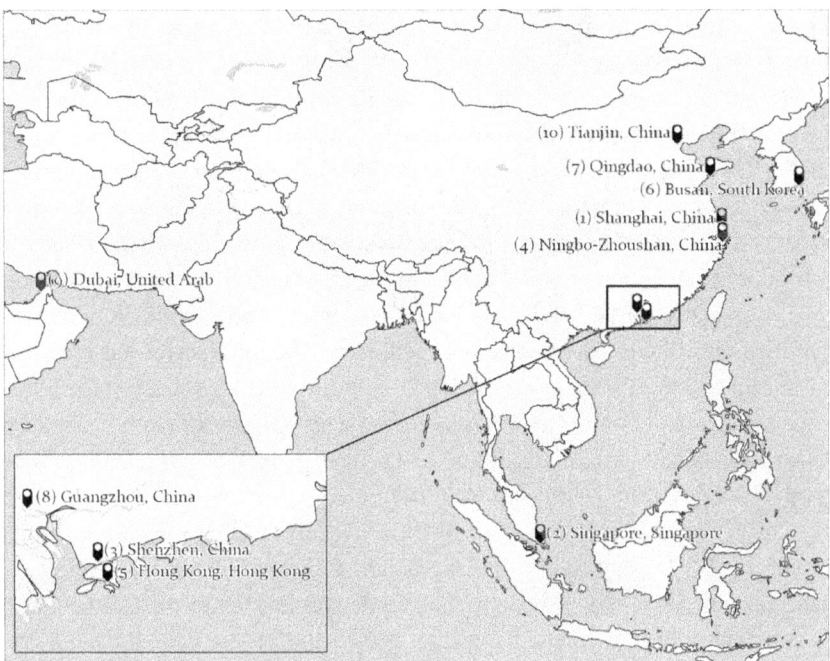

MAP 6.2. The world's busiest container ports.

Source: Adapted by Carson Liesik from batchgeo, "Mapping the Busiest Ports Worldwide," accessed December 7, 2023, https://blog.batchgeo.com/mapping-the-busiest-ports-worldwide/.

connect near and far waters through regional and global economic integration.[71] Again, the purpose of seapower is to achieve economic and political goals on shore. The commercial ports that China is involved in provide access to generative sectors that supply the inputs to its domestic economy and markets to sell products made in China.

To be successful in these economic goals requires establishing "interests" and "influence" in other countries: a common cause across the history of seapowers. But of course the means of establishing interest change. China is using money: the promise of investment in the infrastructure of subsidiary countries is the financial incentive of development with a Chinese flavor. China is also promising to support the regimes of subsidiary countries. In 2022, the security pact with the Solomon Islands came with a promise of troop deployments that could support the ruling government against internal dissent.[72] This is an attractive offer to a country where economic bad times could be just around the corner. The Solomon Islands deal is just one of such intergovernmental connections that China is nurturing along with its brick-and-mortar strategy of port development and infrastructure connection.

When China's presence starts through commercial treaties, Western protests against it can come across as silly. In April 2022, the commandant of the US Marine Corps, General David Berger, voicing his professional concern about an increased Chinese military presence in the South Pacific, said, "This is, in other words, an extension of 'hey we're here with a cheque, we're here with money, we'd like to improve your port or your airfield or your bus station.' And that just sounds so great, until a year later or six months later."[73] On the surface, protest against the building of bus stations seems petty. However, the geopolitics of seapower is one of both infrastructure investment, including innocuous-looking bus stations, and military power. It's hard to make an argument against the former, even though history tells us that the latter may well follow.

China has built a military base in Djibouti to look after its burgeoning "interests." It is very likely that more will follow and that existing commercial port interests will be militarized. The Pakistani port of Gwadar is considered to be a likely candidate, and there was some evidence that a part of the port of Khalifa in the United Arab Emirates was being built as a facility to support Chinese naval activities.[74] Apparently, this construction was halted after the US objected to the UAE. Such protest and concerns, along with the fears voiced by US and Australian officials regarding the (domestic?) security aspects of the Solomon Islands deal, come from an established worldview that economic interests and a military presence are inextricably linked, in terms of both policy and a geographical presence.

This should not come as a surprise. The history of seapower is based on a virtuous cycle of economic gain and the projection of military force.[75] Western commentators are wired to see the taken-for-granted connections in the cycle as, indeed, virtuous when describing the history and contemporary goals of their own countries, while seeing essentially the same process as far from virtuous when the Chinese are at the helm.

Economic ambitions and the establishment of a global network of commercial ports are inseparable from questions of geopolitical competition and competing visions of national security. Competition can lead to war. To try to avoid the horror, cost, and disruption of war, countries describe their actions as peaceful and as beneficial for all humanity, as the current Chinese language of the Doctrine of Peaceful Emergence suggests.[76] Previous hegemons all hoped that creating a particular message of common sense around themes of "peace," "freedom," and "prosperity" would reduce the need for military action. This type of geopolitics is provoked by fears that competition between primary countries will lead to military confrontation in near and far waters. Wars of words over access to far waters that have been taken for granted for decades are especially fierce. That is the case today when such far waters for the US are the near waters of the rising power, China. Hence, the rhetorical geopolitics that frames current geopolitical tensions is the next topic.

SEVEN

The Visions behind Force Projection

The hegemonic power's ability to establish unequal relations with subsidiary countries and to sell its products across the globe does not rely only on container ships and naval task forces. It also requires spreading the idea that these products are what everybody wants—a global advertising campaign, if you like. The hegemonic power tries to sell its way of life, and the products that are needed to live that way, as universally desired and suitable.[1] For example, the US suburban lifestyle has been "sold" as the epitome of modern living that everyone can and should long for. The hegemonic power advertises a sense of what it means to be modern. Who doesn't want to be modern?[2]

Well, historically, it appears that not everyone wants to be modern, or modern as defined by the hegemonic power. Other countries and political movements propose alternative modernities. At the height of its power the hegemonic country's exhibition of modernity has great sway across the globe. In periods of decline challenges become stronger.[3] For example, British hegemony was challenged by anti-imperial visions of modernity, such as that of Indian nationalist and anti-imperialist Mahatma Gandhi. Currently, China is questioning the validity of the US's vision of global society by arguing that it maintains inequalities between countries through the use of military force and is a modern form of empire.

The world is organized around competing ideas of the "modern" through global institutions. Empire was one such form of institution. It was replaced by US-led institutions (such as the World Bank and the International Monetary Fund) designed to manage relations with subsidiary states.[4] These institutions are facing competition from Chinese-led institutions such as the Asian Infrastructure Investment Bank (AIIB).[5] The competition between these institutional engagements with subsidiary countries is echoed in rhetorical battles over who has the best interests of those countries in mind.

The competition of ideas and institutions has always been grand. It has revolved around a hubristic sense of universalism, or the idea that a certain country has *the* vision for how the world should be organized. The hegemonic power tries to convince others that what it is doing is apolitical and for the benefit of everyone.[6] It tries to sell its actions as "common sense" rather than "geopolitics."

The hegemonic country sells the belief that the particular geopolitical relations being maintained by its military might upon the seas, and the trading relations they protect, are for the benefit of all. Whether British imperialism or the US idea of "development," a civilizational project is constructed: one form or another of the White Man's Burden, to use the term coined in 1899 by the pro-British imperialist poet Rudyard Kipling. Though it seems very odd now, imperialism was once seen as a project that would benefit everyone, even imperial subjects in colonies. It was, for a time, seen as the only and obvious way to organize the world. After the Second World War, ideas of "development" replaced those of imperialism. Development was also sold as benefiting everyone. But both imperialism and development seemed to require some coercion to prevent people from proposing and living out alternative modernities.

The universalism of the hegemonic vision of modernity has its time but it becomes challenged with a view toward the control of the global market and the selling of a particular image of how society should be organized. Historically such challenges have led to new conflicts over the control of the seas. Becoming the hegemonic power requires the naval strength to ensure freedom of navigation across the oceans. The naval power required to do this also rests on the ability to convince others that what you are doing is not a matter of a competitive or zero-sum geopolitics. For example, contemporary US-led ideas of development are faced with an alternative in the "South-South cooperation" being proposed by China.[7]

The projection of power across the globe through trade and violence requires justification. Killing indigenous people and changing their economies for the benefit of wealthier people on the other side of the globe requires a "civilizing" mission. Fighting other primary countries is costly, in citizens' lives and state finances. That needs to be justified too. No word has been more useful in such justifications than *freedom*. The Dutch, the British, and the US have spread their economic tentacles, and used violence in the process, for material gain but in the name of freedom. This has been a historical constant. But the precise meaning of *freedom* has, of course, changed over time.[8]

The freedoms of the time have revolved around an evolving understanding of liberalism. The word *liberalism* has become a weapon, or a slur, in current political debates. It is, ironically, used against those to the left of the political center to suggest government overreach. Hence in the US the term is misused to mean a poorly defined "socialism." On the other hand, those on the political left use the term *neoliberalism* to criticize current economic policies of spending cuts and low taxes that have widened income inequalities.

The word *liberalism* should not be thought of in either of these two ways. Instead, it is an umbrella term for political, social, and economic freedoms that favor choices for individuals and groups and a relative lack of government oppression. It also advocates for a tendency to let businesses act with few taxes and tariffs. Free trade is an essential part of this formula, generally known as laissez-faire economics. However, the idea of laissez-faire and the thinking of Adam Smith have themselves become a controversial way to promote neoliberalism and quash criticism.[9] On the contrary, Adam Smith was very aware of the important role governments played in helping businesses thrive at home and merchants gain advantage abroad.[10]

The Radical Enlightenment of the Dutch

The Dutch geopolitical project was a liberal one, a radical enlightenment.[11] It challenged the power of the Catholic Church and gave voice to the idea of religious freedom. This ideological battle cry required the geopolitics of war, notably the Thirty Years' War (1618–48) against Spain and its attempt to stamp out Protestantism. The United Provinces were seen as a haven of religious toleration. Religious freedom generated other freedoms of thought that led to artistic movements and scientific advances. Dutch universities were the driving force of the adoption of Cartesian philosophy after French mathematician and scientist René Descartes moved to the United Provinces in the 1620s.[12] Cartesian philosophy questioned existing religious authority and catalyzed advances in the sciences of physics, astronomy, and medicine[13]—intellectual freedom, in other words.

Crucially, scholarship in Dutch cities exported new liberal ideas as it became the home of the publication of French-language journals that were gaining influence over the Latin-language journals largely published in northern Germany.[14] The period of Dutch seapower was also the Golden Age of Dutch art. Rembrandt (1606–69) and Vermeer (1632–75) are just two of the famous artists of the time. The collection of Dutch artists and their pupils benefited from the growing wealth of Dutch merchants who were eager to fill their new and large houses with the cutting-edge art of the day.[15]

Hugo Grotius (1583–1645) bridged the scholarly, legal, philosophical, and political arenas. Among his other achievements, he is regarded as helping to define and broadcast the philosophy of natural law. In the first half of the seventeenth century he defined the modern sense of republicanism, or "the idea that liberty, stability, virtue, and prosperity are best preserved when government is consultative and reserved to a closed oligarchy, such as the regents, with the resources, time, and education to devote themselves fully to public affairs, reverently abiding by the constitutional procedures of the republic."[16] Simply, let businesses be businesses, and people be people, but always have government force available as needed.

The ideas of Grotius were radical for the time. However, the role of the Dutch as hegemonic power meant that these ideas became accepted as global norms. These norms were meant to allow for domestic economic growth based on patterns of global trade and the inequality of primary-subsidiary relations. Belief in these relations as the basis for economic superiority have persisted. Hence, the essence of what Grotius argued can be found within the policies and attitudes of Britain and the US at the height of their geopolitical power. Basically, liberty allows for social harmony and economic prosperity. But though new forms of liberty are a challenge to the authoritarianism of the time, change is limited. Access to the levers of power remains somewhat restricted to the educated and privileged. That is the domestic basis of liberalism. The Dutch were the first to make sure that new freedoms led to "order and discipline."[17] Freedom was to go only so far. There had to be enough social stability to make sure that the elites who had pushed liberalism were not challenged by more radical ideas from less privileged groups, and, of course, that the money-making cogs of the economic machine turned effectively. The liberalism of the Dutch was radical but limited.[18]

Liberalism, and its counterpart "order," were not limited to home. Grotius applied the idea of liberty to trade—in his classic thesis of *Mare Liberum* (Freedom of the Seas; 1609).[19] This ideology, which has been central to the rules of global politics ever since, maintains the idea of international waters and the freedom of navigation within them. The principle was reinforced in the 1982 UNCLOS. Of course, those with the biggest merchant and military fleets have the most to gain from such freedom.[20] And even the author of the idea, Grotius, readily argued that the principle could be limited if one's own country was likely to suffer negative economic consequences.[21]

The liberalism of the Dutch catalyzed thought and social change. It also helped advance science and the economy. It offered a philosophical basis for the dominance of the world's oceans. Such projection across the globe led to violence. The application of the liberal ideas of Dutch hegemony displayed remarkable geographic flexibility. There was great variation in what was deemed as acceptable behavior for peoples in subsidiary countries compared to home.[22] The pattern of expansive rhetoric that hoped to hide more restrictive and less liberal acts was to be repeated through British and US hegemony.

Britain's "Modern" Empire

As Britain's power grew through the 1700s until its global dominance in the 1800s, it too sold a picture of freedom and liberalism, but it was highly qualified. In the E. M. Forster novel *Howards End* (published in 1910), the socially concerned female character Helen Schlegel is motivated by the chronic inequalities of wealth and opportunity in nineteenth-century Britain. Her concern is focused upon raising the status of one earnest working-class man who is intent on self-improvement to climb the social ladder and join the middle class. Dishonesty and complications mean he fails and is left destitute. Henry Wilcox, the scheming member of the business classes who has betrayed his promises to support the man, dryly remarks, "There always have been rich and poor . . . and there always will be rich and poor . . . and you can't deny that, in spite of all, the tendency of civilisation has on the whole been upward."[23] Perhaps so. But the novel gives a useful illustration of the dominant British social attitudes when it was the global economic and naval power. National wealth was the metric, by which the privileged few would profit handsomely. Inequalities of wealth were the necessary and accepted basis for national success.

There were many connected geographies of this model. There was a growth in industrial cities such as Leeds, Sheffield, Manchester, Newcastle, and Glasgow.[24] These new cities were seen as the most modern way of living. Important dignitaries toured them in awe of the output of steam-powered factories. They were also places of disgraceful living conditions. The new factories required a new workforce. Urban slums were part of the new ways of making money, as Friedrich Engels, Marx's coauthor of the *Communist Manifesto*, was keen to point out.[25]

The growth in industrial cities did create a new wealthy class, the industrial entrepreneurs. Much wealth was made. Industrial titans gained respect and fortunes. Isambard Kingdom Brunel (1806–59) was the world's greatest engineer. His genius was behind the building of railways, bridges, and steamships. He was the Bill Gates or Steve Jobs of his time. William Armstrong (1810–1900), the arms manufacturer and Tyneside-based shipbuilder, entertained foreign rulers, including in 1897 Nasir-ud-Din, the shah of Persia, and in 1889 Rama V, the king of Siam.[26]

Such new men of wealth disrupted but did not destroy the established social system of Britain. The landed aristocracy and their connection to the financial institutions of the City of London remained the dominant force.[27] Their social dominance was upheld by the monarchy, and the Crown was, and has remained, an imperial institution.[28]

The rapidly growing industrial and port cities in Britain constituted one end of an urban network that stretched into Britain's imperial territories.[29] British schoolchildren were taught with atlases showing much of the world map colored imperial red. But these were not just swathes of territory. They were inhabited places that were staffed and policed by those embracing the new career opportunity of colonial officer. The walls of British churches are covered by plaques in memory of the many colonial officers who lost their lives in the subsidiary areas of British empire. Of course, the indigenous died in far greater numbers. Famines were commonplace in an empire that was the institutional form of a vast generative sector.[30] Foodstuffs were shipped out to the metropolis, and as a result the people of Ireland and India, for example, starved to death.

The daily violence of imperial control was damaging to the colonizing and the colonized, especially the latter. In 1936 the novelist and journalist George Orwell reflected on his miserable time as a colonial police officer in British Burma:

> With one part of my mind I thought of the British Raj as an unbreakable tyranny, a something clamped down, *in saecula saeculorum* [forever and ever], upon the will of the prostrate peoples; with another part I thought that the greatest joy in the world would be to drive a bayonet into a Buddhist priest's guts. Feelings like this are normal by-products of imperialism; ask any Anglo-Indian official, if you can catch him off duty.[31]

The primary-subsidiary relationship is necessarily a violent one, especially when it takes the form of empire or colonial relations.

The period of British global power was built upon a system of accepted social inequality within the country and across the globe. The new estates of industrial magnates and the tenements where their workers lived were echoed in the splendor of Indian hill estates and the related squalor of slums in Calcutta and many such places.

And yet, remarkably, in the nineteenth century Britain was also the epicenter of global liberalism. The Houses of Parliament became known as the "Mother of Parliaments."[32] The Dominions built political systems mirroring the mother country. Issues of personal freedom, especially the depravity of slavery and the quest for women's access to the vote and other rights, were driven by British thought. But it was a very limited or peculiar form of liberalism, as its goal was to maintain imperial relations across the globe and the privileges of a landed elite at home.[33] Liberalism and wealth were to be built on limited opportunities for social mobility at home and an assumption of the civilizing benefits of imperialism.

British seapower and economic dominance were built on a liberalism in which "there always will be rich and poor." With such a bleak outlook for the people of the subsidiary countries, it is not surprising that alternative visions would be appealing. Communism and anti-imperialism were one set of alternatives. The US offered another in which being poor was a choice that you could refuse, and wealth for all was an attainable goal. The transition from British to US power meant that empire was seen as a thing of the past, and development as the pathway to the future.

The US Vision of Development

The idea of development was still global in its scope, similar to the visions of empire. But the difference was the belief that global connections would now be made willingly by newly independent countries and that all ships would rise on a tide of global economic growth: the poor would no longer be with us. But there was one caveat. Poor countries had to follow a template of economic activity that was dreamed up within the intermingled conversations of US academia and policymaking. The essence of the idea was Walt Whitman Rostow's *Stages of Economic Growth*, published in 1960.[34] Rostow was an economist and political theorist who was national security adviser for President Lyndon B. Johnson. In Rostow's vision of world politics, the type of society all countries and people should strive for was no longer the grimy and class-ridden industrial cities of Britain, but the sparkling consumer-driven suburbia of the US. As with all good visions, details such as the exclusion of black people from the suburbs were brushed under the carpet as much as possible.

For Rostow, the responsibility for economic growth rested with the poor countries. The era of imperial noblesse oblige, Kipling's "white man's burden," was over. If poor countries followed the template of development they would move through stages from "primitive" to the age of "mass consumption"[35]—presumably, from mud huts to the wealth of the suburbs. Images of what one could or should become were beamed around the world in Hollywood movies and TV shows. The good life was available for all in this vision: it simply required a disciplined approach to national economic growth.

The essence of developmentalism, as described in the *Stages of Economic Growth*, was a set of instructions that countries should follow as if they had freedom of choice. The reality is that countries exist within a web of unequal primary-subsidiary relations that limits what they can do. The message of developmentalism stressed the responsibilities of individual countries, while denying the restrictions imposed by a country's position in the global economy.[36] Developmentalism defined the pathway to success as one of stepping-stones to mass consumption. The world's poorer countries would become export-driven economies, gaining wealth through progressive stages of agricultural and commodity export, then low-value manufacturing, and then higher-value manufacturing and a service economy (figure 7.1).

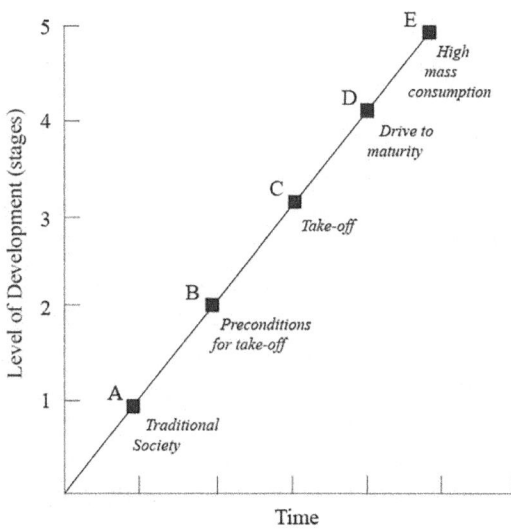

FIGURE 7.1   Rostow's stages of economic growth.

Source: Drawn by Anna Johnson.

There were just a couple of fundamental problems with the vision of development. First, countries trying to go through these stages were in competition with each other. This meant that the prices they could get for their products were lowered by the fact that other countries were trying to do the same thing.[37] Countries undercut each other, so wealth generation was a tough task. This meant that costs within the national economy had to be kept low, especially government expenditures and subsidies. The path to wealth was, apparently, austerity.[38]

Competition and austerity might have worked if it were not for the vagaries of global demand. If the global price of commodities dropped, then pressure was put on the "developing" economies. The pressures often required them to go into further debt managed mainly by US banks. Such debts came with further demands to limit government involvement in national economies and export more. Though Rostow sold development as a visionary carrot, in practice it involved a lot of painful sticks, including warfare.[39]

The second problem was that not everyone was on board with this economic growth. There was an alternative vision out there, communism. Though it's hard for us to picture this now, when communism is associated with the "hermit kingdom" of North Korea, the ideology had global appeal at the time of the transition from British to US global power. Economic hardship made an alternative to capitalism intriguing to workers in the richest economies. Many in the intelligentsia of Western countries were supportive.[40] And the sacrifices made by the Soviet Union in the defeat of Nazism were not lost on the general public, especially in Britain, which was grateful for relief provided by the eastern front of the Second World War.

Despite Winston Churchill's deep dislike of communism and his distrust of Joseph Stalin, the Soviet leader became known as "Uncle Joe": a homely nickname for a ruthless dictator. It's not surprising that Churchill felt a deep grief when he realized that President Franklin D. Roosevelt found Stalin the more relevant statesman in diplomatic discussions regarding the postwar world.[41] But Roosevelt could not manage Stalin. The Cold War was an ideological battle that meant "development" was not to be completely global in scope; some countries chose not to adopt the US model for participation in the global economy.[42]

Internal strife within the poorer countries and the existence of an alternative way to organize society meant that one thing did not change. The poorer countries needed to be policed by the wealthier and more powerful ones. Though empire was no longer the watchword, interference and a military presence across the globe remained. The US developed a system of global control that was largely but only partially successful. It had three components.

One component was the new set of institutions established by the US that were designed to promote free trade, the foundation of Rostow's economic vision. The Bretton Woods Agreement of 1944 established the International Monetary Fund and the World Bank.[43] In combination, the mission of these institutions was to prime the global economy in the wake of the Second World War. The mission established the new economic orthodoxy of development. Investments in infrastructure, especially in the world's poorest countries, were designed for purposes of trade with the wealthier countries.[44] As in periods of Dutch and British global power, the role of the dominant national economy was to strengthen its position through building a global infrastructure network. National transport networks led to ports and the maritime trade networks connecting rich and poor countries.

The second component was a network of observation, control, and interference in countries across the world to ensure that they followed the pathway Rostow had designed. Rather than imperial control, the project of development depended on ostensibly independent governments making national decisions that fell within the policies defined by the Bretton Woods institutions. But sometimes they didn't. People independent of imperial control had their own visions of how their societies and economies should or could be run. When these visions became policies nationalizing key industries or imposing price controls, or other ideas that did not have the Bretton Woods rubber stamp of approval, then the US intervened.[45] The main intervener was the CIA, which channeled funds to support political parties favorable to economic policies deemed to be acceptable.[46] If such support failed, then more drastic measures were imposed, such as instigating coups and supporting authoritarian regimes that would enforce austerity.

Poorer countries apparently needed to have the US police their internal affairs if they were to "develop" in the prescribed way. The policing occurred within the context of a global ideological battle: capitalism versus communism. This was a unique situation for the global power. Neither the Dutch or the British had experienced such a clear ideological challenge at the height of their global power.[47] Their world visions had been largely accepted by other powerful countries, and there was no organized political response from the weaker countries. The potential appeal of communism, in its variety of forms in the settings of different countries, meant that development was a global project in opposition to an alternative. Hence, the subtitle of Rostow's book was *A Non-Communist Manifesto*.[48]

Though framed within the ideals of "democracy" and "freedom," the use of US force, directly or indirectly, was closely tied to economic concerns. The United Fruit Company (UFC) in Guatemala is a cause célèbre. Through the 1950s, under the direction of Allen Dulles, the CIA flew under the radar of congressional oversight. The agency increasingly became more than an intelligence agency and was "intertwined with the armed services" through bureaucratic connections.[49] Military officers would be assigned to a CIA mission and then return to their posts as agency missionaries. If that was not enough interinstitutional empire building, Dulles kept close connections with US businesses, as many were old clients from his time as a D.C. lawyer.[50]

When, in 1952, President Jacobo Arbenz of Guatemala had the audacity to propose land reform in the name of social justice, the UFC cried foul. Seventy percent of the country's farmland was owned by 2 percent of landowners. And the UFC was set to lose vast properties to poor farmers.[51] Also, the UFC owned nearly every mile of Guatemala's railway tracks, its only major Atlantic port, and the telephone system[52]—in other words, the country's infrastructure. The machinations of the CIA soon led to Arbenz's ousting, the trashing of his reputation through a disinformation campaign, and the installation of a friendly government.[53] The example of Guatemala and the UFC echoes the way the Dutch East India and British India Company used political connections at home to embed themselves in political relations abroad to cultivate a friendly setting, while dominating communications networks to allow for an export economy that benefited shareholders but not the local population.[54] Today the Western press is aghast with shock and vocal with accusation as China attempts to construct the same web of far-water relations.

A third component of global control was necessary, the deployment of military strength across the oceans and stationed across the continents. The Cold War was the military expression of the project of development.[55] The US built upon a process of global military reach that began in earnest during the Second World War. It took over British military establishments in Australia and the Pacific and Indian Oceans, while retaining its presence in Britain itself. Instead of heeding the "Yankees go home" graffiti of the war, US forces settled down. After advancing across Germany to help defeat Hitler, they stayed in the country and made their presence an everyday reality within German towns near military bases. The US also became the dominant power in the Mediterranean Sea, ousting what had been established British power and nurturing new alliances, such as the one with Turkey.

On the other side of the globe, the US presence in the western Pacific was both strong and compromised. The defeat of Japan allowed the US to rewrite its constitution.[56] The aim was to make Japan a country that would no longer challenge US power projection in the region but would act as a host to US bases, notably the enormous complexes on Okinawa.[57]

On the other hand, the prewar visions of US influence in China were thwarted by national support for Mao's vision of communism. The US also found itself in an ideological and policy predicament by thwarting anti-imperial ambitions in Korea and Vietnam and embarking on postcolonial military campaigns. If countries did not want Rostowian development, they apparently needed to be bombed "back to the stone age" (in the words of US Air Force general and later armed services' chief of staff Curtis LeMay)[58]—ironically, a condition not unlike the stage of growth Rostow thought they were starting from. War in the periphery could be a precursor for development. Napalm could wipe the slate clean, and once a country had learned the errors of its ways it could embark on the development project. This has worked, to some extent for Vietnam, though not as a US vassal state, and for South Korea. Bluntly, force projection is always partial and, to some degree, negotiated.

The key point is that the project of development required a global political and military presence across the globe.[59] The economic manifesto of US global power required the same export of violence and control that the Dutch and British had found to be necessary. Of course, the way it appeared on the ground was different; technology and political circumstances had changed. But the symbiosis of economic networks and the projection of political control through military strength carried over from previous epochs.

The geopolitics of force projection and the establishment of global economic networks meant that the US now felt the imperative to be present in a swathe of far waters. These far waters were the shores of countries looking to "develop" through the export of commodities and, if they progressed through Rostow's stages, manufactured goods. Oceanic trade networks had to be built and protected. The presence of an alternative, in the form of Soviet- and Chinese-inspired communist projects that connected to nationalist (or anti-imperial) movements across Asia, Africa, and South and Central America, meant that the imperative of far-water presence required an enormous economic and political commitment from the US.[60] This commitment was expressed in the Truman Doctrine to fight communism anywhere in the world.[61]

The commitment lasted for a long time. But it is now unwinding in the face of economic cost, a lack of political will, and allies identifying new opportunities—as well as the emergence of another country with ambitions to control its own near waters and create its own far-water presence. Of course, that would be China.

China's Message of "South-South Cooperation"

China's ongoing attempts to claim to be acting for the good of the world are very different from the rhetoric of the US, Britain, and the Dutch. This is for two reasons. One is that rather than depicting itself as the world's most powerful country, China claims, when it is to its benefit, to be a "developing country." The second reason is that the three previous hegemonic countries have had some basis for saying that they were the leading lights of liberalism in the world. Instead, as a single-party authoritarian country, China has to claim that the political system of the West is in crisis and failing. If China is to use soft power in its strategy of force projection, it is going to have to convince other countries that its model of government and global relations is what is needed at the moment. Though it is unlikely to succeed in convincing primary powers, it may have more success with subsidiary countries.

China is hoping that the mundane phrases of "mutual benefit" and "South-South cooperation" will become as influential as the US's catchphrase of the "American dream." China's strategy is to use a rhetoric that signals China has a similar history to subsidiary countries, understands their position in the world economy, and is sympathetic to their historical difficulties in dealing with primary countries.[62] China is not saying something along the lines of "Look what we've done, why not try to copy us?" Instead, it is saying something like "We understand your pain and we're here to help." Arguably, it is a very appealing call. The participation of some subsidiary countries in the BRI suggests that some countries are receptive to China's rhetoric, though other governments and commentators remain highly skeptical. The jury is still out as to whether it is just another siren call of a powerful country seeking to make primary-subsidiary relations in the same old way, or whether it is truly transformative.

The undoubted economic power of China is being used as an illustration to other subsidiary countries of what can be achieved in a global economy based on competition and inequality. The basis for China's story of what can be done is its own history of emerging from being the punching bag of imperial powers to become an independent country seeking its own power and wealth. Additionally, China is saying that the very nature of global economic relations is ripe for change. The post–Second World War ideology of "development" is attacked as a means to keep subsidiary countries poor.

Instead, China says that the relations it is building through trade and investment are in the spirit of mutual growth, based on a rose-tinted history of the ancient Silk Road.[63] The message is that the investments in infrastructure that China has embarked upon, and the trade they are designed to facilitate, will lead to economic growth for subsidiary countries that will allow them to thrive and become wealthy themselves. Such language is, of course, very similar to that of the US prophets of growth, such as W. W. Rostow.

The key difference is that China is offering a compact between a whole set of countries. China's message is one of "We're all in this together" rather than the developmentalist message of "Everyone for themselves and here's the map to climb to the top." The implication is that a bloc of countries have suffered from primary-subsidiary relations and that China will fix that for good.

This idea was made clear at the early stage of the BRI project when the focus was on cooperation with neighbors, so-called periphery diplomacy based on a sense of a historic "big family of harmonious co-existence," in the words of President Xi Jinping.[64] Since then the geography of the BRI has become indistinct, and any sense of China mapping it precisely has been avoided. Abstract or conceptual maps are preferred.[65] This is seen as a deliberate strategy to portray the BRI as "an unlimited and boundless global campaign."[66]

Shouting the idea of "South-South cooperation" from the rooftops reminds the vast majority of the world's population that their history is one of colonial and postcolonial relations. "South-South cooperation" is a reminder of the cost of the history and legacies of "North-South" inequalities. It is a powerful rhetorical weapon, and one that provides an attractive alternative to the never-ending yet largely ineffective promises of development.

China's agenda of "South-South cooperation" is appealing to subsidiary countries for another reason—the promise of noninterference in their domestic politics. China's rhetoric stands in clear contrast to the direct rule of British imperialism and the indirect control of US interventions in the name of anticommunism and the spread of "democracy." Instead, China has taken a very different line of supporting the sovereign right of governments to do what they want to do within their own borders. Of course, this is an echo of China's own practices within its country, especially the suppression of Uyghur identity in Xinjiang Province and the suppression of political freedom of expression. While Western critics are keen to point this out, China can readily point to the Cold War history of the US suppressing elections and opposition parties across the world.

In sum, China's rhetoric has a lot of appeal to subsidiary countries.[67] It promises a pathway to economic growth without domination or subservience, and without a threat of public harangues on human rights violations or other political crimes and misdemeanors. And any sense of uninvited covert or military intervention is certainly absent from the conversation.

Despite these potential appeals, the attractive power of China's words may well be met with skepticism for three reasons. First, despite all the verbal promises of economic relations being of mutual benefit to China and any subsidiary country, it is generally realized that the overall nature of primary-subsidiary connections is being continued, as described in chapter 5. Second, despite China's "We're all in this together" rhetoric, China has suggested at other times that it is more interested in a hierarchy of geopolitical interests in which "great power" relations take precedence over neighbors and subsidiary countries.[68] Third, China's language does little to disguise its ambition to become a great power itself, leaving room for questions as to whether subsidiary countries are merely the stepping-stones on this ambitious path.[69]

These contradictions should not be surprising. The rhetoric used to justify or excuse actions diverges from the facts of China's economic growth and the necessary force projection that it entails. The question remains as to how much of the world (especially subsidiary countries) will buy into the rhetoric, or at least be willing to overlook the contradictions. There also remains the question of whether China's model of authoritarianism and a large dose of state involvement in the economy will have global appeal. Past hegemonic powers have been liberal in their politics, though they have been involved in the economy to different degrees across sectors and at different times. On the whole, history leads us to expect that China's model will fail, as did other "national socialist" projects such as Hitler's Germany and Japan's imperial modernization. On the other hand, maybe global crises, such as climate change, mean that a new model is required and China is ahead of the game, at least in its rhetoric.

The current moment of geopolitical transition sees the naval geopolitics of seapower and the ideological geopolitics of visions of modernity combining to raise tensions between the US and China. US developmentalism is being challenged by a new Chinese rhetoric of cooperation. Countries now have a choice of which vision of primary-subsidiary relations to follow. But geopolitics is more than just rhetoric. It is also about the friction between competing military presences in a country's near waters. The US no longer has unrestricted access to the western Pacific and the South China Sea—access that was an outcome of the earlier process of force projection culminating in US victory and Japanese unconditional surrender in the Second World War. Islands were important physical features in the competition between the US and Japan. They are at the forefront of today's tensions between the US and China.

The following chapter addresses why the unique physical geographic and geopolitical nature of islands makes them a historic and contemporary flashpoint for the geopolitics of seapower and the underlying geopolitical relations.

EIGHT

No Island Is an Island

Small islands and coral reefs a long way from the shores of the US and Europe have recently drawn a lot of attention from the politicians and media of Western countries. It is often argued that these small islands, located in the South China Sea, could lead to a major war.[1] Such fears cannot be discounted. Why? It is not the islands themselves, and the resources within their EEZs, that are the cause for potential war, but the importance of seapower in the projection of geopolitical force. Islands are especially important geographic and political features that enable the projection of seapower and attempts to resist the projection of seapower by others.

Islands have become a focus for those concerned about an impending global war because of China's new project to change the geography of global trade and challenge the dominance of US visions of primary-subsidiary relations. The Belt and Road Initiative (BRI) is challenging trade and investment patterns that have been largely present and taken for granted since the Second World War. The new options being offered by China are somewhat appealing. Even primary countries allied with the US are finding them hard to resist. China's near waters were once the US's (and before that Britain's) far waters. European, Middle Eastern, and African near waters are becoming China's far waters. This is the current state of the geopolitical dynamics of seapower and trade relations.

The geopolitics of seapower involves the use of oceanic physical features such as choke points and open seas as SLOCs. Islands are a particular physical geographic feature because of their existence as liminal physical spaces that are both territorial and oceanic and that bridge the two.[2] Islands are liminal as they provide access to both land and sea. The control of an island is a form of territorial geopolitics that is about controlling and possessing a piece of *terra firma* and excluding the presence and use of others. The control of an island enables the projection of naval power in the island's vicinity and beyond the horizon (figure 8.1).[3] A period of flux in the geopolitics of seapower is likely to involve conflict over the control of particular islands.

The control of an island enables the projection of seapower in the neighborhood and the ability to help or hinder the flow of trade through adjacent SLOCs.[4] Also, the control of an island in one ocean may enable the projection of force into other oceans. For example, the US switched control of Caribbean islands from Britain to the US at the outset of the Second World War not just to secure the US's Atlantic flank but to organize its national security resources to allow for projection of power in the Pacific.[5] Islands in near waters play a defensive role for a country that, once secured, can enable the projection of power nearby or across the globe.

Of course, the same islands are in the near water of one country, or more, and the far water of other countries. The way islands are crucial for the geopolitics of SLOCs and the projection of power in parts of the oceans that are simultaneously near and far waters means that they are the focus of military strategies. The islands in the South China Sea are in the near

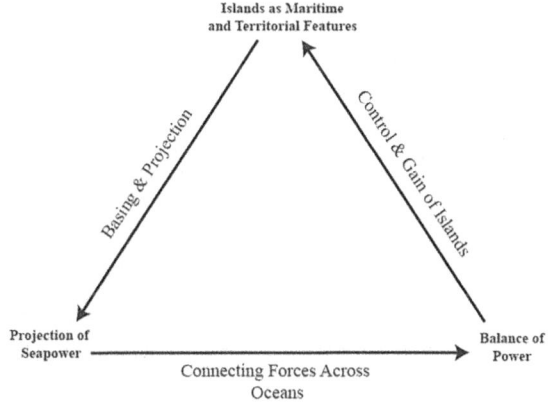

FIGURE 8.1.   The role of islands in force projection.

Source: Created by the author; appeared in C. Flint, "Seapower, Geostrategic Relations, and Islandness: The World War Two Destroyers for Bases Deal," in the open-access *Island Studies Journal* 16, no. 1 (2021): 271–91.

waters of China, the Philippines, Vietnam, and other countries. They are also in the far waters of the US. These islands are physical features that play a role in the intertwined geopolitics of trade and national security. Islands play a key role in the current period of geopolitical change because of the flux in primary-subsidiary and primary-primary relations. The flux in these relations is driven by related economic shifts. The historical cases of the Dutch, Britain, and the US have displayed similar changing geopolitical calculations regarding islands. In the past these economic changes have led to war and/or political negotiations that have transferred control of islands from one country to another.

The Dutch in a Chokehold

The Dutch saw that the control of islands was essential in their projection of seapower. They also recognized that other countries could use the security advantage of choke points to limit their ambition. The Kattegat is the crucial entry into the Baltic Sea with Denmark to the south and west and Sweden to the north and east. The channel becomes particularly narrow as ships must navigate past the island of Zealand, with the city of Copenhagen located on the eastern shore.

The early phase of the Dutch rise to power was based upon the trade in bulk goods in the near waters of the Baltic. The Danish had other ideas and used the constricted channel of the Danish Sound as a choke point that led to tolls being placed on Dutch shipping.[6] This threat to Dutch trade was conquered by diplomatic outreach to the Hanseatic League and Sweden. The Danish backed off, and in 1613–14 the Dutch established a *Pax Neerlandica* in the Baltic and promoted the ideology of the freedom of the seas.[7]

The problem of Dutch access to the Baltic did not go away, though. There is always some challenge to the hegemonic power. In the 1640s the Danes collaborated with the Spanish to challenge the Dutch dominance of the Baltic. The Dutch needed a show of naval strength to fight against a new imposition of tolls and maintain control of their near waters.[8] Yet the problem of the Kattegat choke point persisted, especially with the growing strength of Sweden. In the 1650s the Swedish challenged the Baltic *Pax Neerlandica* by imposing a blockade on Danzig that disrupted the Dutch grain trade. The next step was even more threatening. Sweden took control of the Danish islands in the Sound. The Dutch had to send a naval force to fight the Swedes, who held both sides of the Sound until the Dutch navy overthrew Swedish control of Copenhagen in 1658.[9]

However, the Dutch dominance of trade in the Baltic created resentment from other powers. In 1659 the English joined forces with the Swedes, leading to a confrontation between the Dutch and the combined fleets of England and Sweden in the narrow channels between the Danish islands of Fuenen and Zealand. Tensions were high, but the English backed down and the Dutch avoided conflict. Still, the issue did not go away.[10] Sweden, France, and England continued diplomatic negotiations to try to break the dominance of the Dutch over Baltic trade. Though control of near waters was essential for the Dutch to use trade to become a global power, that control could never be taken for granted, and other countries used choke points in their battles over tolls and freedom of navigation.

Islands were also important for the Dutch projection of power. The presence of resources on islands made them attractive. The very name "Spice Islands" shows the economic value of Amboina, Tidore, and Ternate in what the Dutch called the East Indies. They also became the site for Dutch garrisons.[11] The control of these islands became crucial in battles over the control of Asian trade and the geographic focus upon the choke point of the Moluccan Strait. In the 1640s the Strait and the East Indies were an important theater in the Eighty Years' War with Spain, including control of Manila. The very last battles of that war occurred on the island of Ternate.[12] Just as the Danish Sound was a choke point highlighting the vulnerability of the Dutch in their near waters, the Moluccan Strait was a choke point for the lucrative trade with Asia. The Dutch were able to apply the chokehold in this piece of the ocean, exclude the Portuguese, and gain dominance themselves.[13]

Islands are geographic features that cause strategic headaches and opportunities for seapowers. Dutch control of the Spice Islands restricted the activity of competitors and ensured the profitable functioning of a key generative sector. On the other hand, and closer to home, the ability of the Danes and Swedes to use Zealand as a plug in the Kattegat was an aggravation to the Dutch throughout their reign as the global seapower. The history of Dutch seapower shows that islands play a twin role in the imperatives of offense and defense. The dual role of islands in the defense of near waters and the projection of power in far waters is also seen in the period of British seapower.

Britain's Empire of Islands

Half the size of Gibraltar but with much strategic importance, the island of Heligoland lies three hundred miles off the coast of Britain but just thirty miles off the coast of Germany, and one hundred miles from the port of Hamburg. The small island played a big role in the geopolitical competition between Germany and Britain. Notably, Heligoland was important for Britain's near- and far-waters strategies.

In 1806 the geopolitics of the island was a Continental matter and also a step on the pathway to a global empire built upon seapower. This dual role is an example of how the geopolitics of islands extends beyond the immediate horizon. The French defeat of Prussia at Jena and Auerstedt raised British fears of Napoleonic domination of northern Europe and the end of Danish neutrality.[14] If Denmark were to ally itself with France, the Danes could turn Heligoland into a fortress and allow France to turn its attention to the world's oceans, despite the recent defeat at the Battle of Trafalgar. The British seized the island from Denmark with the recognition that, in the words of British agent and diplomat Edward Thornton, "a squadron of the King's ships could regulate from hence the principal rivers of the North Sea."[15]

Heligoland was "the hinge between empire and Continent," and epitomized the geography of islands that are both territorial and defined entities while also being liminal and unspecific.[16] In other words, such islands are the connective tissue of the tentacles of seapower. The seizure of the island in 1807 provided a vital link between Britain and the Continent as it faced the challenge posed by Napoleon's France. Far from being an "isolated rock," in the words of Sir John Hindmarsh, who became governor in 1840, it enabled British influence on the Continent with a minimal presence.[17]

The island had its own chamber of commerce made up of traders from London, Hull, Bremen, and Hamburg.[18] It was a British offshore entrepôt that funneled the products from British colonies, especially from "East India" on to the Continent.[19] But as we have seen throughout this book, economic endeavors cannot be separated from military exploits. Heligoland served as a base for Hanoverian troops that had escaped from Napoleon's onslaught and as a recruitment station for those wanting to continue the fight.[20] Through the 1800s the government, economy, and culture of Heligoland was a British and German mixture.

In the hands of the British, Heligoland became a means of keeping hostile forces away from British near waters. It was also a means of making sure competitors were at a disadvantage in exploring the far waters in which Britain was becoming ever more dominant. Additionally, Heligoland was a staging post for Britain to continue to trade with Europe in the face of sanctions imposed by Napoleon. But more than that, Heligoland was just one island in a chain coming under British control. The goal was an "insular empire" that allowed for the simultaneous management of the Continent and the projection of power into far waters.[21] This was a singular or combined strategy, not a compartmentalization of separate policies or visions with one more important than the other.

The wars with France at the beginning of the 1800s led to British control of a string of islands: Corsica, Elba, Malta, Sicily, and the Ionian Islands—along with Gibraltar. These islands acted as a barrier to French ambitions and as a means to engage the Continent without being present on the landmass. But these "European possessions," as they were called at the time, also ensured that the Mediterranean Sea was under British control. Further, the islands were to act as "political workshops." They were to be locations of political and constitutional "experiments" modeled on British institutions.[22] The islands were export markets for British visions of development.

The Mediterranean, aptly known at the time as the Middle Sea, was a stretch of waters that achieved three British geopolitical goals: a managerial influence on the European continent, the protection of near waters, and, once the Suez Canal opened in 1869, the ability to reach important Asian far waters. The insular empire involved the construction of island bases to enable these three strategic goals.

Heligoland played a crucial role in establishing Britain as a seapower in the early 1800s. The island also played a role in what was to become the endgame of British hegemony. In 1890 Germany and Britain signed the Heligoland-Zanzibar Treaty. It concerned both near and far waters. The treaty consisted of twelve articles. Only the last one discussed Heligoland. The bulk of the treaty was focused on carving out parts of East and West Africa as imperial spheres of influence for the two countries. Commercial interests in both Britain and Germany were pushing for an aggressive stance. The issue was not so much the East African coast itself but how access to the coast would provide access to the hinterlands of the major African rivers and the Great Lakes region. Though the importance of the Nile River to Britain's imperial strategy made it unlikely that a weaker Germany would force the issue, there was still a lot of haggling to be done.[23] In the end, Britain got all the concessions it had wanted in Africa, in a region in which it held the upper hand. The deal was explicitly connected to the exchange of Heligoland to negate the moves by German imperialists to increase and consolidate their commercial interests in Zanzibar.[24]

Though the hinterlands mattered, it was the position of the island of Zanzibar in far waters that was crucial. The island connected the homeland to the continental interior of Africa, a key British generative sector. The diplomatic benefit for Britain was that German voices proposing to carve out their own generative sector within the same part of the world were muted. Control of the island of Zanzibar helped Britain maintain its presence in far waters.

Without doubt, Britain got the better end of the deal in Africa. The treaty demonstrated that Britain was the dominant country in African far waters. It was because of this that the treaty came under harsh criticism from the political right in Germany. The colonialist Carl Peters coined the pithy retort that Germany had given away three African kingdoms for the "bathtub Heligoland." The British explorer Henry Stanley furthered the sense that Britain had outwitted the Germans with his phrase that Britain had gained a new suit for an old trouser-button.[25] But what else could a country like Germany do, given it had aims to be a global power but was unable to thwart the dominant seapower? Perhaps, in the context of 1890, it could do little but throw in the towel. The 1890 treaty was certainly interpreted this way in German politics.

However, thinking of the dynamics of near and far waters as a historical process allows us to draw a different conclusion. German imperialists could certainly feel aggrieved that their ambitions had been curtailed and that Britain had secured the advantage. But what Germany achieved was the ability to secure its own near waters even in the face of dominant British seapower. The entrance to the Kiel canal was now protected. The industrial base for Germany's naval rearmament and for the arms race with Britain that was a major catalyst for the First World War was protected. In the long game of geopolitics, Germany was securing its near waters.

After 1890 the island became "Germanized." Links between Germany and the British Empire were cut. The island became a site of confrontation. The Kaiser and his fleet made frequent trips to an island that now had German street names and was a part of the Prussian state.[26] It became the "German Gibraltar," and the landscape was transformed. "By 1914, easily half of Heligoland was taken up by military installations. A sixth of the island had been tunneled under or dug into, with bunkers and depots carved fifteen meters deep into the red rock."[27] The island featured heavily in British and German war plans in the buildup to the First World War.

German control would make a British blockade difficult. But there was not only a perceived defensive advantage for Germany. In German emperor Kaiser Wilhelm II's evocative language, the German fleet would be "leaning on Heligoland," from which it could attack the British coast: "Only if the mailed fist is thus held before his face will the British Lion hide his tail."[28]

When war came, the island played a defensive role rather than being the launching pad that the Kaiser had envisioned. In August 1914, the first month of the war, the island became part of a submarine and destroyer picket line that protected Germany's crucial near waters around Wilhelmshaven and the Keil Canal. The artillery on Heligoland complemented Germany's naval forces. Britain's response was also defensive, setting up a line that protected the English Channel and its North Sea coastline.[29] No great battle or breakout into the opponent's near waters happened. Just three major engagements occurred in the North Sea throughout the war. The first became known as the Battle of Heligoland Bight, fought on August 28, 1914. The balance of loss on naval tonnage and personnel allowed this to be chalked up as a British victory, though the imbalance of forces made the outcome almost inevitable.

In the Second World War, Hitler used Heligoland as a symbol of Germany's weakness and humiliation. He rebuilt the fortifications on the island with the goal of making it a naval base, similar to the role of the island in the First World War.[30] But the nature of war had changed, and now attacks on the island came from the air.[31] It was targeted by British and US bombers, as both countries were now invested in protecting British near waters. Near the end of the war the occupants of the island considered overthrowing the German garrison to stop the bombing.[32] It was to no avail, and the rhetoric that the island would become one of the holdout "citadels" of the Nazi regime provoked ferocious bombing attacks. In April 1945 the inhabitants of the island took a few possessions and evacuated the devastated island.[33]

The history of conflicts over Heligoland provides a number of broader lessons about the geopolitical role of islands. Geographical proximity to Britain and the Continent meant that the near waters of rivals overlapped. The island was seen as a "rightful" possession by two countries, and each saw it as vital in the defense of near waters. More importantly, the geopolitical importance of an island rests in its role in allowing for a projection of power. In the case of Heligoland and the rest of the "insular empire," the projection was with an eye to the European continent and far waters. Conflicts and deals between countries over the island were conducted with a view to far waters as much as near waters. Controlling islands is simultaneously about defense and offense. Plus, an island's importance is usually a matter of its connection to other islands. Britain's "insular empire" was the precursor to today's tensions over island chains.

As discussed throughout the book, it was Britain's inability to secure its far waters that highlighted its geopolitical weakness. And that weakness impelled the US to focus on islands in near and far waters, in the Atlantic and Pacific Oceans, in the process of becoming the hegemonic power.

The US Atlantic and Pacific Flanks

Like the Dutch and the British before them, the US was able to project power into multiple oceans. It reached from its eastern and western coastlines across the Atlantic and Pacific oceans. The projection of power across the Atlantic and into the European continent was a necessary strategic move to settle security issues on the eastern flank and create a global context that allowed for US projection of power into the Pacific. These twin movements of force projection required controlling islands and turning them into garrisons.[34] In the Second World War, the Destroyers for Bases deal and Operation Bolero were relatively bloodless advances across the Atlantic that involved Caribbean islands, Newfoundland, Iceland, Ireland, and Britain. The control of these islands secured a US flank that preceded the bloodier island-hopping battles in the Pacific.

After the Second World War the geography of the Atlantic remained a landscape of islands that allowed for the policing of SLOCs and the securing of US presence on the European continent. These maritime and continental strategic achievements prevented a new round of global war, this time with the Soviet Union as the adversary, while ensuring global trade routes. Though there was no new global war, the Cold War provided a host of skirmishes and tensions, and, in the Pacific theater, actual wars. In the Atlantic, the Greenland-Iceland-United Kingdom (GIUK) gap became a key security focus.

The GIUK gap consists of the stretches of the North Atlantic that can use the three islands to prevent or hinder ships from heading into the Atlantic from the north or toward the Arctic from the south (map 8.1).[35] The GIUK gap was an important arena of the Cold War, and the seabed itself became militarized through the deployment of listening devices and mines. The first generation of Soviet nuclear submarines needed to travel through the gap to be able to target the US. Protection of the near waters and homeland of the US required controlling the island barrier chain in the North Atlantic. As nuclear missile technology developed, Soviet submarines did not need to break into the Atlantic to be a threat. However, a change in NATO strategy based on "flexibility" meant that any war on the European continent required shipping military personnel and equipment across the Atlantic. These shipments would be vulnerable to Soviet attack submarines if they were able to break through the GIUK gap. The potential for some sort of a repeat of Operation Bolero and the Battle of the Atlantic required the control of the GIUK islands.

The collapse of the Soviet Union provided a brief respite, but the resurgence of Russian naval expeditions into the Atlantic has led to a new round of tensions. In 2016 Admiral James G. Foggo III, then commander of the US Navy's Sixth Fleet, speculated on a "fourth Battle of the Atlantic."[36] NATO's problems are now compounded by the new technology of long-range anti-ship missiles and anti–access/area denial capability. The ability of the US to operate in far waters that include Russian near waters has been reduced. The renewed tension in the Atlantic led the US in 2018 to reestablish its Second Fleet, reemphasize the North Atlantic as a strategic focus, and refurbish its military base in Keflavik, Iceland.

Russian naval military doctrine still includes the aim to challenge NATO in the Atlantic, the Mediterranean, and the Black Sea.[37] This would require pushing forces through the GIUK gap. Another contemporary threat is to

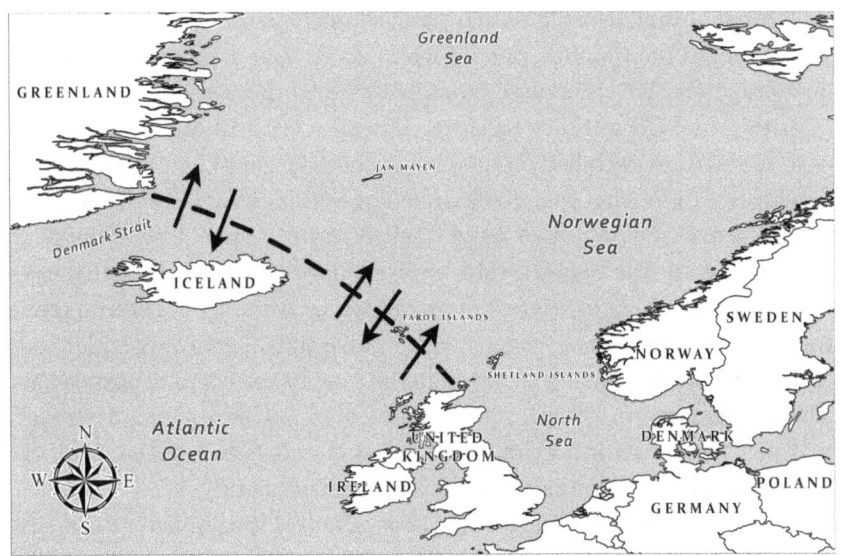

MAP 8.1. The Greenland-Iceland-United Kingdom (GIUK) gap.

Source: Original work by Carson Liesik, using multiple sources freely available on the internet.

the seabed cables that span the Atlantic. Influence and interests require broadband communication, a new form of force projection. In sum, the US and its NATO allies remain vulnerable to Russian submarine attack. The GIUK gap continues to be a crucial geographic landscape of blockade. The islands of the North Atlantic that were used in US force projection across the Atlantic remain relevant in protecting those far-water interests and, to some extent, US near waters.

The Pacific Ocean theater of the Second World War was a battleground of islands. The need to control islands to secure victory was made clear by two opening moments of the war. Japan attacked Pearl Harbor in Hawaii, the archipelago that was essential for US control of its Pacific near waters. The first riposte by the US, a symbolic response to perk up the American public, was the so-called Doolittle raid. The operation was led by US Army Lieutenant Colonel James (Jimmy) H. Doolittle. It required B-25 bombers to launch from an aircraft carrier, the USS *Hornet*, fly over Japan to target cities, and then fly on to the China to land, hopefully, in friendly territory. On April 17, 1942, the sixteen bombers took off from aircraft carrier, each carrying just four bombs, but none reached Chinese airfields as planned. Most crash-landed after running out of fuel; one crew made it to Vladivostok, where they were interned by the Soviets (officially neutral in the Pacific theater). Eight of the planes were captured by the Japanese, leading to either execution or imprisonment for the crew.[38] Despite these losses, the operation has been hailed as a successful example of US military bravado ever since.

Looking at the Doolittle raid with a focus on near and far waters shows how desperate the action was. Japan remained a threat to US near waters after the raid. US military bases on Hawaii were still at risk, and Japanese submarines patrolled off the Pacific coast. In February 1942 one even launched a futile shelling attack aimed at fuel tanks at Ellwood Airfield in California.[39] On the other hand, the US was not even close to the near waters of Japan. The Doolittle raid required sacrificing aircraft, with the acceptance of the high likelihood of casualties, because the US had no other way to enter Japan's near waters. At the same time, Japan was rapidly advancing from island to island, through the established colonial possessions of European powers. For example, carrier-based Japanese planes destroyed British naval bases in Ceylon (Sri Lanka) just days before the Doolittle raid.[40] The invasion of Australia was a distinct possibility.

Preventing the fall of Hawaii and Australia was the immediate concern after the Pearl Harbor attack. Securing these territories was essential to maintaining a line of communication between US near waters and the far waters that were to be the site of decisive battles. The Philippines, Malaya and Singapore, Burma, and the Dutch East Indies would all soon fall to Japan. The story of how the tide of war was turned is well known. The Battle of Midway in June 1942 was a new type of sea battle in which carrier-based bombers and torpedo planes tried to sink the opposition's aircraft carriers. Without these "mother ships" force could not be projected. The US sank or otherwise put out of action four Japanese aircraft carriers, a heavy cruiser, a cruiser, and several destroyers.[41] In comparison, Admiral King stated that "US losses are inconsiderable," though they included the aircraft carrier USS *Yorktown* and a destroyer, the USS *Hammann*.[42]

Though the Battle of Midway was a crucial victory, it only ushered in a new phase of the war: a war of attrition that required battles over islands and atolls. This was the strategy of "island-hopping" to push the Japanese back from the far waters they had controlled in the South Pacific all the way to New Guinea. The process now became one in which the US regained control of islands it had previously used to project its power into the Pacific, especially the Philippines, and those once controlled by its allies, such as New Guinea. The final and very costly battle was over control of Okinawa,[43] an island that had once been independent but was colonized by Japan to solidify the security of its near waters. It is now a massive US military outpost in US Pacific far waters.

The US waged the Second World War in the Pacific against a foe it described as imperialist and militaristic. These two labels were quite accurate. The irony is that after the victory they imposed their own military presence in the far waters that were, of course, simultaneously other people's near waters.[44] Japan rejected the imperialism that had provoked the war and "embraced defeat" by acquiescing to US demands for demilitarization while accepting the establishment of US bases across the archipelago.[45] Okinawa was the key island in this strategy and became the home to over thirty US bases covering about 20 percent of the island.[46] The Kadena Airbase alone is home to over fourteen thousand US troops. The local neighborhoods look like parts of American suburbia, and the US military presence has distorted the cost of housing to the detriment of the locals. Okinawa neighborhoods have also become districts for the selling of sex to US military personnel. The US presence remains a point of political contention with residents who are furious about the risks they face from aircraft accidents and the sexual violence of US troops.[47] The Japanese and US arguments are that these are relatively minor and occasional aberrations and that the costs are worth negating a greater risk. The message is that the people of Okinawa, Japan, the Philippines, Guam, et cetera should see the benefits of the US presence in their towns.

Such "benefits," if they do indeed exist, are because of the role of islands in projecting power and providing points of resistance to the counterprojection of power by enemies. In the post–Second World War period the Cold War provided the geopolitical context in which a "greater risk" could be identified and used to justify US presence in Pacific far waters. The island bases of Okinawa and the Philippines were the launching pads for military operations in the Korean and Vietnam Wars. No Doolittle-esque operations were needed. Permanent bases on islands allowed for the projection of force through Asian near waters and on to the continent itself.

The US strategy was not just about its own force projection. The goal was also to prevent the force projection of others, namely the Soviet Union and China. US policy in the Cold War was a continuation of the "quarantine" idea evoked by President Franklin D. Roosevelt in the Second World War.[48] In a speech given in January 1950, Secretary of State Dean Acheson defined a defensive line that ran along the Aleutian Islands, through the Japan archipelago, and to the Ryukyus.[49] This island-based line was the outer limit of US Pacific near waters. It was a line not to be crossed without a direct US military response. Though the term was not used at the time, Acheson's statement was the definition of what is now known as area denial.[50] The Pacific near waters of the US were denied as far waters for other countries.

In contrast, the status of the Asian far waters on the other side of the perimeter was ambiguous. Countries beyond the perimeter were initially treated on the basis of the postwar principle that independent countries were able to make their own decisions. This strategic stance matched the idea of anti-imperialism and Rostow's developmentalism. But the geography of the Cold War in Asia had yet to become clear. Secretary of State Acheson was loath to commit the US to military action beyond the defensive perimeter. In fact, in January 1950 he said, "It must be clear that no person can guarantee these areas against military attack. But it must also be clear that such a guarantee is hardly sensible or necessary within the realm of practical relationship."[51] For many, this statement has been interpreted as giving a green light to Soviet support for the start of the Korean War.[52]

The conflict in Korea was just one of a set of Cold War battles over the littoral countries of Korea, Vietnam and Malaysia, and the island of Taiwan. In a change of strategy, the far waters and countries beyond Acheson's perimeter were not, as he had said in 1950, to be allowed to choose their friends and make their own decisions. They became lands adjoining far waters that were to be fought over in a zero-sum game of competing visions: capitalist developmentalism versus communist statism. US seapower became the way to access far waters to gain influence in Southeast and East Asian countries.

The Cold War twin-geographies of accessing other's near waters while denying access to the US's near waters are no longer stable. China has disrupted the maritime geopolitics of near and far waters that had been taken for granted for so long. The disruption is occurring because China wants to establish control of its near waters and reach out to far waters. Island chains in the western Pacific are again the basis for the tensions involved in creating a new maritime geopolitical order.

China's Island Building

The port city of Guangzhou in southern China is a key node in China's growing seapower and engagement with the wider world. It also has a history of being the access point for foreign countries into the Chinese economy. It was a site of the Opium Wars. It has been an important area of foreign far waters and the presence of other countries in Chinese near waters. The Guangzhou neighborhood of Shamian Island is a beautiful spot. It is the location of shady squares surrounded by large European-style buildings that were once embassies and consulates. These were the necessary bureaucracies to ensure European countries had favorable access to Chinese near waters and the hinterlands of the Pearl (or Zhujiang) River. Now the area is a tourist spot, and a favorite site for Chinese couples to pose for wedding photos. I have enjoyed my times walking in this peaceful area where I can step away from the noise and bustle of the city by crossing over a small bridge.

Bridge? Yes. Shamian Island is separated from the rest of the city by a narrow canal, dug by the British and French in 1859. The man-made feature ensured that the European elites gained physical distance from the Chinese to emphasize the social distance gained by their colonial status. European access to Chinese near waters was achieved, but access for the Chinese to parts of their own city was controlled. Such small-scale urban geography, a reflection of the global geography of primary and subsidiary countries, was done by making an island within the city. How ironic, then, that the process of global geopolitics that could lead us to global war is focused on the Chinese making islands over the horizon from Guangzhou in the South China Sea. The pendulum of geopolitical power has swung, but the means of achieving power remain very much the same.

Similar to the history of other powerful countries, China's seapower requires influence in islands in far waters. For example, as the archipelago of Zanzibar was relevant in the geopolitical context of declining British power, it is of renewed interest as China changes the geopolitical landscape.[53] Zanzibar remained a British protectorate until 1963 and soon after merged with Tanganyika to form the independent country of Tanzania. The combination of an archipelago in the Indian Ocean, making it one of the closest African locations to East Asia, and a coastal country whose ports give access across the African continent is very appealing to China. The relevance of seapower as the ability to build influence and interest on land is evident yet again. The east coast of Africa is also of importance to China for the harvesting of fish and squid. Yet it is the access from Tanzania through the infrastructure of the BRI that cements (if you excuse the pun) the influence into a generative sector in far waters.

Access to African countries, and other continents, requires the functioning of SLOCs, and these have always been vulnerable to military seapower. Interests on land can be maintained and fulfilled only if oceanic links to the homeland are secure. Islands are vital in this role, and China has been active in developing this part of the geopolitical equation.

No island is an island. Its geopolitical relevance involves its connection to other islands and seas. Like the ancient Greeks looking up to the night sky and drawing lines to connect separate stars to make constellations, modern strategists have connected islands to create a geography of island chains. These chains have played a role in defense policy, especially since the Second World War. And just as with the constellations of the ancient Greeks, the chains that are made by drawing straight lines between them come with their own stories—ones of who has the right, and the right reason, for controlling them. The current geopolitical context is one in which the efficacy of some of the island chains that were secured by the US as they became the hegemonic power is now being usurped or bypassed by China's efforts to control existing and new island chains.

US security and force projection were based upon three island chains. The first or most western island chain was the defensive perimeter as stated by Secretary of State Dean Acheson (map 8.2). Behind this was a second island chain extending from the northwestern tip of Papua New Guinea through Guam and the Mariana Islands to the eastern coast of the largest island of the Japanese archipelago, Honshu. Behind that was the third island chain extending from the northern tip of New Zealand through Hawaii to the western end of the Aleutian Islands, which had been the one part of the US where the Japanese had been able to land troops in the Second World War. In combination, these island chains were a barricade to protect US Pacific near waters that had proven vulnerable in the

Second World War. They were also the means to protect vital Pacific Ocean SLOCs.[54]

On the other hand, the island chains provided the launching pads for force projection. Naval bases in southern California and Hawaii were homes for aircraft carrier task forces, and not just defensive ships. Subic Bay in the Philippines, the island of Guam, and the bases on Okinawa and in other parts of Japan were all part of a scheme that fused protection of near waters with force projection into far waters; near and far waters were inseparable.

Inseparable but, hopefully, delineated. Acheson's perimeter speech attempted to create a geography in which near waters (even if they were not geographically near to the US west coast) were seen as inviolable. Waters to the west of the first island chain were described in a more nuanced way.[55] The combination of nationalist and communist sympathies meant that the US military became heavily involved in land wars: Korea, Vietnam, and Cambodia. Seapower, in the form of control of the three island chains, al-

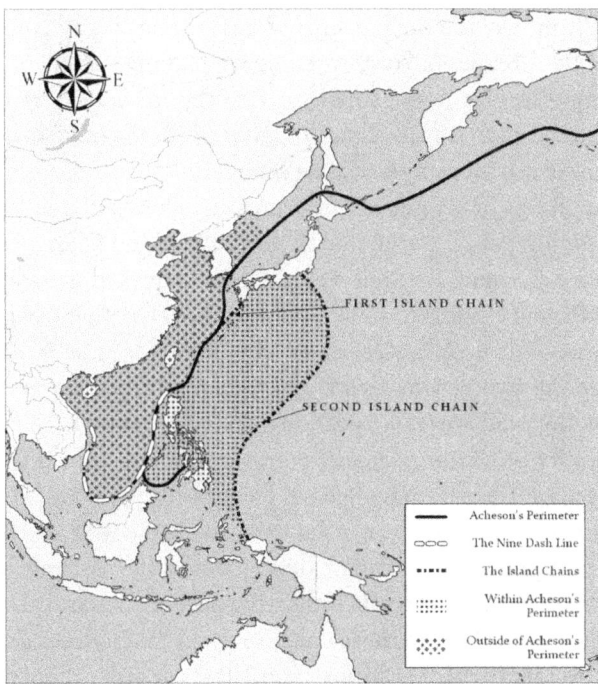

MAP 8.2. The Acheson perimeter and the nine-dash line.

Source: Original work by Carson Liesik, using multiple sources freely available on the internet.

lowed for force projection into Southeast Asia in what became defining wars in the Cold War battles with the Soviet Union and China. Though the US experienced a tie in the Korean War and a loss in Vietnam, its seapower was never in question. The defense of near waters was successful, and the ability of the Soviets and Chinese to project power across the Pacific was limited—until now.[56]

Now new sets of island chains are being made. Of course, this is not the new eruption of islands from the seabed. Rather, it is the identification of new islands as strategic resources in the context of a changing balance of power. A fourth and fifth set of island chains are now discussed within strategic circles.[57] The first of these extends southwards from the Pakistan port of Gwadar to Sri Lanka and then on to the island of Diego Garcia (legally a British territory, in effect a US military outpost). Notably, this chain is an arena in which both China and the US have a strong presence, China in the northern portion and the US in the southern portion. Hence, it is ripe for conflict.

The fifth island chain extends from Djibouti in the Horn of Africa down the eastern coast of Africa, including the perpetually relevant islands of Zanzibar. China has the most energy in this arena. Many commentators believe that the US and its Western allies are playing a game of "catch-up" in the competition for naval superiority in the far waters of the Indian Ocean.[58] The competition is not just a matter of SLOCs but one of access to the countries of Africa as a generative sector.

Drawing chains of islands involves creating stories of new geopolitical situations. Identification of the fourth and fifth island chains has led to a new geopolitical arena: the Indo-Pacific.[59] The physical geography of the Indian and Pacific Oceans has not changed. However, there is a concerted effort by some security analysts, especially those based in India and Australia, to see the two oceans as a single conjoined security arena. A geopolitics of action and reaction is driving this new context. The blue-water naval capability of China may still be much smaller than that of the US and its allies. But Chinese naval power is certainly growing. The Western response has been the creation of alliances such as AUKUS and the Quad.[60]

The new geopolitics of island chains relates to the separate but related need to defend near waters while projecting power into far waters. Taiwan is the most relevant island in these dual processes. Though the same chains of islands are identified by Chinese and US strategists, their meaning is different. For the US, the first island chain is the westernmost presence in Pacific far waters. For China the same chain of islands is the first line of defense for their near waters. For both countries the importance of the islands extends beyond their immediate location. Control of these islands, or lack of such control, allows for or prevents force projection across the oceans, control of SLOCs, and access to the generative sector and markets.

Though China has considerable influence along most of the first island chain, its inability to control the "breakaway province" of Taiwan means that such control is incomplete. The US alliance with Taiwan is a potential threat to Chinese near waters. This situation complicates, though it does not prevent, China's ongoing ambitions for force projection. If any island is to be the spark for a new global conflagration, it is likely to be Taiwan.[61]

Any such battle would not be limited to the vicinity of Taiwan, or to a US-China confrontation. The region of the first and second island chains contains numerous disputes over national ownership of islands. In the northernmost part of the contentious region, the Kuril Islands, stretching from Kamchatka Province to the northern tip of Japan's Hokkaido Island, remain disputed between Russia and Japan. This dispute is still unresolved from the Second World War. Further south, Korea and Japan are in dispute over the rock outcrop (the term *island* would be generous) of Dokdo/Takeshima. In the South China Sea the Paracel and Spratly Islands, many uninhabitable and barely above the ocean waves, are the focus of a conjunction of claims to sovereignty between Malaysia, the Philippines, Vietnam, and China. In 2016 an international tribunal in The Hague ruled that there was no basis for Chinese claims to sovereignty, a decision enthusiastically endorsed by the US.[62]

Though the range of islands under dispute are relevant because of nearby oil and gas deposits, and fisheries, their main importance extends beyond their immediate location. The resources within the EEZs of the disputed islands are not insignificant, but the issue is also about SLOCs and force projection. This is especially the case for the Paracel and Spratly Islands, which straddle the SLOC connecting China to oil supplies from the Middle East, imports from Africa, and access to a number of markets. The islands are vital in the geopolitics of primary-subsidiary relations, the generative sector, and building an economy that makes and sells highly profitable goods.

These concerns are so vital that new physical geographies are being made. The construction of Shamian Island in 1859 was a sign that China was a subsidiary country with no control of its near waters. In contrast, it is now building islands in the South China Sea. It has been dumping ballast and pouring concrete to turn reef outcrops into usable islands. For the past ten years or so China has created 3,200 acres of new land in the Paracel and Spratly Islands. Places such as Fiery Cross Reef and Subi Reef are now sites of long runways and harbor facilities. There is evidence that some have missile launching sites.[63]

This wave of island building reflects China's new status as one of the strongest primary countries, perhaps with the ambition to be the hegemonic power. The geopolitical influence of the islands spans across one horizon to protect near waters—and the geopolitics of area denial. Across another horizon, the influence spreads into the far waters of the Indian Ocean. Both are an expression of seapower—one defensive, the other offensive. The offensive expression is to achieve the purpose of seapower: influence on land, namely, the construction of a generative sector in Africa and the maintenance of the established generative sector of Middle Eastern oil and gas.

No island is an island. No island chain is a chain without the separate islands that are linked; no island chain is of relevance without its relationship to near and far waters; and near and far waters have meaning and relevance only within a broader geopolitical context. Some features of the broader context will remain the same: namely, the unequal relations between primary and subsidiary countries, the need for access to the generative sector to drive economic competition between primary countries, and the imperative to secure near waters before force projection into far waters can be considered. However, the geography of these constant features is dynamic, and particular moments of that dynamism lead to increased tension between primary countries, an intense search for access to existing and emerging generative sectors, and shuffling of geopolitical alliances and rivalries.

England was a seapower with imperial appendages within the island of Britain and just across the Irish Sea. Yet its proximity to the continent of Europe, the home to the great powers of the modern age until the rise of the US, meant that Continental geopolitics could not be ignored. English, and subsequently British, seapower had to be achieved through the management of Continental geopolitics. Britain did not become the hegemonic power by avoiding Continental geopolitics. Instead, it had to balance Continental and oceanic geopolitics, and it became successful by controlling islands. Perhaps, rather than talking of Britain as a seapower we should think of it as an island power.

The strategy of Britain's island geopolitics was practiced by the US, and currently China is taking similar steps. The difference is that, through the BRI, China is embarking upon a continental strategy at the same time. Could this twin-pronged strategy lead to a form of hegemony yet to be seen, or is it a pathway that will overstretch China's resources and lead it away from a focus on the up-to-now historically successful pursuit of seapower? Will it result in war?

CONCLUSION

The Gathering Storm Clouds of War

Geopolitics is a combination of economic and political relations that change over time. Though the approach of this book is more complex than the nationally biased and simple proscriptions of classic geopolitics, such complexity is important for two reasons. First, it is a more accurate explanation of how the world works. Second, the approach is not meant to advocate for one country over another; it is not meant to be a voice for arguing why *we* are right and just, and *they* are wrong and immoral. It is meant to be a guide to why the world is facing a dangerous situation that could lead to global war.

The potential Chinese invasion of Taiwan is a conflict over Chinese near waters/US far waters. The explanation of the dangers of war over Taiwan emphasized the underlying economic relations that drive near-water/far-water competition. In 2023, then NATO secretary general Jens Stoltenberg responded to US encouragement to switch focus from the Russia-Ukraine War and turn the alliance's attention toward China. The stated imperative was "our dependencies on other authoritarian regimes, not least China, for our supply chains, technology, and infrastructure."[1] Though the national focus was upon China, the geography of primary and subsidiary countries and the means to connect them was the foundation for this strategic statement. In sum, it was all about SLOCs and seapower.

For the US and its allies, the potential conflict was about preventing disruption to existing, and taken-for-granted, primary-subsidiary relations. For China, the goal of creating a new set of primary-subsidiary relations to its benefit required control of Taiwan to secure near waters. China saw a detrimental presence of a hostile power in its near waters. The US saw threats to its long-standing presence in Asian far waters.

For *The Economist*, the policy to "avoid a third world war" is to maintain the status quo:[2] specifically, to deter China from invading Taiwan without provoking it. This is a simple military calculation in which the US "should keep modernizing its armed forces and rallying its allies. . . . And it should be prepared to break a future blockade, by stockpiling fuel, planning an airlift, providing backup internet links and building an allied consensus on sanctions."[3] Avoid war by preparing for war, in other words. We've been here before, and war has often resulted.

Not only is the response reminiscent of the past, so is the rhetoric. The defense of Taiwan is portrayed as justified on ideological grounds of protecting a country that "is admirably liberal and democratic."[4] Other than allusions to a regional "American-led order" being replaced by a "Chinese-led one," the importance of the island in primary-subsidiary relations is not emphasized.[5] The role of Taiwan in the projection of US seapower into far waters for economic benefits is not identified as the main reason for the conflict. As usual, the geography of global inequality, and competition for advantageous relations with subsidiary countries, is hidden in the shadows when discussions of geopolitics come to the fore.

China and the View of Its Rising Seapower

The scope and ambition of China's actions are increasingly global. Three parallel initiatives are in motion to try to transform the global web of relations to China's advantage.[6] The "Global Development Initiative" is focused on developing new primary-subsidiary relations that will benefit China's economy. The "Global Civilisation Initiative" is the political partner of the economic goals. It aims to create friendly relations with subsidiary countries by allowing them to be autocratic if they so wish. Western newspapers decry this, while conveniently forgetting the pervasive support of autocracies they have provided with an eye to maintaining favorable economic relations (see chapter 7). What is good for the goose is, apparently, unacceptable for the gander.

China's economic goals will be protected by its "Global Security Initiative." Interestingly, this aspect of China's strategy is described by *The Economist* as "opposing efforts to contain China's military threat."[7] Agreed. However, the key is how to think about this. The use of the word *contain* is illuminating. It shows that the dominant view, as expressed by *The Econo-*

mist, is to see China's attempt to move into far waters as aggressive and the US presence in China's near waters as taken for granted, defensive, or even "natural." From the perspective of the near-waters/far-waters framework, China is frustrated by US attempts to restrict its actions to near waters and sees US presence off its coastline as aggressive. To simply label the situation as aggression by one country or the other, depending upon your nationality, misses the point. The immediacy of national security concerns is a function of a historical and global process of projecting power into others' near waters for economic gain. Continuing this pattern of might to enable economic gain at the expense of others is a form of Einstein's definition of lunacy, with war as the likely outcome.[8]

Sadly, there is ample evidence that the process toward global war is well advanced. There is increased competition and nervousness about access to new technology. There is also the related competition over new and existing generative sectors. The current context is made up of the same situations and actions that have, in the past, been the precursors to global war.[9] And the precursors are expressions of seapower. Namely, they are the combination of an emerging primary country building a blue-water navy, that same country trying to push the existing seapower out of its near waters, and a flurry of alliances as most countries in the world are drawn into this competition (whether they like it or not) to either maintain or change the post–Second World War geography of seapower. It is these processes that keep me awake at night, literally.

The virtuous cycle of seapower is the means and goal of China's current policy.[10] China's declaration in November 2012 of its aim to become a maritime power was reinforced by a defense white paper released in April 2013 that said: "China is a maritime as well as land country. The seas and oceans provide immense space and abundant resources for China's sustainable development, and thus are of vital importance to the people's well-being and China's future. It is an essential national development strategy to exploit, utilize and protect the seas and oceans, and build China into a maritime power. It is an important duty for the PLA to resolutely safeguard China's maritime rights and interests."[11] In other words, economic development and the ability to project military power are part and parcel of the same dynamic of geopolitical change.

China's passage through the virtuous cycle has led to its development. Ironically, yet troublingly, China's development is seen as a threat rather than a success story. We are not embracing the tenets of Rostow's developmentalism by congratulating China on going through the prescribed stages of economic growth.[12] Instead, the West is fearful. China's virtuous cycle of seapower is seemingly not virtuous when established patterns of power, and oceanic geography, are being disrupted (figure C.1).[13] China's rise is a mixture of economics, in the form of national technological prowess and the need to establish a generative sector, and political connections supported by growing naval power. It is déjà vu all over again.

Needs and intentions like China's were once expressed by the Dutch, the British, and the US. For example, in the 1920s the influential US geographer Isiah Bowman, in his arrogantly titled textbook *The New World*, argued in favor of US global leadership through economic prowess: "With a rapidly increasing rate of farm production in the United States and an even more rapid growth of city population bent on increasing industrial output and trade, the foreign commerce of the United States has grown to striking proportions. The process, though not new, has been greatly hastened in recent years. Since the beginning of the World War [World War I] the United States has increased its foreign investments fourfold, doubled its foreign commerce, and become the creditor of sixteen European nations. It was hardly an accident that the reparation problem was at least partly solved by the adoption of a plan of American origin."[14]

The economic and military projection of power through the course of US hegemony was to follow. China is trying to chart a similar course. Bowman wrote with national hubris but also a genuine sense that a better and fairer world was possible. China's economic proclamations have the same tone. However, Bowman's vision for the US emerged through participation in the First World War. The Second World War was soon to follow, and victory

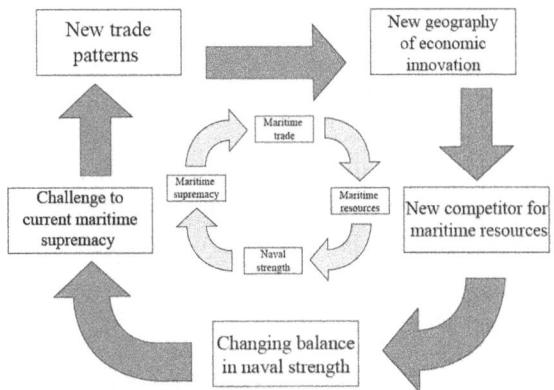

FIGURE C.1. The nonvirtuous cycle of seapower.

Source: Drawn by Anna Johnson, adapted from figure 1.3 (p. 17) in Geoffrey Till's *Seapower*, 3rd ed. (London: Routledge, 2013).

secured the global economic presence that Bowman had advocated for. Participation in global war was crucial to the rise of the US as a global power. Once achieved, US hegemony required different forms of violence, as discussed in chapter 5. Perhaps the best intentions cannot avoid the imperatives of primary-subsidiary relations and primary-primary competition.

China's goal is clear, and its development of a blue-water navy is not in question. The question I would like to emphasize is, How should we approach the dramatic geopolitical shift that is involved in China becoming a seapower? The traditional approach is through a realist national perspective, a reaction of "How dare they!" This reaction is one of belief in the rightness of one's own country, and it requires ignoring historical processes—in other words, not considering what it took for the established geography of seapower to come about. Such a reaction is likely to demand that the US and its allies push back against China's ambitions using force. If that is the case, the immediate future will likely hold modern-day equivalents of Dutch raids on Copenhagen, Britain's victory over France at Trafalgar and the Nile, and US triumph at the Battle of Midway. Such past battles, and the broader wars of which they were part, are the geopolitical manifestation of action and reaction. A historical approach shows that all geographies of seapower are shaped by a combination of economic and military power, and, ultimately, are enforced by violence. Sometimes that violence takes the form of a global war.

Three Takeaways

I hope the framework offered by this book leads to three seemingly simple takeaways that will help you understand the current geopolitical moment. The main point is that we've been here before. Contemporary geopolitics has a specific flavor because of the uniqueness of China and the US as countries with their own history and culture, and reason to be in conflict with each other. But the uniqueness of the situation is a particular expression of a geopolitical context of competition over near and far waters that has recurred on a regular basis. That should lead us to conclude that any attempts to arrest a move toward global war need to address the underlying causes behind the contexts rather than the specificities of foreign policy or military doctrine.

The next point is to consider the implications of geopolitical action and reaction. The book brings attention to the history of countries that have been unable to control their near waters. Readers in Western and primary countries are likely to assume that their near waters have always been theirs and that any incursions by, say, Russian submarines are clearly wrong and must be countered. I agree with the belief that near waters should not be infringed upon without agreement. The historical contexts outlined in this book emphasize that infringement of near waters has been a constant form of geopolitics. Countries that have been able to infringe on others have first had to push out other countries from their own near waters. The projection of force into far waters will, at some time, produce a reaction from those wishing to control their own near waters. Now is such a time, as China reacts to the established presence of the US in its near waters.

Without considering history, the current situation could easily be seen as something in which only one player, China, is at fault. The presence of the US in Asian far waters is usually told as a story of common sense that gets portrayed, by the powerful, as somehow "natural." Mainstream emphasis is upon the reaction to the current US-led geopolitical order and not the basis for why China wants to change it. Global war is more likely to be avoided if the West reflects on how its actions have led to the current moment of geopolitical tension and how its own history was similar.

Such reflection could lead to two outcomes. One is a recognition of the imperatives of primary-subsidiary relations, especially the competition over access to the generative sector and the need to protect SLOCs connecting near and far waters. This is the persistent historical pattern of the geopolitics of seapower and the likely resort to war to redefine the pattern of global geopolitics. It would behoove the US and its allies to ponder the history of this process: the primary country that has been the dominant seapower has never been able to retain control of the far waters it dominated. And in the case of Britain its own near waters became threatened.

The other possible reflection, and the third takeaway from this book, is to consider how an unequal world based on primary-subsidiary relations leads to the need for seapower and the geopolitics of near and far waters. The pathway to war is built on the foundations and imperatives of primary-subsidiary relations. Preventing another global war, perhaps one fought with nuclear weapons, requires addressing the foundation and not just the pathway.

Global inequalities may seem to be a topic separate from geopolitics, and a call to think about them may seem naive. Chapter 1 outlined a set of building blocks to help clarify the dynamics of the geopolitics of seapower. Primary-subsidiary relations are an essential part of this foundation. Geopolitics and economics are not separate fields but intertwined sets of power relations.[15] The way university teaching and research are organized into separate disciplines is designed to hide the nature of power in economics.[16] A scholar or student can decide to look at development and not geopolitics, or vice versa, as if browsing separate floors in a department store. Instead, this book shows that they are inseparable. And the reason to consider primary-subsidiary relations, perhaps just out of self-interest for those living in a rich and powerful country, comes from the likelihood that the weak may make the strong weak.

The near-/far-waters framework leads us to see that a battle over SLOCs in the Indo-Pacific is certainly a possibility. But that is a secondary manifestation of the driver of the conflict: control of generative sectors. Hence, looking for the gathering storm clouds of a next global war requires focus upon the competition between primary countries for influence in subsidiary countries. The African continent is the most likely arena. If the US and its allies try to defend their interests in African countries, but from a position of catch-up with China, there may be another example of how the weak may make the strong weak—though more accurately, what would weaken the strong would be the inability of strong countries to maintain established interests in weak countries. The past few years have provided ample and stark examples of the weakness of the US, the current seapower, to police its far-water interests.

Lessons for the Geopolitical Moment

Policy is made within contexts, and we need to understand those contexts to consider the range of policy options for countries in a particular moment.[17] The context limits the options that countries have, but it doesn't determine those options. If actions were determined there would be no point in writing this book. We would just have to let history take its course. That is the exact opposite of my motivation. Instead, I believe that the context we live in constrains choices for countries, and that similar contexts in the past have led to decisions that have led to war. Understanding that context allows us to be informed about the likely political choices that are going to be made. To be forewarned is to be forearmed in a way that we can voice our concerns and consider the adaptations and humility necessary to avoid global war.

The book is a historical discussion of the combination of economic and political relations that are the reason behind, and the result of, the development of seapower to control near waters and project force into far waters. Specifically, six lessons have been highlighted throughout the book:

1) The gain and loss of seapower is a historic process.

2) The dominant seapower is the country that leads in technology and trade.

3) The need to trade is built on the inequality of primary-subsidiary relations, and violence is necessary to maintain these relations.

4) Though a country may become the dominant seapower or hegemon, it still faces constant challenges and competition.

5) Some of these challenges may be tackled without resort to violence, but violence and war have been ever present to some degree.

6) Becoming the global seapower/hegemon involves cooperation and tensions between merchants, entrepreneurs, and government within the emerging power.

In each chapter I have described historical patterns that illustrate these lessons. Each chapter has concluded with a discussion of the contemporary situation and how the patterns of the past seem to be repeating, in a general rather than a specific sense. Of course, the current situation is about competition in the US far waters/Chinese near waters of the Western Pacific and China's growing presence in far waters. The historical lessons resonate because of that competition and its potential to escalate into war.

Prospects for a Third World War

This is a period of economic competition and conflict between the US and China. As in similar historic periods, this shift in relative economic strength manifests itself in "trade wars," which are really a competition over which country is the dominant host of companies manufacturing the newest and most profitable products. Competition over new technology requires access to the generative sector, and that requires access to far waters. Competition between the US and China in Africa, the Middle East, and SLOCs is the outcome.

China's emergence as a seapower does not threaten US near waters. Nor is China likely to play a role in the defense of US near waters against another challenger. A scenario could be constructed in which Russian threats in the Arctic, an increasingly important arena for SLOCs because of climate change, would provide mutual benefits for Chinese-US cooperation. This scenario is unlikely because it is unclear whether Russia is strong enough to provide such a challenge. There seems to be no future need for the US to seek help defending its near waters in a similar way to Britain's need for US support. This difference is probably a positive, as it makes a pathway to global war less likely.

Second, as with Britain's decline, the threat will be most obvious and have the greatest impact in US far waters. Britain attempted to put together a coalition of common interests (India, Australia, and New Zealand) to negate Japan's threat to Britain's Asian far waters. Ultimately, the US became the dominant player, and victory over Japan led to the diminishing role of Britain, and other European countries, in what had been established far waters. Today, the US is trying to arrange a similar coalition of interests in the same oceans. Again, Australia and India are important players. Japan is now an ally. China has done little to build friendships in the same region. Rather, it has antagonized its neighbors.[18] But in the Pacific the US is at a disadvantage because the contested waters are China's near waters.

Third, the nature of primary-subsidiary relations has changed from the formal relations of colonies and empires to a global network of economic relations that meshes with spheres of political influence. The generative sector was once defined by the territorial delineation of colonies and protectorates. Now the generative sector is a matter of influence. Both forms of primary-subsidiary relations were competitive, but perhaps today's arrangements are less likely to lead to war. Today's battle for control of the generative sector is not a zero-sum game of annexation and territorial control as it was in the buildup to the Second World War. For example, Japan's increasing economic presence in China in the 1920s and 1930s was accepted, as that was what the Western countries were doing themselves. It was the territorial annexation of Manchuria and the creation of the Manchukuo state that changed the geopolitical balance. Wars over territory are the bloodiest and hardest to resolve.[19] Battles over influence, such as those in Africa and the Pacific, have the potential to be a less bloody form of geopolitical transition.

Just as the average Briton in the 1930s was unlikely to view Burma or Singapore as the Achilles' heel in the geography of their country's global power, most Americans today do not have Somalia, Tanzania, or Ghana in the forefront of their concerns. History suggests that is wrong. Competition in the generative sector is where a declining power's weaknesses are most exposed. As history suggests, far waters are the most dangerous waters in the possible pathway to war. To recognize the risks of war does not mean being fatalistic. Pathways to peaceful outcomes exist.

Reasons to Be Cheerful

The contextual setting of the imminence of a third world war is a weighty and rather depressing conclusion. But looking back to history gives us some room for optimism. A country may regain control of its near waters without using violence. The US achieved this goal without a major war, though not a complete absence of violence. SLOCs and choke points have been managed by international cooperation, though this has often been motivated by a shared concern over piracy. Countries have, at times, recognized that conversation and compromise is better than fighting. The media and other influence makers, such as educators, play a key role here by trying to create a political space in which politicians feel comfortable or obliged to focus upon dialogue rather than defaulting to militarized responses. Sadly, the tone of debate in the US, China, and other countries appears to be reinforcing a sense of the inevitability of war. And so it has been in similar historical contexts. Alternative voices and agendas are essential.

These reasons to be cheerful focus on how powerful countries have agreed to work together rather than fight each other. But sometimes they have fought, in fact quite often. And even though powerful countries have sometimes found ways to avoid war, the unequal and often violent relations with weaker and poorer countries have remained.

The danger of global war suggests that rather than a national perspective that promotes *our* might and *our* right, an approach is needed that understands the current situation as a moment in a historical process. Similar contexts have occurred in history, and perhaps historical wisdom can be used to avoid the rising heat of national and militaristic chest-thumping. Instead, nationalist viewpoints may be transcended to see the global connections that are driving the geopolitical process of seapower. History should give us cause for concern but also reasons for optimism. The history of Dutch, British, and US seapower shows that peaceful pathways have been possible. Understanding seapower as a matter of entwined global relations between and among primary and subsidiary relations is the first step in setting the agenda for a contemporary conversation.

That conversation must include subsidiary countries as equal partners. The powerful have had no interest in making the weak strong. Talk of China's development of an "unequal partnership" between China and Africa may not be wrong, but it conveniently sweeps the debris of centuries of unequal primary-subsidiary relations under the carpet.[20] Rather, the possibility that the weak can make the strong weak should be emphasized. Rising tensions between the British, French, and Germans in Africa at the turn of the nineteenth century were the canaries in the coal mine in that geopolitical context. Seapower, or force projection, was the means and end of these tensions.

Concern about the needs and goals of the subsidiary countries, the bulk of the world's population, may well be the best way to avoid another round of global war. Rather than fueling an arms race of new technologies, we need to reflect on how to reform the world economy to reduce competition for control of the generative sector. If seapower is an unvirtuous cycle of guns and butter, we need to be considering global inequities in wealth rather than national abilities to wage war.

I Have to Stop and Others Must Start

It is hard to conclude a book that is about geopolitics as a process. The geopolitics of seapower is an ongoing process, and not something that lends itself to a definitive statement. Rather than providing a conclusion about what will happen, and certainly avoiding pointing fingers to identify a simple "us versus them" of good and bad guys, I emphasize two things.

First, the book is primarily a call to look at the world in a certain way: specifically, to see geopolitics as a web of economic and political relations between and among primary and subsidiary countries that are in a constant state of change. Focusing on seapower is a way to make sense of these relations. Second, seeing the world in this way provides avenues for political decision-making that are different from the narrow "us versus them" attitudes of national geopolitics, a form of thinking that has in the past led to nothing but zero-sum competitions to be resolved by military force.

The process of peacebuilding is very different from the practices of classic geopolitics. Peacebuilding requires seeing conflict as the product of complexity in the form of many actors (countries and businesses, mainly), each with a multitude of interests.[21] Even one country has multiple needs, goals, and issues that it must wrestle with at a particular time. Classic geopolitics, on the other hand, wants to simplify the world. It leads to an "us versus them" mentality that believes the "them" to be unscrupulous and unreasonably vindictive.[22] Classic geopolitics is a mapping of the world based on a set of simple good and evil binaries. The tedious parade of superhero movies is a cultural support for this worldview.[23] Recognizing the position, needs, and arguments of others is seen as hopelessly naive and as guaranteeing you'll get eaten in the jungle. But that is the pathway to war.

Peacebuilding offers an alternative path. It is not naive. In fact, successful peacebuilding involves recognizing how hard any problem is to solve. It does not simply ask us to sit in a circle and sing kumbaya. It is not the coward's path. The exact opposite is true. It is the braver path. Why? Because it requires swimming against the tide of policy, academic, and cultural preferences that glorify war. Can you imagine *Top Gun,* or a superhero movie about resorting to violence in the name of good, being displaced from the box-office records list by a peacebuilding blockbuster movie? Cheerleading for militarism is the easier path, the path that is usually demanded of us.

Peacebuilding is brave for another reason too. It requires peacebuilders to be vulnerable by considering their own attitudes and actions and how they are contributing to the problem. In other words, it requires people in the US and allied countries to figure out how their actions are provoking reactions. And it requires us to consider how we use violence to prevent those reactions. It also requires us to challenge dominant narratives of why the current unequal world is either "natural" or something that just needs a little tinkering while the power relations remain largely the same. In peacebuilding language, it requires those of us in primary countries to "turn first."[24] Specifically, it requires a consideration of how the geopolitics of near and far waters has been constructed for the benefit of a minority of the world's population.

The process of "turning first" is hard. Once you're ready to turn, the challenge is to be brave and strong enough to face the dominant and taken-for-granted arguments of today's classic geopolitics. Dominant voices will argue that might equals right and that we're right anyway, regardless of our might. I wish you the best if challenging the dominance of nationally based geopolitics and the seeming effectiveness of military "solutions" is the pathway you choose. I can only hope that this book is of some help in that journey.

ACKNOWLEDGMENTS

Writing a book requires a certain amount of ego and of faith. When a book project takes years to unfold, as this one has, then a host of people are needed to sustain one's confidence and belief. The foundation of my education and the early stages of finding a way to interpret the world and speak about it began at the University of Newcastle-Upon-Tyne. I am grateful to the Department of Geography for taking a chance on admitting me to their undergraduate degree despite the attainment of just two A-levels. Peter J. Taylor and Mark Overton goaded and guided me into having something to say and being able to say it. At the University of Colorado-Boulder John O'Loughlin fostered an analytical approach. Though crises of confidence were rife, all the professors (other than one economic historian) nurtured and enabled me. They taught me the value of classroom leadership.

Numerous colleagues have inspired and sustained me through my academic career. Special mention is due to Bob Denemark, Ray Dezzani, Klaus Dodds, Lorraine Dowler, Jeannie Johnson, Scott Kirsch, Virginie Mamadouh, Tom Mayer, Bob Pois, Steve Sharp, James D. Sidaway, Lynn Staeheli, James Tyner, David Wilson, and Xiaotong Zhang.

I am grateful for the financial support of the College of Humanities and Social Sciences at Utah State University through the grant of a CARE award. USU has a long tradition of excellence in undergraduate research, and I have certainly benefited from that, especially the research and editing work performed by Christina Anderson and Anna Johnson. USU alum Carson Liesik was an indispensable aid in creating the maps. Thanks to Jade Bartnicki and Marie-Catherine Pavel for editorial help.

Richard Mason has offered support, persuasion, humor, and questions throughout this project. Michael Spooner has endured many conversations about this book and offered sage advice. An author needs an editor who can sharpen your view of your own book and share the belief that it is worth publishing; I couldn't ask for more from an editor than the support and advice Dan LoPreto has given.

The undergraduate students I have had the privilege to share a classroom with have been a constant inspiration, especially at USU. I am impressed by your commitment to pursuing knowledge, and your bravery in tackling the daunting issues we face. Special mention to the Aggies GO students—you make it all real and worthwhile.

At the end of the day, sustenance and faith come from my family. This book is in print because of the life's foundation, scaffold, roof, walls, and garden they have given to me. Thank you with love to Courtney, Doug, and Jack.

SUGGESTED READINGS

References to the foundational academic work can be found in the endnotes. The following is a small selection of books that may be of interest for further exploration of some topics in the book. Though referenced throughout the book, a broader view of seapower can be found in the key text by Geoffrey Till, *Seapower: A Guide for the Twenty-First Century*, 3rd ed. (London: Routledge, 2013).

The book focuses on the waxing and waning of seapower of just four countries: the Dutch Republic, Great Britain, the United States of America, and contemporary China. The geopolitical process of seapower began before the rise of the Dutch Republic with the transoceanic competition between Portugal and Spain, driven by the economic imperative of plunder, especially of gold and silver. George Modelski identifies both countries as seapowers in his framework of world leadership. See George Modelski, *Long Cycles in World Politics* (Seattle: University of Washington Press, 1987). The early history of China's oceanic exploration is presented by Louise Levathes, *When China Ruled the Seas: The Treasure Fleet of the Dragon Throne, 1405–1433* (Oxford: Oxford University Press, 1994). For discussion of maritime trade in the premodern period and the transition to capitalism, see Janet Abu-Lughod, *Before European Hegemony, the World-System A.D. 1250–1350* (New York: Oxford University Press, 1992), and Immanuel Wallerstein, *The Modern World-System: Capitalist Agriculture and the Origins of the European World-Economy in the Sixteenth Century* (New York: Academic Press, 1976).

The process of near-water defense and far-water projection for the four countries highlighted in this book involved cooperation and conflict with several countries that could be termed "middle powers." I am indebted to Jonathan Israel for his outstanding scholarship on the history of the Dutch Republic. Dutch seapower, and details on the interaction with middle powers through the process of trade and power projection, are discussed in detail in Jonathan I. Israel, *Dutch Primacy in World Trade, 1585–1740* (Oxford: Clarendon Press, 1989).

For more on the role of middle powers in the transition from British to US seapower prior to the Second World War, see Bert Becker, *France and Germany in the South China Sea, c. 1840–1930: Maritime Competition and Imperial Power* (Cham, Switzerland: Palgrave Macmillan/Springer Nature, 2021), and Alessio Patalano, *Post-war Japan as a Sea Power: Imperial Legacy, Wartime Experience and the Making of a Navy* (London: Bloomsbury, 2015). For the naval arms race preceding the First World War, I recommend Robert K. Massie, *Dreadnought: Britain, Germany, and the Coming of the Great War* (New York: Ballantine Books, 1991). For further discussion of seapower in the Second World War, see Craig L. Symonds, *World War II at Sea: A Global History* (New York: Oxford University Press, 2018).

The process of seapower geopolitics continues today with, for example, Russia, Indonesia, India, Australia, and the European Union playing important roles as competition between the US and China unfolds. The current period of near-/far-waters tension between China and the US has, and continues to, generate much debate. An even-handed approach to China's rise can be found in David Shambaugh, *China Goes Global: The Partial Power* (Oxford: Oxford University Press, 2013). For particular focus on naval tensions, see David Brewster, ed., *India and China at Sea: Competition for Naval Dominance in the Indian Ocean* (New Delhi: Oxford University Press, 2018), and Rory Medcalf, *Indo-Pacific Empire: China, America and the Contest for the World's Pivotal Region* (Manchester: Manchester University Press, 2020). For a discussion of maritime power as a combination of trade and military power that begins with China's rise but involves all the world's major seas, see Geoffrey F. Gresh, *To Rule Eurasia's Waves: The New Great Power Competition at Sea* (New Haven, CT: Yale University Press, 2020).

NOTES

Preface

1. David Pepper and Alan Jenkins, eds., *The Geography of Peace and War* (New York: Blackwell, 1985); Nurit Kliot and Stanley Waterman, eds., *The Political Geography of Conflict and Peace* (London: Belhaven, 1991).

2. Derek Gregory and Allan Pred, eds., *Violent Geographies: Fear, Terror, and Political Violence* (London: Routledge, 2006).

3. Colin Flint, *Introduction to Geopolitics*, 4th ed. (London: Routledge, 2022).

4. Klaus Dodds and David Atkinson, eds., *Geopolitical Traditions: A Century of Geopolitical Thought* (London: Routledge, 2000); Virginie Mamadouh, "Geopolitics in the Nineties: One Flag, Many Meanings," *Geojournal* 46, no. 4 (December 1998): 237–53.

5. Klaus Dodds, *Geopolitics: A Very Short Introduction*, 3rd ed. (Oxford: Oxford University Press, 2019).

6. Colin Flint, "Putting the 'Geo' into Geopolitics: A Heuristic Framework and the Example of Australian Foreign Policy," *Geojournal* 87, no. 4 (December 2022): 2577–92.

7. Jennifer Hyndman, "Mind the Gap: Bridging Feminist and Political Geography through Geopolitics," *Political Geography* 23, no. 3 (March 2004): 307–22.

8. Jeremy Black, *Naval Power* (London: Red Globe Press, 2009), 1.

9. Quoted in Dan Jackson, *The Northumbrians: North-East England and Its People. A New History* (London: Hurst, 2019), 86.

Introduction

1. Cited in Admiral Sir Herbert Richmond, *Statesmen and Sea Power* (London: Clarendon Press, 1946), 109.

2. George Modelski, *Long Cycles in World Politics* (Seattle: University of Washington Press, 1987).

3. Geoffrey Till, *Seapower: A Guide for the Twenty-First Century*, 3rd ed. (London: Routledge, 2013), 25.

4. Till, *Seapower*, 17. The virtuous cycle of power requires a consideration of power. Power can be thought of in a material sense: things and indices such as the size of the navy, the number of aircraft carriers, the size of the economy (and the relative mix of primary, secondary, and tertiary sectors), the size of the population and their level of education, and so on. But material power has an impact only when it is mobilized in relation to other actors. Seapower is all about relational power, with the ability to create unequal terms of trade or the ability to project power into another country's near waters being just two key examples. For a discussion of material and relational power, see John Allen, *Lost Geographies of Power* (Oxford: Blackwell, 2003).

5. Till, *Seapower*, 6.

6. Jeremy Black, *Naval Power* (London: Red Globe Press, 2009), 1.

7. Sir Julian Corbett, *Some Principles of Maritime Strategy*, 2nd ed. (London: Longmans, Green, 1911), reprinted with introduction by Eric Grove (Annapolis, MD: Naval Institute Press, 1988), 67, quoted in Till, *Seapower*, 25. Though Corbett wrote over one hundred years ago, he remains an influential strategist.

8. Till, *Seapower*, 37, emphasis in original.

9. The work of Alfred Thayer Mahan is discussed later. His writing about seapower reinforces the idea that control of the seas is important for what it allows a country to do in another country's territory. The penultimate sentence of *The Influence of Sea Power upon History, 1660–1783* (London: Sampson, Low, Marston, 1890), 541, says, "In any coming war their [territories'] permanency would depend wholly upon the balance of sea power, upon that empire of the seas concerning which nothing conclusive had been established by the war." In other words, the oceans were legitimate arenas of contestation for seapowers and were ripe for an increased US presence as the twentieth century was about to begin. Mahan's conclusion implied that US seapower would enable control of territories both near and far from its shores. Intriguingly, Mahan is not cited in Bruce D. Jones, *To Rule the Waves: How Control of the World's Oceans Shapes the Fate of the Superpowers* (New York: Scribner, 2021). However, Jones's reading of the intersection of contemporary global trade, naval power competition, and global climate change has echoes of Mahan's political concerns. Jones highlights the duality of US coastal centers based on global trade and "a non-coastal population disconnected from that global enterprise" (305). This division is a contemporary challenge to Mahan's unity of national character and political will.

10. Peter J. Taylor, "Understanding Global Inequalities: A World-Systems Approach," *Geography* 77, no. 1 (1992): 10–21; Immanuel Wallerstein, *The Capitalist World-Economy* (Cambridge: Cambridge University Press, 1979), 66–94. The role of trade and its connection to competition over control of the oceans are the focus of Geoffrey F. Gresh, *To Rule Eurasia's Waves: The New Great Power Competition at Sea* (New Haven, CT: Yale University Press, 2020).

11. Modelski, *Long Cycles*.

12. Modelski, *Long Cycles*; Mahan, *Influence of Sea Power*, 26.

13. Colin S. Gray, *Modern Strategy* (Oxford: Oxford University Press, 1999), cited in Till, *Seapower*, 48. Also, the means of navigation have changed dramatically, from hopes of clear skies to enable navigation by the stars to today's precise satellite navigation systems. Nonetheless, since the rise of Dutch seapower traders and admirals have been able to travel from near to far waters. See Dag Pike, *The History of Navigation* (Barnsley: Pen and Sword Maritime, 2018). Interestingly, Till's *Seapower* does not spend much time on the topic.

14. Colin Flint, "Putting the 'Geo' into Geopolitics: A Heuristic Framework and the Example of Australian Foreign Policy," *Geojournal* 87, no. 4 (2021): 2580–83.

15. Colin Flint, *Geopolitical Constructs: The Mulberry Harbours, World War Two, and the Making of a Militarized Transatlantic* (Lanham, MD: Rowman and Littlefield, 2016), 33–34; Peter J. Martin and Alex Dennis, "Introduction: The Opposition of Structure and Agency," in *Human Agents and Social Structures*, ed. Peter J. Martin and Alex Dennis (Manchester: Manchester University Press, 2010), 14.

16. Modelski, *Long Cycles*.

17. Giovanni Arrighi, "The Three Hegemonies of Historical Capitalism," *Review* 13, no. 3 (Summer 1990): 365–408.

18. Peter J. Taylor, *Modernities: A Geohistorical Interpretation* (Cambridge: Polity Press, 1998), 30–34.

19. The ability to trade across oceans has been a feature of human activity for centuries. See Jerry H. Bentley, "Cross-cultural Interaction and Periodization in World History," *American Historical Review* 101, no. 3 (June 1996): 749–70. My approach focuses upon seapower within the social system of the capitalist world-economy. The distinction is important because the emergence of capitalism created a system based upon inequalities between regional societies and economies that is the economic foundation of the ability to, and the need to, project power into far waters; see Immanuel Wallerstein, "The West, Capitalism, and the Modern World-System," *Review* 15, no. 4 (Fall 1992): 561–619. An academic debate exists between two prominent scholars regarding the nature of the precapitalist regional subsystems and the role they played in the formation of a capitalist global economy. See Janet Abu-Lughod, *Before European Hegemony: The World-System A.D. 1250–1350* (New York: Oxford University Press, 1989), and Wallerstein, "West, Capitalism." For a summary of the debate, see Elson E. Boles, "Assessing the Debate between Abu-Lughod and Wallerstein over Thirteenth-Century Origins of the Modern World-System," in *Routledge Handbook of World-Systems Analysis*, ed. Salvatore J. Babones and Christopher Chase-Dunn (Abingdon: Routledge, 2012), 21–29.

Without doubt there were many regional subsystems of trade prior to the emergence of capitalism in Europe in the mid-1400s. See David Wilkinson, "Power Polarity in the Far Eastern World System, 1025 BC–AD 1850: Narrative and 25-Year Interval Data," *Journal of World-Systems Research* 5, no. 3 (1999): 501–617. He lists eighteen "macrosystems" that include a Far Eastern system lasting from 1025 BC to AD 1850 and what he calls the central social system centered on Mesopotamia and Northeast Africa and interacting with societies across Europe and into the Far East. He also highlights the Far Eastern social system that emerged in the Yellow River basin over three thousand years ago and interacted with the Central and Indic systems. The Far Eastern system was destroyed by the projection of Dutch and British seapower into Asian far waters that is discussed in this book. For a slightly different mapping of these systems, see Leonid Grinin and Andrey Korotayev, "The Afroeurasian World-System: Genesis, Transformations, Characteristics," in Babones and Chase-Dunn, *Routledge Handbook*, 30–38. They describe an Afroeurasian system emerging in the Fertile Crescent in the tenth to eight millennia BCE. Notably, they point to an Indian Ocean Basin system beginning in the first millennium BCE that was "a prototype of an oceanically connected world-system" (34). The Indian Ocean Basin system included trade in luxury and bulk goods.

These civilizations were the basis for trade and political networks that continued into the capitalist world-economy; see David Wilkinson, "Civilizations as Networks: Trade, War, Diplomacy, and Command-Control," *Complexity* 8, no. 1 (September-October 2002): 82–86. The civilizations subsequently took the form of far-water/near-water competition. Networks of bulk goods exchange, political/military interactions, trade in prestige or luxury goods, and information exchange were features of these civilizations, with the network of bulk goods trade having the narrowest geographical scope, and the last two the widest networks; see Thomas D. Hall, "Frontiers, Ethogenesis, and World-Systems: Rethinking the Theories," in *A World-Systems Reader: New Perspectives on Gender, Urbanism, Cultures, Indigenous Peoples, and Ecology,* ed. Thomas D. Hall (Lanham, MD: Rowman and Littlefield, 2000), 237–70. Interestingly, and as a precursor to the near-/far-water tensions that are the focus of this book, change and competition were most prevalent at the frontiers of these precapitalist social systems (Hall, "Frontiers, Ethogenesis," 239). In other words, interaction between societies across the globe has been an ever-present form of cooperation and competition between societies, with the Indian Ocean region playing an early and continuous role (Bentley, "Cross-cultural Interaction," 754).

20. Modelski, *Long Cycles.*

21. Gregory B. Poling, *On Dangerous Ground: America's Century in the South China Sea* (Oxford: Oxford University Press, 2022); James C. Hsiung, *The South China Sea Disputes and the U.S.-China Contest: International Law and Geopolitics* (Hackensack, NJ: World Scientific Press, 2018).

22. Colin Flint and Peter J. Taylor, *Political Geography: World-Economy, Nation-State, and Locality,* 7th ed. (London: Routledge, 2018), 22–25.

23. Paul S. Ciccantell and Stephen G. Bunker, "The Economic Ascent of China and the Potential for Restructuring the Capitalist World-Economy," *Journal of World-Systems Research* 10, no. 3 (Fall 2004): 570–71.

24. Modelski, *Long Cycles.*

25. Till, *Seapower,* 21.

26. Saul Bernard Cohen, *Geopolitics of the World System* (Lanham, MD: Rowman and Littlefield, 2003), 34.

27. My use of the labels *primary* and *subsidiary* is a simplified use of the terms *core* and *periphery* that are foundational within the body of knowledge known as world-systems analysis. These concepts are discussed more fully in chapter 2 and are revisited in chapters 5 and 6. The simplification is to enable accessibility, and the use of *primary* and *subsidiary* emphasizes the relationality between the concepts; the wealth of primary/core countries is a function of the poverty of subsidiary/periphery countries. And seapower is essential for establishing and maintaining this connection. For more on world-systems analysis, see Wallerstein, *Capitalist World-Economy*, Immanuel Wallerstein, *World-Systems Analysis: An Introduction* (Durham, NC: Duke University Press, 2004), and summaries and applications in Flint and Taylor, *Political Geography*, 12–28. I also use the more familiar term *country* rather than the term *state*. Though they may seem to be synonymous, the term *state* is useful in exploring the links between businesses (or economic actors) and government bureaucracy (or political actors), and the relative autonomy of the latter from the former. This is a complex theoretical discussion and not the focus of the book. For a quick introduction, see Flint and Taylor, *Political Geography*, 150–65.

28. Taylor, "Understanding Global Inequalities."

29. Arrighi, "Three Hegemonies"; Flint and Taylor, *Political Geography*, 53–61.

30. Ciccantell and Bunker, "Economic Ascent of China."

31. Though this book is not written from the perspective of international relations theory, the process of a country moving from near waters to far waters can be seen as a progression of a state's strategy from the basic realist tenet of security or survival (Hans J. Morgenthau, *Politics among Nations: The Struggle for Power and Peace* [New York: Knopf, 1948]; Robert O. Keohane, "Theory of World Politics: Structural Realism and Beyond," in *Political Science: State of the Discipline*, edited by A. W. Finifter [Washington, DC: American Political Science Association, 1983], 503–40; Stephen M. Walt, "The Renaissance of Security Studies," *International Studies Quarterly* 35, no. 2 [June 1991]: 211–39) to power through prestige (Robert Gilpin, *War and Change in World Politics* [Cambridge: Cambridge University Press, 1981]). The projection of power through alliances may also be interpreted through the lens of realism; see Glenn H. Snyder, *Alliance Politics* (Ithaca, NY: Cornell University Press, 1997). Moments of competition over near and far waters may be an expression of the transfer of hegemonic power; see A. F. K. Organski and Jacek Kugler, *The War Ledger* (Chicago: University of Chicago Press, 1980).

32. H. S. K. Kent, "The Historical Origins of the Three-Mile Limit," *American Journal of International Law* 48, no. 4 (October 1954): 537–53.

33. For the full text of the relevant part of the Convention, see UN Convention on the Law of the Sea, Part V: Exclusive Economic Zone, accessed April 9, 2023, https://www.un.org/depts/los/convention_agreements/texts/unclos/part5.htm.

34. For the full text of the relevant part of the Convention, see UN Convention on the Law of the Sea, Part VII, High Seas, accessed April 9, 2023, https://www.un.org/depts/los/convention_agreements/texts/unclos/part7.htm.

35. The seminal text is Mahan, *Influence of Sea Power*. Mahan wrote at the

turn of the nineteenth century, but his work is still cited today (for example, see Office of the Historian, US Department of State, "Mahan's *The Influence of Sea Power upon History*: Securing International Markets in the 1890s," accessed April 11, 2023, https://history.state.gov/milestones/1866-1898/mahan). Mahan's writing is commonly used to advance US foreign policy from a realist perspective; see Greg Russell, "Alfred Thayer Mahan and American Geopolitics: The Conservatism and Realism of an Imperialist," *Geopolitics* 11, no. 1 (2006): 119–40. As is the case with many historical geopoliticians, contemporary usage of their writings often skips over the complexity of what they actually said and distills it into a commonsense essence that is mobilized for the purposes of contemporary policy arguments (for a discussion of the complexity of Mahan's writing, see Jon Sumida, "Alfred Thayer Mahan, Geopolitician," *Journal of Strategic Studies* 22, nos. 2–3 [1999]: 39–62, and Jon (Tetsuro) Sumida, *Inventing Grand Strategy and Teaching Command: The Classic Works of Alfred Thayer Mahan Reconsidered* [Washington, DC: Woodrow Wilson Center Press; Baltimore: Johns Hopkins University Press, 1997]). The realist reading of Admiral James Stavridis, *Sea Power: The History and Geopolitics of the World's Oceans* (New York: Penguin, 2017) acknowledges Mahan's consideration of economics/commerce (and his imperialist perspective!) but still focuses on the geographic features—though "updated" (309–21)—and the difference between land and seapower (314).

36. Mahan's writing has been adopted by the Chinese foreign policy community to advocate for the construction of a blue-water navy; see James R. Holmes and Toshi Yoshihara, "The Influence of Mahan upon China's Maritime Strategy," *Comparative Strategy* 24, no. 1 (2005): 23–51; James R. Holmes, "China's Way of Naval War: Mahan's Logic, Mao's Grammar," *Comparative Strategy* 28, no. 3 (2009): 217–43. For analysis of the change in policy, see Nan Li, "The Evolution of China's Naval Strategy and Capabilities: From 'Near Coast' and 'Near Seas' to 'Far Seas,'" *Asian Security* 5, no. 2 (2009): 144–69; Srikanth Kondapalli, "China's Naval Strategy," *Strategic Analysis* 23, no. 12 (2000): 2037–56. And for an updated and realist perspective, see Michael A. McDevitt, *China as a Twenty First Century Naval Power: Theory, Practice, and Implications* (Annapolis, MD: Naval Institute Press, 2020).

Chapter One

1. For example, *The Economist* offers an online course, for a princely sum, that equates international relations with geopolitics.

2. Robert D. Kaplan, *The Revenge of Geography: What the Map Tells Us about Coming Conflicts and the Battle against Fate* (New York: Random House, 2013); Tim Marshall, *Prisoners of Geography: Ten Maps That Explain Everything about the World* (New York: Simon and Schuster, 2015).

3. Robert D. Kaplan, *Balkan Ghosts: A Journey through History* (New York: Random House, 1996).

4. Gearóid Ò Tuathail, *Critical Geopolitics* (New York: Routledge, 1997); David Atkinson and Klaus Dodds, eds., *Geopolitical Traditions: A Century of Geopolitical Thought* (London: Routledge, 2000).

5. Atkinson and Dodds, *Geopolitical Traditions*.

6. Geoffrey Parker, *Western Geopolitical Thought in the Twentieth Century* (London: Routledge, 1985).

7. Zbigniew Brzezinski, *The Grand Chessboard: American Primacy and Its Geostrategic Imperatives* (New York: Basic Books, 1997); Henry Kissinger, *World Order* (New York: Penguin Press, 2014).

8. Atkinson and Dodds, *Geopolitical Traditions*.

9. Gerry Kearns, *Geopolitics and Empire: The Legacy of Halford Mackinder* (Oxford: Oxford University Press, 2009); Brian W. Blouet, *Halford Mackinder: A Biography* (College Station: Texas A&M University Press, 1987).

10. H. J. Mackinder, "The Geographical Pivot of History," *Geographical Journal* 23, no. 4 (April 1904): 436–37; Gearóid Ò Tuathail, "Putting Mackinder in His Place: Material Transformations and Myth," *Political Geography* 11, no. 1 (January 1992): 101.

11. Alfred Thayer Mahan, *The Influence of Sea Power upon History, 1660–1783* (London: Sampson, Low, Marston, 1890), 28.

12. Mahan, *Influence of Sea Power*, v.

13. Mahan, *Influence of Sea Power*, 58.

14. For Mahan, geographical determinism can be a constraint, but if read the right way it is an opportunity at a given moment. His first "principal condition" of seapower is *geographical position*: namely, if a country needs to defend itself by land or seek territorial gain, "it has, by the very unity of its aim directed upon the sea, an advantage as compared with a people one of whose boundaries is continental" (*Influence of Sea Power*, 29). Peace with Canada and the assumptions of the Monroe Doctrine were coupled with the strategic importance of the Suez Canal so that the US would exert geopolitical control through its strategic advantage of a "base of permanent operations . . . understood [as] a country whence come all the resources, where are united the great lines of communication by land and water, where are the arsenals and armed posts" (34): in other words, US money, infrastructure, and military power. The location between east and west, Atlantic and Pacific, was enhanced by the second principal condition of *physical conformation*, or territorial coherence not divided by waterways (35), and a long coastline suitable for ports connecting the country's hinterland to the oceans, the third principal condition (42).

These physical features may have been deemed natural by Mahan, but they were not exclusively so. The length of a single US coastline was a product of the North's victory in the Civil War. The Central American Isthmus is a thin barrier between the Atlantic and the Pacific, but the Panama Canal could only be completed once President Theodore Roosevelt had instigated a revolution and carved out Panama as a new country separate from Colombia. And physical conformation, or control of coastlines on three sides of the North American continent, was a product of the genocide of indigenous peoples and wars with Mexico and the British. Hence, the "national will" that Mahan's writing sought to exhort had already been in action.

15. Mackinder, "Geographical Pivot of History," 421–37.

16. George F. Kennan, "The Sources of Soviet Conduct," *Foreign Affairs* 25, no. 4 (July 1947): 566–82. The zone of conflict between landpowers and seapowers was identified as the "Rimland." See Nicholas J. Spykman, *The United States and the Balance of Power* (New York: Harcourt, Brace, 1942).

17. Gearóid Ò Tuathail and John Agnew, "Geopolitics and Discourse: Practical Geopolitical Reasoning in American Foreign Policy," *Political Geography* 11, no. 2 (March 1992): 190–204.

18. Nicholas John Spykman, *The Geography of the Peace* (New York: Harcourt, Brace, 1944): 16; Erik D. Weiss, "Cold War under the Ice: The Army's Bid for a Long-Range Nuclear Role, 1959–1963," *Journal of Cold War Studies* 3, no. 3 (Fall 2001): 32; Ò Tuathail, "Putting Mackinder in His Place," 102.

19. Patrick O'Sullivan, "Antidomino," *Political Geography Quarterly* 1, no. 1 (January 1982): 57–64.

20. John Agnew, *Geopolitics: Re-visioning World Politics*, 2nd ed. (London: Routledge, 2003), 4.

21. Sun Tzu, *The Art of War: The Denma Translation* (Boston: Shambhala, 2002), 5.

22. Colin Flint, *Introduction to Geopolitics*, 4th ed. (London:, 2022), 42–43.

23. Peter J. Taylor, "Understanding Global Inequalities: A World-Systems Approach," *Geography* 77, no. 1 (1992): 10–21; Immanuel Wallerstein, *The Capitalist World-Economy* (Cambridge: Cambridge University Press, 1979), 66–94.

24. Giovanni Arrighi, "The Three Hegemonies of Historical Capitalism," *Review* 13, no. 3 (Summer 1990): 365–408.

25. Arrighi, "Three Hegemonies," 372; Sami Moisio, "Re-thinking Geoeconomics: Towards a Political Geography of Economic Geographies," *Geography Compass* 13, no. 10 (October 2019): 3–4.

26. Giovanni Arrighi, *The Long Twentieth Century: Money, Power, and the Origins of Our Times* (London: Verso, 1994), 1–2.

27. Geoffrey Till, *Seapower: A Guide for the Twenty-First Century*, 3rd ed.(London: Routledge, 2013), 17. For an interpretation of the cycle as geoeconomics, see Geoffrey F. Gresh, *To Rule Eurasia's Waves: The New Great Power Competition at Sea* (New Haven, CT: Yale University Press, 2020), 9–14.

28. Till, *Seapower*, 61.

29. Till, *Seapower*, 219.

30. Colin Flint and Peter J. Taylor, *Political Geography: World-Economy, Nation-State, and Locality*, 7th ed. (London: Routledge, 2018), 59–61.

31. Colin Flint, "Putting the 'Geo' into Geopolitics: A Heuristic Framework and the Example of Australian Foreign Policy," *Geojournal* 87, no. 4 (2022): 2580–83.

32. Flint, *Introduction to Geopolitics*, 15. Culture is an important part of geopolitics: the representations of different places and regions are used to justify actions against them. This is discussed in the sense of grand world visions in chapter 7. In other words, they create maps of threat and risk that are used to justify military actions, and maps of economic opportunity and need that are used to justify the economic relations. The use of culture in geopolitics is the remit of critical geopolitics. Key texts include Gearóid Ó Tuathail, *Critical Geo-*

politics (Minneapolis: University of Minnesota Press, 1996), and Jason Dittmer and Daniel Bos, *Popular Culture, Geopolitics and Identity*, 2nd ed. (Lanham, MD: Rowman and Littlefield, 2019).

33. Till, *Seapower*, 17 and 23; Jeremy Black, *Naval Power* (London: Red Globe Press, 2009), 1; Weiqiang Lin, "Transport Geography and Geopolitics: Visions, Rules and Militarism in China's Belt and Road Initiative and Beyond," *Journal of Transport Geography* 81 (2019): 5.

34. Colin Flint, *Geopolitical Constructs: The Mulberry Harbours, World War Two, and the Making of a Militarized Transatlantic* (Lanham, MD: Rowman and Littlefield, 2016), 33–34; Peter J. Martin and Alex Dennis, "Introduction: The Opposition of Structure and Agency," in *Human Agents and Social Structures*, ed. Peter J. Martin and Alex Dennis (Manchester: Manchester University Press, 2010), 14.

35. Robert Denemark, "Pre-emptive Decline," *Journal of World-Systems Research* 27, no. 1 (2021): 150.

36. Flint, "Putting the 'Geo' into Geopolitics," 2579–80.

37. Flint, "Putting the 'Geo' into Geopolitics," 2580–83.

38. Flint and Taylor, *Political Geography*, 59–61.

39. Agnew, *Geopolitics*, 85–114.

40. Arrighi, *Long Twentieth Century*, 1–2; Wallerstein, *Capitalist World-Economy*, 66–94; Immanuel Wallerstein, *Historical Capitalism* (Cambridge: Cambridge University Press, 1983), 13–43.

Chapter Two

1. Geoffrey Parker, *Western Geopolitical Thought in the Twentieth Century* (London: Routledge, 1985).

2. Peter J. Taylor, "Understanding Global Inequalities: A World-Systems Approach," *Geography* 77, no. 1 (1992): 10–21; Immanuel Wallerstein, *The Capitalist World-Economy* (Cambridge: Cambridge University Press, 1979), 66–94; Giovanni Arrighi, "The Three Hegemonies of Historical Capitalism," *Review* 13, no. 3 (Summer 1990): 365–408.

3. The book's focus on seapower tends toward studying interactions (economic and military, and peaceful and conflictual) between countries. It should be noted that *core* and *periphery* in world-systems analysis refer to economic processes and not to countries or regions. However, core and periphery processes tend to be clustered in territorial spaces. Hence, as a shorthand, we can refer to core (primary) and peripheral (subsidiary) countries as those in which core or periphery processes tend to dominate the economy. For a critical engagement, see John Agnew, "The Territorial Trap: The Geographical Assumptions of International Relations Theory," *Review of International Political Economy* 1, no. 1 (Spring 1994): 53–80.

4. Raymond J. Dezzani, "Measuring Transition and Mobility in the Hierarchical World-Economy," *Journal of Regional Science* 42, no. 3 (2002): 595–625.

5. Christopher Chase-Dunn, *Global Formation: Structures of the World-Economy* (Oxford: Blackwell, 1989), 23; Colin Flint and Ray Dezzani, "State

Maneuver in the Capitalist World-Economy: A Political Geography of Contextualized Agency," *Environment and Planning A* 50, no. 8 (November 2018): 1580–1601.

6. Geoffrey Till, *Seapower: A Guide for the Twenty-First Century*, 3rd ed. (London: Routledge, 2013), 17.

7. George Modelski, *Long Cycles in World Politics* (Seattle: University of Washington Press, 1987).

8. Immanuel Wallerstein, *The Politics of the World-Economy* (Cambridge: Cambridge University Press, 1984), 4.

9. Colin Flint and Peter J. Taylor, *Political Geography: World-Economy, Nation-State, and Locality*, 7th ed. (London: Routledge, 2018), 20–21; Chase-Dunn, *Global Formation*, 25.

10. Peter J. Taylor, *Britain and the Cold War: 1945 as Geopolitical Transition* (London: Pinter, 1990), 13–17; Hew Strachan, *The Direction of War: Contemporary Strategy in Historical Perspective* (Cambridge: Cambridge University Press, 2013), 34.

11. Robert O. Keohane, *After Hegemony: Cooperation and Discord in the World Political Economy* (Princeton, NJ: Princeton University Press, 1984).

12. Colin Flint and Ghazi-Walid Falah, "How the United States Justified Its War on Terrorism: Prime Morality and the Construction of a 'Just War,'" *Third World Quarterly* 25, no. 8 (2004): 1379–99.

13. Andre Gunder Frank, *Dependent Accumulation and Underdevelopment* (London: Macmillan Press, 1978); Flint and Taylor, *Political Geography*, 20–21.

14. David A. Lake, *Hierarchy in International Relations* (Ithaca, NY: Cornell University Press, 2009).

15. Enrico Augelli and Craig Murphy, *America's Quest for Supremacy and the Third World* (London: Pinter, 1988), 138–41.

16. Michael Klare, *Rogue States and Nuclear Outlaws: America's Search for a New Foreign Policy* (New York: Hill and Wang, 1995), 9–10.

17. Flint and Dezzani, "State Maneuver," 1587.

18. International Institute for Strategic Studies, "The Arab Gulf States and the Geopolitics of the Energy Transition," *Strategic Comments* 28, no. 2 (2002): i–iii.

19. Gerard Toal, *Near Abroad: Putin, the West, and the Contest over Ukraine and Caucasus* (Oxford: Oxford University Press, 2017), 3.

20. K.-H. Shin and P. S. Ciccantell, "The Steel and Shipbuilding Industries of South Korea: Rising East Asia and Globalization," *Journal of World-Systems Research* 15, no. 2 (2009): 167–92. For a current example of competition for the most valuable and profitable economic activities, see Chris Miller, *Chip War: The Fight for the World's Most Critical Technology* (New York: Scribner, 2022).

21. Charles Tilly, *Coercion, Capital, and European States, AD 990–1990* (Cambridge, MA: Blackwell, 1990).

22. Flint and Dezzani, "State Maneuver," 1587–88.

23. Frank, *Dependent Accumulation and Underdevelopment*; Paul S. Ciccantell and Stephen G. Bunker, "The Economic Ascent of China and the Potential for Restructuring the Capitalist World-Economy," *Journal of World-Systems Research* 10, no. 3 (Fall 2004): 570–71.

24. Ciccantell and Bunker, "Economic Ascent of China," 570–71; Julie Michelle Klinger, *Rare Earth Frontiers: From Terrestrial Subsoils to Lunar Landscapes* (Ithaca, NY: Cornell University Press, 2017), 4–7.

25. Flint and Dezzani, "State Maneuver," 1589–90; Flint and Taylor, *Political Geography*, 17–18.

26. Tobias Vestner, "The New Geopolitics of the Arms Trade," Arms Control Association, December 2020, https://www.armscontrol.org/act/2020-12/features/new-geopolitics-arms-trade-treaty.

27. Keller Easterling, *Extrastatecraft: The Power of Infrastructure Space* (London: Verso, 2014); Jean-Paul Addie, Michael R. Glass, and Jen Nelles, "Regionalizing the Infrastructure Turn: A Research Agenda," *Regional Studies, Regional Science* 7, no. 1 (2020): 10–26; Jean-Marc Blanchard and Colin Flint, "The Geopolitics of China's Maritime Silk Road Initiative: Introduction," *Geopolitics* 22, no. 2 (2017): 232–35.

28. Peter J. Taylor, "The Error of Developmentalism," in *Horizons in Human Geography*, ed. Derek Gregory and Rex Walford (London: Palgrave Macmillan, 1989), 303–19; Faheem Ur Rehman, Abul Ala Noman, and Yibing Ding, "Does Infrastructure Increase Exports and Reduce Trade Deficits? Evidence from Selected South Asian Countries Using a New Global Infrastructure Index," *Journal of Economic Structures* 9, no. 10 (2020), https://doi.org/10.1186/s40008-020-0183-x.

29. Johannes Petry, "Beyond Ports, Roads and Railways: Chinese Economic Statecraft, the Belt and Road Initiative and the Politics of Financial Infrastructures," *European Journal of International Relations* 29, no. 2 (October 2022), https://doi.org/10.1177/13540661221126615.

30. Henry W. Yeung, *Strategic Coupling: East Asian Industrial Transformation in the New Global Economy* (Ithaca, NY: Cornell University Press, 2016); Emily T. Yeh and Elizabeth Wharton, "Going West and Going Out: Discourses, Migrants, and Models in Chinese Development," *Eurasian Geography and Economics* 57, no. 3 (2016): 286–315.

31. See James Walvin, *A World Transformed: Slavery in the Americas and the Origins of Global Power* (London: Robinson, 2022), and Milton Meltzer, *Slavery: A World History*, updated ed. (Chicago: Da Capo Press, 1993).

32. Bruno Maçães, *Belt and Road: A Chinese World Order* (London: C. Hurst, 2018); James Sidaway and Chi Yuan Woon, "Chinese Narratives on 'One Belt, One Road' (一带一路) in Geographical and Imperial Contexts," *Professional Geographer* 69, no. 4 (2017): 591–603. The actual impact of the BRI and whether its promises will come to fruition are still unclear and a matter of debate. See Jean-Marc Blanchard, "Belt and Road Initaitive (BRI) Blues: Powering BRI Research Back on Track to Avoid Choppy Seas," *Journal of Chinese Political Science* 26 (2021): 235–55.

33. Seth Schindler, Jessica DiCarlo, and Dinesh Paudel, "The New Cold War and the Rise of the 21st-Century Infrastructure State," *Transactions, Institute of British Geographers* 47, no. 2 (June 2022): 331–46.

34. Dan Sabbagh and Julian Borger, "NATO Summit: Leaders Declare China Presents a Security Risk," *The Guardian*, June 14, 2021. https://www.theguardian.com/world/2021/jun/14/nato-summit-china-russia-biden-cyber-attacks.

35. Sasha Davis, "The US Military Base Network and Contemporary Colonialism: Power Projection, Resistance and the Quest for Operational Unilateralism," *Political Geography* 30, no. 4 (May 2011): 216.

36. Augelli and Murphy, *America's Quest*, 8; Flint and Falah, "How the United States Justified Its War," 1388.

37. A. F. K. Organski and Jacek Kugler, *The War Ledger* (Chicago: University of Chicago Press, 1980); Robert Gilpin, "The Theory of Hegemonic War," *Journal of Interdisciplinary History* 18, no. 4 (Spring 1988): 591–92; Arrighi, "Three Hegemonies"; Modelski, *Long Cycles*.

38. Peter J. Taylor, *Modernities: A Geohistorical Interpretation* (Cambridge: Polity Press, 1998), 38–39.

39. Catherine Weaver, *Hypocrisy Trap: The World Bank and the Poverty of Reform* (Princeton, NJ: Princeton University Press, 2008), 8–10.

40. Weaver, *Hypocrisy Trap*, 8–10; Richard Peet, *Unholy Trinity: The IMF, World Bank and WTO*, 2nd ed. (London: Zed Books, 2009).

41. Colin Flint and Madeleine Waddoups, "South-South Cooperation or Core-Periphery Contention? Ghanaian and Zambian Perceptions of Economic Relations with China," *Geopolitics* 26, no. 3 (2021): 889–918.

42. Fiona McConnell and Chih Yuan Woon, "Mapping Chinese Diplomacy: Relational Contradictions and Spatial Tensions," *Geopolitics* 28, no. 2 (2021): 593–618.

43. Taylor, "Understanding Global Inequalities."

44. Flint and Taylor, *Political Geography*, 20–21; Flint and Dezzani, "State Maneuver," 1588.

45. Steven Radil, Colin Flint, and Sang-Hyun Chi, "A Relational Geography of War: Actor-Context Interaction and the Spread of World War I," *Annals of the Association of American Geographers* 103, no. 6 (2013): 1468–84; Zeev Maoz, *Networks of Nations: The Evolution, Structure and Impact of International Networks, 1816–2001* (Cambridge: Cambridge University Press, 2011).

Chapter Three

1. Nicholas Mulder, *The Economic Weapon: The Rise of Sanctions as a Tool of Modern War* (New Haven, CT: Yale University Press, 2022).

2. Mulder, *Economic Weapon*, 17 and 291.

3. Peter J. Taylor, *Britain and the Cold War: 1945 as Geopolitical Transition* (London: Pinter, 1990), ix; Colin Flint and Ray Dezzani, "State Maneuver in the Capitalist World-Economy: A Political Geography of Contextualized Agency," *Environment and Planning A* 50, no. 8 (November 2018): 1580–1601.

4. Geoffrey Till, *Seapower: A Guide for the Twenty-First Century*, 3rd ed. (London: Routledge, 2013), 17.

5. Jonathan I. Israel, *The Dutch Republic: Its Rise, Greatness, and Fall, 1477–1806* (Oxford: Oxford University Press, 1995), 179–205.

6. Israel, *Dutch Republic*, 205–20.

7. Israel, *Dutch Republic*, 241–53.

8. Israel, *Dutch Republic*, 2.

9. Till, *Seapower*, 17.
10. Jonathan I. Israel, *Dutch Primacy in World Trade, 1585–1740* (Oxford: Clarendon Press, 1989), 80–86.
11. Jeremy Black, *Naval Power* (London: Red Globe Press, 2009), 36.
12. Till, *Seapower*, 23–25.
13. Sir Julian Corbett, *Some Principles of Maritime Strategy*, 2nd ed. (London: Longmans, Green, 1911), 67, cited in Till, *Seapower*, 25.
14. Israel, *Dutch Primacy*, 68.
15. Israel, *Dutch Primacy*, 86.
16. Israel, *Dutch Primacy*, 102–3.
17. Israel, *Dutch Primacy*, 269.
18. Elena Conde Pérez and Zhaklin Valerieva Yaneva, "Unequal Treaties in International Law," *Oxford Bibliographies: International Law*, March 25, 2020, https://doi.org/10.1093/OBO/9780199796953-0131.
19. Black, *Naval Power*, 37.
20. Israel, *Dutch Primacy*, 95.
21. Israel, *Dutch Republic*, 861.
22. Black, *Naval Power*, 36.
23. Israel, *Dutch Primacy*, 68.
24. Israel, *Dutch Primacy*, 67–73.
25. Israel, *Dutch Primacy*, 62.
26. The name of the country we know as Great Britain, but commonly and erroneously refer to as England, is complicated. England, especially the city of London and the surrounding "home counties," is the center of the country's financial and political power. It is an imperial entity that spread control through northern England and Wales, Scotland, and Ireland. In essence, England is an imperial country that colonized its Celtic neighbors and used that base to create a global empire. I tend to use *Britain* when referring to events after 1707, the Union of England and Scotland. Nationalists in Wales, Scotland, and Ireland still view the country of the United Kingdom of Great Britain and Northern Ireland as a collection of colonies controlled by England. In this book I refer to *Britain* as shorthand for the country as a whole but use *England* when the interests of the financial and political elite are in focus. Of course, many Scots, Welsh, and Irish embraced and energized the construction of the British Empire, profited from the empire, and laid down their lives for the cause. See Michael Hechter, *Internal Colonialism: The Celtic Fringe in British National Development* (Berkeley: University of California Press, 1975), and Tom Nairn, *The Break-Up of Britain* (London: Verso, 1977).
27. Black, *Naval Power*, 49.
28. Black, *Naval Power*, 51.
29. Black, *Naval Power*, 69.
30. Black, *Naval Power*, 111.
31. Lawrence James, *The Rise and Fall of the British Empire* (New York: St. Martin's Griffin, 1994), 156–57.
32. Black, *Naval Power*, 85.

33. Ian W. Toll, *Six Frigates: The Epic History of the Founding of the U.S. Navy* (New York: W. W. Norton, 2006), 331–54.

34. James, *Rise and Fall,* 190, 198.

35. James, *Rise and Fall*, 226–31; Douglas M. Peers, "Britain and Empire," in *A Companion to 19th-Century Britain*, ed. Chris Williams (Malden, MA: Blackwell, 2006), 63.

36. James, *Rise and Fall*, 170–71.

37. C. M. Law, "Population in England and Wales, 1801–1911," *Transactions, Institute of British Geographers* 41, no. 1 (June 1967): 134.

38. Peter Mathias, *First Industrial Nation: The Economic History of Britain, 1700–1914* (London: Methuen, 1969); Martin J. Wiener, *English Culture and the Decline of the Industrial Spirit, 1850–1980*, 2nd ed. (Cambridge: Cambridge University Press, 2004).

39. James, *Rise and Fall,* 259–60.

40. James, *Rise and Fall,* 173.

41. William Dalrymple, *The Anarchy: The East India Company, Corporate Violence, and the Pillage of an Empire* (London: Bloomsbury, 2019), 382.

42. Quoted in James, *Rise and Fall,* 177.

43. Fred Halliday, *The Making of the Second Cold War* (London: Verso, 1983), 3–5.

44. Halliday, *Making of the Second Cold War*, 5.

45. Catherine Weaver, *Hypocrisy Trap: The World Bank and the Poverty of Reform* (Princeton, NJ: Princeton University Press, 2008), 8–10.

46. Enrico Augelli and Craig Murphy, *America's Quest for Supremacy and the Third World* (London: Pinter, 1988), 67.

47. Gabriel Kolko, *Another Century of War?* (New York: New Press, 2002), 91–94; Barry Gewen, *The Inevitability of Tragedy: Henry Kissinger and His World* (New York: W. W. Norton, 2020); Halliday, *Making of the Second Cold War*, 245–46.

48. Black, *Naval Power*, 90.

49. Toll, *Six Frigates*, 21–24.

50. Black, *Naval Power*, 89.

51. Toll, *Six Frigates*, 331–54.

52. Black, *Naval Power*, 89.

53. Seward W. Livermore, "American Naval-Base Policy in the Far East, 1850–1914," *Pacific Historical Review* 13, no. 2 (June 1944): 113–35.

54. James R. Reckner, *Teddy Roosevelt's Great White Fleet* (Annapolis, MD: Naval Institute Press, 1988).

55. Fred Anderson and Andrew Cayton, *The Dominion of War: Empire and Liberty in North America, 1500–2000* (New York: Viking, 2005), 344.

56. Waldo Heinrichs, *Threshold of War: Franklin D. Roosevelt and American Entry into World War II* (New York: Oxford University Press, 1988), 6–8.

57. Rana Mitter, *Forgotten Ally, China's World War II, 1937–1945* (Boston: Houghton Mifflin Harcourt, 2013), 51–52.

58. Isaiah Bowman, *The New World: Problems in Political Geography*, 4th ed. (New York: World Book, 1928).

59. Louis Morton, "American and Allied Strategy in the Far East," *Military Review* 29, no. 9 (December 1949): 22–39; Maurice Matloff and Edwin M. Snell, *Strategic Planning for Coalition Warfare, 1941–1942* (1953; repr., Washington, DC: Center of Military History, United States Army, 1999), 76–78.

60. Mark Skinner Watson, *Chief of Staff: Prewar Plans and Preparations* (1950; repr., Washington, DC: Center of Military History, United States Army, 1991), 376.

61. Michael Howard, *The Mediterranean Strategy in the Second World War* (1968; repr., London: Greenhill Books, 1993), 9–12.

62. Watson, *Chief of Staff*, 105.

63. Halliday, *Making of the Second Cold War*, 7–9.

64. Mitter, *Forgotten Ally*, 14, 373–77.

65. Colin Flint and Zhang Xiaotong, "Historical-Geopolitical Contexts and the Transformation of Chinese Foreign Policy," *Chinese Journal of International Politics* 12, no. 3 (Autumn 2019): 310.

66. Flint and Zhang, "Historical-Geopolitical Contexts," 312.

67. Flint and Zhang, "Historical-Geopolitical Contexts," 313.

68. Flint and Zhang, "Historical-Geopolitical Contexts," 313.

69. Xu Guoqi, *China and the Great War: China's Pursuit of a New National Identity and Internationalization* (Cambridge: Cambridge University Press, 2005), 114–17.

70. Mitter, *Forgotten Ally*, 240–44.

71. Jay Taylor, *The Generalissimo: Chiang Kai-shek and the Struggle for Modern China* (Cambridge, MA: Harvard University Press, 2011), 194–244.

72. Flint and Zhang, "Historical-Geopolitical Contexts," 314.

73. Philip Short, *Mao: The Man Who Made China* (London: I. B. Tauris, 2017), 418–19.

74. Ezra F. Vogel, *Deng Xiaoping and the Transformation of China* (Cambridge, MA: Harvard University Press, 2011), 424–25, 688.

75. Yongsheng Zhou, "A Review: Economic Diplomacy of Three Generations of Communist Leaders Since the Founding of the PRC," in *Chinese Economic Diplomacy*, ed. Xiaotong Zhang and Hongyo Wang (London: ACA Publishing, 2015), 11, quoted in Flint and Zhang, "Historical-Geopolitical Contexts," 314.

76. Flint and Zhang, "Historical-Geopolitical Contexts," 314.

77. Neil Coe and Henry W. Yeung, *Global Production Networks: Theorizing Economic Development in an Interconnected World* (Oxford: Oxford University Press, 2015).

78. Flint and Zhang, "Historical-Geopolitical Contexts," 316; Deborah Brautigam, *The Dragon's Gift: The Real Story of China in Africa* (Oxford: Oxford University Press, 2009), 41–42.

79. Flint and Zhang, "Historical-Geopolitical Contexts," 323; Andrew Small, *The China-Pakistan Axis: Asia's New Geopolitics* (Haryana, India: Random House, 2015), 76.

80. Taylor, *Generalissimo*, 419–21; Kolko, *Another Century of War?*, 92–94 and 97–100.

81. Small, *China-Pakistan Axis*, 37.

82. Small, *China-Pakistan Axis*, 37.
83. Quoted in Small, *China-Pakistan Axis*, 39.
84. Small, *China-Pakistan Axis*, 39.
85. Russell Ong, "China and the U.S. War on Terror," *Korean Journal of Defense Analysis* 18, no. 2 (2006): 95–96.
86. North Atlantic Treaty Organization, "NATO and China Cooperate to Fight Piracy," January 20, 2012, https://www.nato.int/cps/en/natolive/news_83585.htm?selectedLocale=en. It is notable that most NATO websites describing this operation do not mention China's participation.
87. Brautigam, *Dragon's Gift*; Pádraig R. Carmody and James T. Murphy, "Chinese Neoglobalization in East Africa: Logics, Couplings and Impacts," *Space and Polity* 26, no. 1 (2022): 20–43; David G. Landry, "Comparing the Determinants of Western and Chinese Development Finance Flows to Africa," Working Paper No. 2018/21, SAIS-CARI Policy Briefs, China-Africa Research Initiative, School of Advanced International Studies, Johns Hopkins University, Washington, DC, https://ideas.repec.org/p/zbw/caripb/292018.html.
88. Quoted in Charlotte Gao, "China Officially Sets Up Its First Overseas Base in Djibouti," *The Diplomat*, July 12, 2017, https://thediplomat.com/2017/07/china-officially-sets-up-its-first-overseas-base-in-djibouti/.
89. Benjamin Barton, *The Doraleh Disputes: Infrastructure Politics in the Global South* (Singapore: Springer Nature, 2023), 2–6.
90. Emily T. Yeh and Elizabeth Wharton, "Going West and Going Out: Discourses, Migrants, and Models in Chinese Development," *Eurasian Geography and Economics* 57 no. 3 (2016): 286–315.
91. Quoted in Bruno Maçães, *Belt and Road: A Chinese World Order* (London: Hurst, 2018), 86.
92. Jean-Marc Blanchard, "Chinese Outward Foreign Direct Investment (COFDI): A Primer and Assessment of the State of COFDI Research," in *Handbook on the International Political Economy of China*, ed Ka Zeng (Cheltenham: Edward Elgar, 2019), 82.
93. Maçães, *Belt and Road*, 9–37; Carmody and Murphy, "Chinese Neoglobalization," 21–22.

Chapter Four

1. Rory Medcalf, *Indo-Pacific Empire: China, America and the Contest for the World's Pivotal Region* (Manchester: Manchester University Press, 2020); Bruno Maçães, *Belt and Road: A Chinese World Order* (London: Hurst, 2018).
2. Jonathan I. Israel, *Dutch Primacy in World Trade, 1585–1740* (Oxford: Clarendon Press, 1989), 18.
3. Israel, *Dutch Primacy*, 50.
4. Israel, *Dutch Primacy*, 60.
5. Israel, *Dutch Primacy*, 62–66.
6. Israel, *Dutch Primacy*, 172.
7. Israel, *Dutch Primacy*, 269.
8. Israel, *Dutch Primacy*, 259.

9. Israel, *Dutch Primacy*, 27–28.
10. Israel, *Dutch Primacy*, 41–48.
11. Israel, *Dutch Primacy*, 97.
12. Israel, *Dutch Primacy*, 103.
13. Israel, *Dutch Primacy*, 105.
14. Israel, *Dutch Primacy*, 73.
15. Israel, *Dutch Primacy*, 103.
16. Israel, *Dutch Primacy*, 103.
17. Israel, *Dutch Primacy*, 104.
18. Israel, *Dutch Primacy*, 66.
19. Israel, *Dutch Primacy*, 123.

20. Sir Julian Corbett, *Some Principles of Maritime Strategy*, 2nd ed. (London: Longmans, Green, 1911), 67, cited in Geoffrey Till, *Seapower: A Guide for the Twenty-First Century*, 3rd ed. (London: Routledge, 2013), 25.

21. This quote is from Mahan's 1890 essay "The United States Looking Forward," first published in the *Atlantic Monthly* in December 1890 and republished in Captain A. T. Mahan, *The Interest of America in Sea Power, Present and Future* (London: Sampson Low, Marston, 1897), https://www.gutenberg.org/files/15749/15749-h/15749-h.htm#II. The Gutenberg version provides no page numbers.

22. Mahan, "United States Looking Forward."

23. This quote is from Mahan's 1893 essay "The Isthmus and Sea Power, first published in the *Atlantic Monthly* in September 1893 and republished in Mahan, *Interest of America*.

24. Mahan, "Isthmus and Sea Power."

25. Michael Howard, *The Mediterranean Strategy in the Second World War* (London: Greenhill Books, 1993), 9.

26. Howard, *Mediterranean Strategy*, 9.

27. Howard, *Mediterranean Strategy*, 33.

28. Mark Skinner Watson, *Chief of Staff: Prewar Plans and Preparations* (1950; repr., Washington, DC: Center of Military History, United States Army, 1991), 29.

29. Louis Morton, "American and Allied Strategy in the Far East," *Military Review* 29, no. 9 (December 1949): 24.

30. Alfred Thayer Mahan, *The Influence of Seapower upon History, 1660–1783* (London: Sampson, Low, Marston, 1890), 49, 83.

31. Phil Butler, *Air Arsenal North America: Aircraft for the Allies, 1938–1945. Purchases and Lend-Lease*, with Dan Hagedorn (Hinckley, UK: Midland Press, 2004), 8.

32. Antony Beevor, *The Second World War* (New York: Little, Brown, 2012), 96.

33. Colin Flint, "Seapower, Geostrategic Relations, and Islandness: The World War II Destroyers for Bases Deal," *Island Studies Journal* 16, no. 1 (2021): 273; Steven High, *Base Colonies in the Western Hemisphere, 1940–1967* (New York: Palgrave Macmillan, 2009), 1–2.

34. Arnold Hague, *Destroyers for Great Britain: A History of 50 Town Class Ships Transferred from the United States to Great Britain in 1940* (Annapolis, MD: Naval Institute Press, 1990), 7.

35. High, *Base Colonies*, 1.

36. H. Duncan Hall, *North American Supply* (London: HMSO and Longmans, Green, 1955), 44.

37. 1939 Declaration of Panama, quoted in Hall, *North American Supply*, 44.

38. Flint, "Seapower, Geostrategic Relations," 6–7.

39. Stetson Conn and Byron Fairchild, *The Western Hemisphere: The Framework of Hemisphere Defense* (Washington, DC: Center of Military History, United States Army, 1960), 100, 138.

40. Richard M. Leighton and Robert W. Coakley, *Global Logistics and Strategy: 1940–1943* (Washington, DC: Center of Military History, United States Army, 1955), 360–61.

41. Watson, *Chief of Staff*, 376.

42. Watson, *Chief of Staff*, 376.

43. Watson, *Chief of Staff*, 123, emphasis added.

44. Maurice Matloff and Edwin M. Snell, *Strategic Planning for Coalition Warfare, 1941–1942* (1953; repr., Washington, DC: Center of Military History, United States Army, 1999), 26.

45. Dan van Der Vat, *The Atlantic Campaign: World War II's Great Struggle at Sea* (New York: Harper and Row, 1988), 151.

46. Samuel Eliot Morison, *Operations in North African Waters, October 1942–June 1943: History of United States Naval Operations in World War II*, vol. 2 (Boston: Little, Brown, 1947), 3.

47. Matloff and Snell, *Strategic Planning*, 98.

48. Matloff and Snell, *Strategic Planning*, 103 quoting JB 355, ser. 707, September 11, 1941, "JB Estimate of U.S. Over-all Pdn Reqmts," Sec. II, Part II, p. 14.

49. Quoted in Morison, *Operations*, 8.

50. Quoted in Morison, *Operations*, 7.

51. George F. Howe, *The Mediterranean Theater of Operations: Northwest Africa: Seizing the Initiative in the West* (Washington, DC: Center of Military History, United States Army, 1957), 271.

52. Howe, *Mediterranean Theater of Operations*, 272.

53. Leighton and Coakley, *Global Logistics and Strategy*, 117.

54. Matloff and Snell, *Strategic Planning*, 57.

55. Matloff and Snell, *Strategic Planning*, 57.

56. Maurice Matloff, *Strategic Planning for Coalition Warfare, 1943–44* (Washington, DC: Center of Military History, United States Army, 1957), 339.

57. Matloff, *Strategic Planning*, 339.

58. As one of countless examples of these assumptions, see Kate Lyons, "A Pivotal Moment: Pacific Faces a Choice over China That Will Shape It for Decades," *The Guardian*, May 27, 2022. https://www.theguardian.com/world/2022/may/28/a-pivotal-moment-pacific-faces-a-choice-over-china-that-will-shape-it-for-decades.

59. Louise Levathes, *When China Ruled the Seas: The Treasure Fleet of the Dragon Throne, 1405–1433* (New York: Oxford University Press, 1996), 20–21.

60. Levathes, *When China Ruled*, 20.

61. Levathes, *When China Ruled*, 173–80.
62. Xu Guoqi, *China and the Great War: China's Pursuit of a New National Identity and Internationalization* (Cambridge: Cambridge University Press, 2005), 114–17.
63. Rana Mitter, *Forgotten Ally, China's World War II, 1937–1945* (Boston: Houghton Mifflin Harcourt, 2013), 4–12.
64. Mitter, *Forgotten Ally*, 370–71.
65. Jay Taylor, *The Generalissimo: Chiang Kai-shek and the Struggle for Modern China* (Cambridge, MA: Harvard University Press, 2011), 403.
66. Taylor, *Generalissimo*, 404.
67. Taylor, *Generalissimo*, 412–13.
68. Taylor, *Generalissimo*, 421.
69. Taylor, *Generalissimo*, 457.
70. Michael A. McDevitt, *China as a Twenty First Century Naval Power: Theory, Practice, and Implications* (Annapolis, MD: Naval Institute Press, 2020), 7–9.
71. McDevitt, *China*, 73–74.
72. Caitlin Byrne, "Securing the 'Rules-Based Order' in the Indo-Pacific: The Significance of Strategic Narrative," *Security Challenges* 16, no. 3 (2020): 10.
73. McDevitt, *China*, 9–11.
74. McDevitt, *China*, 11–16.
75. Anthony J. Blinken, Secretary of State, "Fifth Anniversary of the Arbitral Tribunal Ruling on the South China Sea," US Department of State, July 11, 2021, https://www.state.gov/fifth-anniversary-of-the-arbitral-tribunal-ruling-on-the-south-china-sea/.
76. McDevitt, *China*, 41–71.
77. Julian Borger and Dan Sabbagh, "US, UK and Australia Forge Military Alliance to Counter China," *The Guardian*, September 16, 2021, https://www.theguardian.com/australia-news/2021/sep/15/australia-nuclear-powered-submarines-us-uk-security-partnership-aukus.
78. Medcalf, *Indo-Pacific Empire*, 16–17.
79. Till, *Seapower*, 17.

Chapter Five

1. Geoffrey Till, *Seapower: A Guide for the Twenty-First Century*, 3rd ed. (London: Routledge, 2013), 17.
2. George Modelski, *Long Cycles in World Politics* (Seattle: University of Washington Press, 1987).
3. Till, *Seapower*, 290.
4. Nicholas Mulder, *The Economic Weapon: The Rise of Sanctions as a Tool of Modern War* (New Haven, CT: Yale University Press, 2022), 38–46.
5. Peter J. Taylor, "Understanding Global Inequalities: A World-Systems Approach," *Geography* 77 no. 1 (1992): 10–21; Immanuel Wallerstein, *The Capitalist World-Economy* (Cambridge: Cambridge University Press, 1979), 66–94; Giovanni Arrighi, "The Three Hegemonies of Historical Capitalism," *Review* 13, no. 3 (Summer 1990): 365–408.

6. Raymond J. Dezzani, "Measuring Transition and Mobility in the Hierarchical World-Economy," *Journal of Regional Science* 42, no. 3 (2002): 595–625; Andre Gunder Frank, *Dependent Accumulation and Underdevelopment* (New York: Monthly Review Press and Macmillan Press, 1978).

7. Gary Gereffi, *Global Value Chains and Development: Redefining the Contours of 21st Century Capitalism* (Cambridge: Cambridge University Press, 2018), 1–2; Henry Wai-Chun Yeung, *Interconnected Worlds: Global Electronics and Production Networks in East Asia* (Stanford, CA: Stanford Business Books, 2022), 10–11.

8. K.-H. Shin and P. S. Ciccantell, "The Steel and Shipbuilding Industries of South Korea: Rising East Asia and Globalization," *Journal of World-Systems Research* 15, no. 2 (2009): 167–92.

9. Andrew J. Bacevich, *America's War for the Greater Middle East: A Military History* (New York: Random House, 2016), 1–32.

10. Julie Michelle Klinger, *Rare Earth Frontiers: From Terrestrial Subsoils to Lunar Landscapes* (Ithaca, NY: Cornell University Press, 2017), 70.

11. Sir Julian Corbett, *Some Principles of Maritime Strategy*, 2nd ed. (London: Longmans, Green, 1911), reprinted with an introduction by Eric Grove (Annapolis, MD: Naval Institute Press, 1988), 67, cited by Till, *Seapower*, 25.

12. Mahan spoke of how all people "love money" if wealth is pursued in what he deemed the right way, not through plunder and avarice but through commerce (Alfred Thayer Mahan, *The Influence of Sea Power upon History, 1660–1783* [London: Sampson, Low, Marston, 1890], 50). The Portuguese and Spanish were bad examples, in their plunder of gold and silver in the Americas. The attitude of the French was questionable. The Dutch and the English were extolled as good role models. Notably, the pursuit of wealth was assumed to require the establishment of colonies, if it was done in what Mahan classified as a matter of "national genius" as part and parcel of acquiring seapower (*Influence of Sea Power*, 50). Effortlessly, the unquestioned right to overseas possessions is described by Mahan: "Of colonization, as of all other growths, it is true that it is most healthy when it is most natural. Therefore colonies that spring from the felt wants and natural impulses of a whole people will have the most solid foundations; and their subsequent growth will be surest when they are least trammelled from home, if the people have the genius for independent action" (*Influence of Sea Power*, 55). One wonders how "trammelled" Native Americans felt in the 1880s when Mahan was writing his book.

13. Jonathan I. Israel, *Dutch Primacy in World Trade, 1585–1740* (Oxford: Clarendon Press, 1989), 64.

14. Israel, *Dutch Primacy*, 7.

15. Shin and Ciccantell, "Steel and Shipbuilding Industries," 167–68.

16. Colin Flint and Peter J. Taylor, *Political Geography: World-Economy, Nation-State, and Locality*, 7th ed. (London: Routledge, 2018), 20–21.

17. Israel, *Dutch Primacy*, 14.

18. Israel, *Dutch Primacy*, 19.

19. Israel, *Dutch Primacy*, 166.

20. Israel, *Dutch Primacy*, 182–83.

21. Israel, *Dutch Primacy*, 27, 390.

22. Israel, *Dutch Primacy*, 27.
23. Israel, *Dutch Primacy*, 395–96.
24. Israel, *Dutch Primacy*, 397.
25. Jeremy Black, *Naval Power* (London: Red Globe Press, 2009), 117.
26. Keith Middlemas, *The Strategy of Appeasement: The British Government and Germany, 1937–39* (Chicago: Quadrangle Books, 1972), 2.
27. B. H. Liddell Hart, *History of the Second World War* (New York: G. P. Putnam, 1970), 8.
28. Hart, *History of the Second World War*, 9.
29. Hart, *History of the Second World War*, 10.
30. John Darwin, *The Empire Project: The Rise and Fall of the British World-System, 1830–1970* (Cambridge: Cambridge University Press, 2009), 493.
31. Darwin, *Empire Project*, 493.
32. Darwin, *Empire Project*, 493.
33. Darwin, *Empire Project*, 493.
34. Darwin, *Empire Project*, 424.
35. Darwin, *Empire Project*, 424.
36. Darwin, *Empire Project*, 493.
37. Darwin, *Empire Project*, 426.
38. Darwin, *Empire Project*, 426.
39. Darwin, *Empire Project*, 426.
40. Brian Farrell, *The Defence and Fall of Singapore* (Singapore: Monsoon Books, 2015), 11.
41. Farrell, *Defence of Singapore*, 11.
42. Farrell, *Defence of Singapore*, 11.
43. Farrell, *Defence of Singapore*, 11.
44. Black, *Naval Power*, 116.
45. Farrell, *Defence of Singapore*, 13.
46. Farrell, *Defence of Singapore*, 15; Greg Kennedy, *Anglo-American Strategic Relations and the Far East, 1933–1939: Imperial Crossroads* (Abingdon: Routledge, 2011), 3.
47. Farrell, *Defence of Singapore*, 14–15.
48. Farrell, *Defence of Singapore*, 13.
49. Farrell, *Defence of Singapore*, 16.
50. Farrell, *Defence of Singapore*, 27.
51. Kennedy, *Anglo-American Strategic Relations*, 5.
52. Kennedy, *Anglo-American Strategic Relations*, 10.
53. Kennedy, *Anglo-American Strategic Relations*, 10.
54. Kennedy, *Anglo-American Strategic Relations*, 265.
55. Kennedy, *Anglo-American Strategic Relations*, 113.
56. Kennedy, *Anglo-American Strategic Relations*, 262.
57. S. C. M. Paine, *The Wars for Asia, 1911–1949* (Cambridge: Cambridge University Press, 2012), 4.
58. Antony Beevor, *The Second World War* (New York: Little, Brown, 2012), 248.

59. Waldo Heinrichs, *Threshold of War: Franklin D. Roosevelt and American Entry into World War II* (New York: Oxford University Press, 1988), 10.

60. Heinrichs, *Threshold of War*, 5.

61. Heinrichs, *Threshold of War*, 36.

62. Ronald H. Spector, *Eagle against the Sun: The American War with Japan* (New York: Free Press, 1985), 20.

63. US Department of State, "Stimson Doctrine, 1932," information released online from January 20, 2001, to January 20, 2009, https://2001-2009.state.gov/r/pa/ho/time/id/16326.htm.

64. Waldo H. Heinrichs, "The Role of the U.S. Navy," in *Pearl Harbor as History*, ed. Dorothy Borg and Shumpei Okamato (New York: Columbia University Press, 1973), 199, quoted in Spector, *Eagle against the Sun*, 21.

65. Franklin D. Roosevelt, "October 5, 1937: Quarantine Speech," Miller Center, University of Virginia. https://millercenter.org/the-presidency/presidential-speeches/october-5-1937-quarantine-speech#dp-expandable-text.

66. Fred Anderson and Andrew Cayton, *The Dominion of War: Empire and Liberty in North America, 1500–2000* (New York: Viking, 2005), xxi.

67. Quoted in Anderson and Cayton, *Dominion of War*, 329.

68. Quoted in Anderson and Cayton, *Dominion of War*, 330.

69. David J. Sibley, *A War of Frontier and Empire: The Philippine-American War, 1899–1902* (New York: Hill and Wang, 2007).

70. General James Rusling, "Interview with President William McKinley," *Christian Advocate*, January 22, 1903, 17, https://www.digitalhistory.uh.edu/disp_textbook.cfm?smtID=3&psid=1257.

71. Anderson and Cayton, *Dominion of War*, 330.

72. Anderson and Cayton, *Dominion of War*, 344.

73. Quoted in Anderson and Cayton, *Dominion of War*, 345.

74. Jeremy Black, *War since 1945* (London: Reaktion Books, 2005), 80.

75. Black, *War since 1945*, 81.

76. For one of countless examples, see Maggie Fitzgerald, "China Accuses the US of 'Bullying Behavior,'" CNBC, May 17, 2019, https://www.cnbc.com/2019/05/17/china-accuses-the-us-of-bullying-behavior.html.

77. Israel, *Dutch Primacy*, 168.

78. Emily T. Yeh and Elizabeth Wharton, "Going West and Going Out: Discourses, Migrants, and Models in Chinese Development," *Eurasian Geography and Economics* 57, no. 3 (2016): 286–315.

79. Bruno Maçães, *Belt and Road: A Chinese World Order* (London: Hurst, 2018).

80. Thomas P. Narins and John Agnew, "Missing from the Map: Chinese Exceptionalism, Sovereignty Regimes and the Belt Road Initiative," *Geopolitics* 25, no. 4 (2020): 809–37.

81. Amitendu Palit, "India's Economic and Strategic Perceptions of China's Maritime Silk Road Initiative," *Geopolitics* 22, no. 2 (2017): 292–309.

82. Khalid Mehmood Alam, Xuemei Li, and Saranjam Baig, "Impact of Transport Cost and Travel Time on Trade under China-Pakistan Economic Corridor

(CPEC)," *Journal of Advanced Transportation*, February 25, 2019, 1, https://doi.org/10.1155/2019/7178507.

83. Alam et al., "Impact of Transport Cost," 4.
84. Alam et al., "Impact of Transport Cost," 6.
85. Ben Hubbard and Amy Qin, "As the U.S. Pulls Back from the Mideast, China Leans In," *New York Times*, February 2, 2022, https://www.nytimes.com/2022/02/01/world/middleeast/china-middle-east.html.
86. Gedaliah Afterman, head of the Asia Policy Program, Abba Eban Institute of International Diplomacy at Reichman University, Israel, quoted in Hubbard and Qin, "As the U.S. Pulls Back."
87. Hubbard and Qin, "As the U.S. Pulls Back."
88. Howard W. French, *China's Second Continent: How a Million Migrants Are Building a New Empire in Africa* (New York: Vintage Books, 2014), 3–8.
89. President Xi Jinping, "Full Text: Keynote Speech by Chinese President Xi Jinping at Opening Ceremony of 8th FOCAC Ministerial Conference," November 29, 2021, http://focac.org.cn/focacdakar/eng/zxyw_1/202112/t20211202_10461076.htm.
90. Pádraig R. Carmody and James T. Murphy, "Chinese Neoglobalization in East Africa: Logics, Couplings and Impacts," *Space and Polity* 26, no. 1 (2022): 23–25.
91. President Xi Jinping, "Full Text."

Chapter Six

1. Geoffrey Till, *Seapower: A Guide for the Twenty-First Century*, 3rd ed. (London: Routledge, 2013), 17.
2. Colin Flint and Peter J. Taylor, *Political Geography: World-Economy, Nation-State, and Locality*, 7th ed. (London: Routledge, 2018), 58–60.
3. Paul S. Ciccantell and Stephen G. Bunker, "The Economic Ascent of China and the Potential for Restructuring the Capitalist World-Economy," *Journal of World-Systems Research* 10, no. 3 (Fall 2004): 570–71.
4. Jonathan I. Israel, *Dutch Primacy in World Trade, 1585–1740* (Oxford: Clarendon Press, 1989), 115.
5. Israel, *Dutch Primacy*, 79.
6. Israel, *Dutch Primacy*, 187.
7. Israel, *Dutch Primacy*, 188.
8. Israel, *Dutch Primacy*, 71.
9. Israel, *Dutch Primacy*, 119.
10. Israel, *Dutch Primacy*, 386.
11. Israel, *Dutch Primacy*, 392.
12. C. M. Law, "Population in England and Wales, 1801–1911," *Transactions, Institute of British Geographers* 41, no. 1 (June 1967): 134.
13. Law, "Population in England," 130.
14. Law, "Population in England," 135.
15. John Darwin, *The Empire Project: The Rise and Fall of the British World-System 1830–1970* (Cambridge: Cambridge University Press, 2009), 36.

16. Darwin, *Empire Project*, 37.
17. Darwin, *Empire Project*, 37.
18. Darwin, *Empire Project*, 37.
19. Darwin, *Empire Project*, 59.
20. Darwin, *Empire Project*, 59.
21. Quoted in Lawrence James, *The Rise and Fall of the British Empire* (New York: St. Martin's Griffin, 1994), 183.
22. Edward Said, *Orientalism* (New York: Vintage Books, 1979).
23. David Harvey, *The Limits to Capital* (Oxford: Basil Blackwell, 1982), 431–38.
24. Flint and Taylor, *Political Geography*, 23–25.
25. Flint and Taylor, *Political Geography*, 276–79.
26. Louis H. Orzack, "The Düsseldorf Agreement: A Study of the Organization of Power and Planning," *Political Science Quarterly* 65, no. 3 (September 1950): 393.
27. Stephen G. Walker, "Solving the Appeasement Puzzle: Contending Historical Interpretations of British Diplomacy during the 1930s," *British Journal of International Studies* 6, no. 3 (October 1980): 220.
28. Keith Middlemas, *The Strategy of Appeasement: The British Government and Germany, 1937–39* (Chicago: Quadrangle Books, 1972), 18–20.
29. Sir Basil Henry Liddell Hart, *The British Way in Warfare* (London: Faber and Faber, 1932). For a discussion of Hart's idea, see Brian Holden Reid, "The British Way in Warfare," *RUSI Journal* 156, no. 6 (December 2011): 70–76.
30. David Edgerton, *Britain's War Machine: Weapons, Resources, and Experts in the Second World War* (Oxford: Oxford University Press, 2011), 6–10.
31. Middlemas, *Strategy of Appeasement*, 17, and his reference to F. S. Northedge, *The Troubled Giant: Britain among the Great Powers, 1916–1939* (London: Praeger, 1966), 619.
32. Hideaki Miyajima, "Japanese Industrial Policy during the Interwar Period: Strategies for International and Domestic Competition," *Business and Economic History* 21 (1992): 270–79.
33. Carl Mosk, "Japanese Industrialization and Economic Growth," *EH.net*, accessed September 24, 2022, https://eh.net/encyclopedia/japanese-industrialization-and-economic-growth/.
34. Jeffrey C. Guarneri, "Cartographies of Global Connectivity in Interwar Japan," *Global Urban History* (blog), November 14, 2019, https://globalurbanhistory.com/2019/11/14/cartographies-of-global-connectivity-in-interwar-japan/.
35. Ciccantell and Bunker, "Economic Ascent of China," 575.
36. John W. Dower, *Embracing Defeat: Japan in the Wake of World War II* (New York: W. W. Norton, 2000), 20–22.
37. Dower, *Embracing Defeat*, 29–30.
38. Jean-Paul Rodrigue, Theo Notteboom, and Athanasios Pallis, *Port Economics, Management and Policy* (New York: Routledge, 2021), 477–82.
39. For a discussion of national psychological and related policy shifts in a time of hegemonic decline, see Robert Denemark, "Pre-emptive Decline," *Journal of World-Systems Research* 27, no. 1 (2021), 149–76.

40. Flint and Taylor, *Political Geography*, 22–25.

41. Kai-Fu Lee, *AI Superpowers: China, Silicon Valley and the New World Order* (Boston: Houghton Mifflin Harcourt, 2018), 4–6, 14–17.

42. Lee, *AI Superpowers*, 17–19. For a discussion of the general pattern of state support for economic development, see Erik S. Reinert, *How Rich Countries Got Rich and Why Poor Countries Stay Poor* (New York: Public Affairs, 2008). For the link to national security, see Mark Duffield, *Global Governance and the New Wars: The Merger of Development and Security* (London: Zed Books, 2001).

43. Jason Miller, "DoD Rips Wrapping Paper Off of New Joint AI Center," February 13, 2019, Federal News Network, https://federalnewsnetwork.com/artificial-intelligence/2019/02/dod-rips-wrapping-paper-off-of-new-joint-ai-center/.

44. Paul Scharre and Michael C. Horowitz, "Congress Can Help the United States Lead in Artificial Intelligence," *Foreign Policy*, December 10, 2018.

45. Congressional Research Service, "The Made in China 2025 Initiative: Economic Implications for the United States," In Focus report, April 12, 2019, https://crsreports.congress.gov/product/pdf/IF/IF10964/4.

46. Congressional Research Service, "Made in China 2025 Initiative."

47. Farhad Manjoo, "Biden Just Clobbered China's Chip Industry," *New York Times*, October 20, 2022, https://www.nytimes.com/2022/10/20/opinion/biden-china-semiconductor-chip.html.

48. Catie Edmondson and Ana Swanson, "House Passes Bill Adding Billions to Research to Compete with China," *New York Times*, February 4, 2022, https://www.nytimes.com/2022/02/04/us/politics/house-china-competitive-bill.html.

49. Blake D. Moore and Khosrow B. Semnani, "Opinion: Confronting Made in China is Crucial to America's Leadership," April 1, 2021, https://blakemoore.house.gov/media/in-the-news/opinion-confronting-made-china-crucial-americas-leadership.

50. Till, *Seapower*, 17.

51. R. O. Goss, "Economic Policies and Seaports: The Economic Functions of Seaports," *Maritime Policy and Management* 17, no. 3 (1990): 207–8.

52. Till, *Seapower*, 17.

53. Robert E. Harkavy, *Strategic Basing and the Great Powers, 1200–2000* (New York: Routledge, 2007); Weiqiang Lin, "Transport Geography and Geopolitics: Visions, Rules and Militarism in China's Belt and Road Initiative and Beyond," *Journal of Transport Geography* 81 (2019): 5.

54. Sir Julian Corbett, *Some Principles of Maritime Strategy*, 2nd ed. (London: Longmans, Green, 1911), reprinted with an introduction by Eric Grove (Annapolis, MD: Naval Institute Press, 1988), 67, cited in Till, *Seapower*, 25.

55. Darwin, *Empire Project*, 126.

56. Darwin, *Empire Project*, 126.

57. Darwin, *Empire Project*, 128.

58. Vincent Ni, "China Funnels Its Overseas Aid Money into Political Leaders' Home Provinces," *The Guardian*, May 29, 2002, https://www.theguardian.com/world/2022/may/29/china-funnels-overseas-aid-money-political-leaders-home-provinces.

59. Darwin, *Empire Project*, 128.

60. Sasha Davis, *The Empire's Edge: Militarization, Resistance, and Transcending Hegemony in the Pacific* (Athens: University of Georgia Press, 2015), 5–8.

61. Jim Glassman and Young-Jin Choi, "The Chaebol and the US-Military Industrial Complex: Cold War Geopolitical Economy and South Korean Industrialization," *Environment and Planning A: Society and Space* 46, no. 5 (2014): 1160–80.

62. Michael Beckley, Yusaku Horiuchi, and Jennifer M. Miller, "America's Role in the Making of Japan's Economic Miracle," *Journal of East Asian Studies* 18, no. 1 (2018): 1–21.

63. Olaf Merk, "Geopolitics and Commercial Seaports," *Revue Internationale et Stratégique* 107, no. 3 (2017): 73–83; John Xie, "China's Global Network of Shipping Ports Reveal Beijing's Strategy," *VOA News*, September 13, 2021, https://www.voanews.com/a/6224958.html.

64. Hassan Noorali, Colin Flint, and Seyyed Abbas Ahmadi, "Port Power: Towards a New Geopolitical World Order," *Journal of Transport Geography* 105 (2022), https://doi.org/10.1016/j.jtrangeo.2022.103483.

65. Merk, "Geopolitics and Commercial Seaports," 73; Degang Sun and Yahia Zoubir, "'Development First': China's Investment in Seaport Constructions and Operations along the Maritime Silk Road," *Asian Journal of Middle Eastern and Islamic Studies* 11, no. 3 (2017): 41.

66. Eleanor Albert, "China's Global Port Play," *The Diplomat*, May 11, 2019, https://thediplomat.com/2019/05/chinas-global-port-play; Jiatao Li, Ari van Assche, Lee Li, and Gongming, "Foreign Direct Investment along the Belt and Road: A Political Economy Perspective," *Journal of International Business Studies* 53 (2022): 902–19; Jean-Marc Blanchard, "China's MSRI in Africa and the Middle East: Political Economic Realities Continue to Shape Results and Ramifications," in *China's Maritime Silk Road Initiative, Africa, and the Middle East: Feats, Freezes, and Failures*, ed. Jean-Marc Blanchard (Singapore: Palgrave Macmillan, 2021), 1–4; Mohid Iftikhar and Jing Vivian Zhan, "The Geopolitics of China's Overseas Port Investments: A Comparative Analysis of Greece and Pakistan," *Geopolitics* 27, no. 3 (2022): 826–51.

67. Xie, "China's Global Network."

68. John Gallagher, "Experts Warn of China's Influence at U.S. Ports," *Freight Waves*, October 22, 2019, 1–2, https://www.freightwaves.com/news/experts-warn-of-chinas-influence-at-us-ports.

69. Merk, "Geopolitics and Commercial Seaports"; Xie, "China's Global Network."

70. Rodrigue, Notteboom, and Pallis, *Port Economics*, 130–32.

71. Jihong Chen, Yijie Feia, Paul Tae-Woo Lee, and Xuezong Tao, "Overseas Port Investment Policy for China's Central and Local Governments in the Belt and Road Initiative," *Journal of Contemporary China* 28, no. 116 (2019): 196–215; David Mitchell, "Making or Breaking Regions: China's Belt and Road Initiative and the Meaning for Regional Dynamics," *Geopolitics* 26, no. 5 (2021): 1400; Tim Winter, "Geocultural Power: China's Belt and Road Initiative," *Geopolitics* 26, no. 5 (2021): 1376.

72. Edward Wong, "Solomon Islands Suspends Visits by Foreign Miliary Ships, Raising Concerns in U.S.," *New York Times*, August 30, 2022, https://www.nytimes.com/2022/08/30/us/politics/solomon-islands-us-military-china.html.

73. Daniel Hurst, "US Military Leader Warns Chinese Security Deal with Solomon Islands Sounds 'Too Good to Be True,'" *The Guardian*, April 13, 2022, https://www.theguardian.com/world/2022/apr/13/us-military-leader-warns-chinese-security-deal-with-solomon-islands-sounds-too-good-to-be-true.

74. Julian Borger, "Work on 'Chinese Military Base' in UAE Abandoned after US Intervenes—Report," *The Guardian*, November 19, 2021, https://www.theguardian.com/world/2021/nov/19/chinese-military-base-uae-construction-abandoned-us-intelligence-report.

75. Till, *Seapower*, 17.

76. Zheng Bijian, "China's 'Peaceful Rise' to Great-Power Status," *Foreign Affairs* 84, no. 5 (September/October 2005): 18–24.

Chapter Seven

1. Peter J. Taylor, *Modernities: A Geohistorical Interpretation* (Cambridge: Polity Press, 1998), 30–34.

2. Disseminating a dominant culture has been a prominent component of becoming a world power. This process is covered in a historically comparative way by Peter J. Taylor in *Modernities* as well as his *The Way the Modern World Works: World Hegemony to World Impasse* (Chichester: John Wiley and Sons, 1996). This book does not comprehensively cover culture, though the various discussions of what were deemed "Enlightenment," "civilizing missions," and "development" across Dutch, British, and US power are grand worldviews that are supported by elite and popular cultural representations. China is currently hoping to foster a similar worldview with its messages of renewing the Silk Road. See Tim Winter, *Geocultural Power: China's Quest to Revive the Silk Roads for the Twenty-First Century* (Chicago: University of Chicago Press, 2019).

3. Robert Denemark, "Pre-emptive Decline," *Journal of World-Systems Research* 27, no. 1 (2021): 149–76.

4. Richard Peet, *Unholy Trinity: The IMF, World Bank and WTO*, 2nd ed. (London: Zed Books, 2009), 16–18.

5. Zhang Xiaotong and Colin Flint, "Why and Whither the US-China Trade War? Not Realist 'Traps' but Political Geography 'Capture' as Explanation," *Journal of World Trade* 55, no. 2 (2021): 358.

6. Colin Flint and Ghazi-Walid Falah, "How the United States Justified Its War on Terrorism: Prime Morality and the Construction of a 'Just War,'" *Third World Quarterly* 25, no. 8 (2004): 1388.

7. Colin Flint and Madeleine Waddoups, "South-South Cooperation or Core-Periphery Contention? Ghanaian and Zambian Perceptions of Economic Relations with China," *Geopolitics* 26, no. 3 (2021): 892; Marcus Power and Giles Mohan, "Towards a Critical Geopolitics of China's Engagement with African Development,' *Geopolitics* 15, no. 3 (2010): 476–77.

8. Taylor, *Modernities*, 39–40.

9. Peet, *Unholy Trinity*, 4–14.
10. Giovanni Arrighi, *Adam Smith in Beijing: Lineages of the Twenty-First Century* (London: Verso, 2007).
11. Jonathan I. Israel, *The Radical Enlightenment: Philosophy and the Making of Modernity, 1650–1750* (Oxford: Oxford University Press, 2001).
12. Israel, *Radical Enlightenment*, 24.
13. Israel, *Radical Enlightenment*, 25.
14. Israel, *Radical Enlightenment*, 145.
15. Israel, *Radical Enlightenment*, 350–51.
16. Israel, *Radical Enlightenment*, 421–22.
17. Jonathan I. Israel, *The Dutch Republic: Its Rise, Greatness, and Fall, 1477–1806* (Oxford: Oxford University Press, 1995), 677.
18. Israel, *Dutch Republic*, 677–99.
19. Jonathan I. Israel, *Dutch Primacy in World Trade, 1585–1740* (Oxford: Clarendon Press, 1989), 104.
20. Eric Wilson, "Making the World Safe for Holland: 'De Indis' of Hugo Grotius and International Law as Geoculture," *Review* 32, no. 3 (2009): 253.
21. Israel, *Dutch Primacy*, 104.
22. Israel, *Dutch Republic*, 951–56.
23. E. M. Forster, *Howards End* (New York: G. P. Putnam's Sons, 1911), 233.
24. C. M. Law, "Population in England and Wales, 1801–1911," *Transactions, Institute of British Geographers* 41, no. 1 (June 1967): 134.
25. Friedrich Engels, *The Condition of the Working Class in England in 1844, with Preface Written in 1892* (1892; repr., London: G. Allen and Unwin, 1926).
26. Jeremy Black, *Naval Power* (London: Red Globe Press, 2009), 142.
27. Martin J. Wiener, *English Culture and the Decline of the Industrial Spirit, 1850–1980*, 2nd ed. (Cambridge: Cambridge University Press, 2004).
28. Tom Nairn, *The Enchanted Glass: Britain and Its Monarchy* (London: Radius, 1989).
29. Peter J. Taylor, "The Error of Developmentalism," in *Horizons in Human Geography*, ed. Derek Gregory and Rex Walford (London: Palgrave Macmillan, 1989), 303–19.
30. Mike Davis, *Late Victorian Holocausts: El Niño Famines and the Making of the Third World* (London: Verso Press, 2001), 6–9.
31. George Orwell, "Shooting an Elephant," in *George Orwell* (1936; repr., London: Secker and Warburg/Octopus, 1980), 418.
32. This phrase is attributed to British politician and reformer John Bright from a speech in 1865. See UK Parliament, "A Beacon of Democracy," accessed September 26, 2022, https://www.parliament.uk/about/living-heritage/building/palace/big-ben/much-more-than-a-clock/a-beacon-of-democracy/.
33. David Brown, *Palmerston: A Biography* (New Haven, CT: Yale University Press, 2010), 237–38.
34. W. W. Rostow, *The Stages of Economic Growth: A Non-Communist Manifesto* (London: Cambridge University Press, 1960), 4–16.
35. Rostow, *Stages of Economic Growth*, 4–16.

36. Taylor, "Error of Developmentalism"; Erik S. Reinert, *How Rich Countries Got Rich and Why Poor Countries Stay Poor* (New York: Public Affairs, 2008).

37. Taylor, "Error of Developmentalism."

38. Catherine Weaver, *Hypocrisy Trap: The World Bank and the Poverty of Reform* (Princeton, NJ: Princeton University Press, 2008), 76, 83.

39. Rostow, *Stages of Economic Growth*, 106–22.

40. Fred Inglis, *The Cruel Peace: Everyday Life and the Cold War* (New York: Basic Books, 1991), 194–96. Christopher Andrew, *Defend the Realm: The Authorized History of MI5* (New York: Alfred A. Knopf, 2009), 170.

41. Richard Toye, *Churchill's Empire: The World That Made Him and the World He Made* (New York: Henry Holt, 2010), 244–45.

42. Fred Halliday, *The Making of the Second Cold War* (London: Verso, 1983), 44–45.

43. Peet, *Unholy Trinity*, 16–17.

44. Arghiri Emmanuel, *Unequal Exchange: A Study of the Imperialism of Trade* (New York: Monthly Review Press, 1972).

45. Max Boot, *The Savage Wars of Peace: Small Wars and the Rise of American Power* (New York: Basic Books, 2002), 348–52.

46. David Talbot, *The Devil's Chessboard: Allen Dulles, the CIA, and the Rise of America's Secret Government* (New York: HarperCollins, 2015), 241.

47. Halliday, *Making of the Second Cold War*, 44–45.

48. Rostow, *Stages of Economic Growth*.

49. Talbot, *Devil's Chessboard*, 251.

50. Talbot, *Devil's Chessboard*, 68.

51. Talbot, *Devil's Chessboard*, 257.

52. Talbot, *Devil's Chessboard*, 257.

53. Talbot, *Devil's Chessboard*, 251–54.

54. Talbot, *Devil's Chessboard*, 259.

55. Halliday, *Making of the Second Cold War*, 3–7.

56. John W. Dower, *Embracing Defeat: Japan in the Wake of World War II* (New York: W. W. Norton, 2000), 364–70.

57. Takashi Yamazaki, "The US Militarization of a 'Host' Civilian Society: The Case of Postwar Okinawa, Japan," in *Reconstructing Conflict: Integrating War and Post-war Geographies*, ed. Scott Kirsch and Colin Flint (Farnham: Ashgate, 2011), 253–55.

58. Nick Cullather, "Bomb Them Back to the Stone Age: An Etymology," History News Network, accessed September 26, 2022, https://historynewsnetwork.org/article/30347.

59. Jeremy Black, *War since 1945* (London: Reaktion Books, 2005), 57; Gabriel Kolko, *Another Century of War?* (New York: New Press, 2002), 19–22; Halliday, *Making of the Second Cold War*, 3–7.

60. Boot, *Savage Wars of Peace*, 336–41.

61. Talbot, *Devil's Chessboard*, 570.

62. Flint and Waddoups, "South-South Cooperation," 892; Marcus Power and Giles Mohan, "Towards a Critical Geopolitics of China's Engagement with African

Development," *Geopolitics* 15, no. 3 (2010): 476–77; James Sidaway and Chi Yuan Woon, "Chinese Narratives on 'One Belt, One Road' (一带一路) in Geographical and Imperial Contexts," *Professional Geographer* 69, no. 4 (2017): 591–603; Fiona McConnell and Chih Yuan Woon, "Mapping Chinese Diplomacy: Relational Contradictions and Spatial Tensions," *Geopolitics* 28, no. 2 (2021): 593–618.

63. Tim Winter, *Geocultural Power: China's Quest to Revive the Silk Roads for the Twenty-First Century* (Chicago: University of Chicago Press, 2019), 17–18.

64. McConnell and Woon, "Mapping Chinese Diplomacy," 14.

65. McConnell and Woon, "Mapping Chinese Diplomacy," 14.

66. Jianwei Wang, Xi Jingping's 'Major Country Diplomacy': A Paradigm Shift," *Journal of Contemporary China* 28, no. 115 (2019): 28, quoted in McConnell and Wang, "Mapping Chinese Diplomacy," 14.

67. Benjamin Barton, *The Doraleh Disputes: Infrastructure Politics in the Global South* (Singapore: Springer Nature, 2023), 1–2.

68. McConnell and Woon, "Mapping Chinese Diplomacy," 15.

69. McConnell and Woon, "Mapping Chinese Diplomacy," 16.

Chapter Eight

1. Robert D. Kaplan, *Asia's Cauldron: The South China Sea and the End of Stable Pacific* (New York: Random House, 2014); James C. Hsiung, *The South China Sea Disputes and the U.S.-China Contest: International Law and Geopolitics* (Singapore: World Scientific Publishing, 2018).

2. Colin Flint, "Seapower, Geostrategic Relations, and Islandness: The World War II Destroyers for Bases Deal," *Island Studies Journal* 16, no. 1 (2021): 275–76. Unsurprisingly, Mahan was very much alive to the strategic value of islands. He wrote: "The sea, until it approaches the land, realizes the ideal of a vast plain unbroken by obstacles. On the sea, says an eminent French tactician, there is no field of battle, meaning that there is none of the natural conditions which determine, and often fetter, the movements of the general. But upon a plain, however flat and monotonous, causes, possibly slight, determine the concentration of population into towns and villages, and the necessary communications between the centres create roads. Where the latter converge, or cross, tenure confers command, depending for importance upon the number of routes thus meeting, and upon their individual value. It is just so at sea. While in itself the ocean opposes no obstacle to a vessel taking any one of the numerous routes that can be traced upon the surface of the globe between two points, conditions of distance or convenience, of traffic or of wind, do prescribe certain usual courses. Where these pass near an ocean position, still more where they use it, it has an influence over them, and where several routes cross near by that influence becomes very great,—is commanding." This quote is from Mahan's 1893 essay "Hawaii and Our Future Sea Power," first published in *Forum* in March 1893 and republished in Captain A. T. Mahan, *The Interest of America in Sea Power, Present and Future* (London: Sampson Low, Marston, 1897), and available at https://www.gutenberg.org/files/15749/15749-h/15749-h.htm#II. The Gutenberg version provides no page numbers.

3. Flint, "Seapower, Geostrategic Relations," 276.

4. Christian Wirth, "Solidifying Sovereign Power in Liquid Space: The Making and Breaking of 'Island Chains' and 'Walls' at Sea," *Political Geography* 103 (2023), https://doi.org/10.1016/j.polgeo.2023.102889.

5. Flint, "Seapower, Geostrategic Relations," 277–82.

6. Jonathan I. Israel, *Dutch Primacy in World Trade, 1585–1740* (Oxford: Clarendon Press, 1989), 94.

7. Israel, *Dutch Primacy*, 95.

8. Israel, *Dutch Primacy*, 140–49.

9. Israel, *Dutch Primacy*, 219.

10. Israel, *Dutch Primacy*, 221.

11. Israel, *Dutch Primacy*, 73.

12. Israel, *Dutch Primacy*, 185.

13. Israel, *Dutch Primacy*, 184–85.

14. Jan Rüger, *Heligoland: Britain, Germany, and the Struggle for the North Sea* (Oxford: Oxford University Press, 2016), 7–8.

15. Rüger, *Heligoland*, 9.

16. Jan Rüger, "Sovereignty and Empire in the North Sea, 1807–1918," *American Historical Review* 119, no. 2 (April 2014): 318.

17. Rüger, "Sovereignty and Empire," 317.

18. Rüger, "Sovereignty and Empire," 318.

19. Rüger, "Sovereignty and Empire," 318.

20. Rüger, "Sovereignty and Empire," 318.

21. Gould Francis Leckie, *Historical Survey of the Foreign Affairs of Great Britain* (London: J. Bell, 1808), quoted in Rüger, *Heligoland*, 9.

22. Diletta D'Andrea, "Great Britain and the Mediterranean Islands in the Napoleonic Wars: The 'Insular Strategy' of Gould Francis Leckie," *Journal of Mediterranean Studies* 16, nos. 1–2 (2006): 79.

23. D. R. Gillard, "Salisbury's African Policy and the Heligoland Offer of 1890," *English Historical Review* 75, no. 297 (October 1960): 631.

24. Gillard, "Salisbury's African Policy," 651–52.

25. Earl Thomas Brassey, *Consideration on the Causes and the Conduct of the Present War* (London: Spottiswoode, 1915), 16, cited in Rüger, *Heligoland*, 84.

26. Rüger, "Sovereignty and Empire," 326–27.

27. Rüger, "Sovereignty and Empire," 327.

28. Quoted in Rüger, *Heligoland*, 113.

29. Rüger, *Heligoland*, 134.

30. Rüger, *Heligoland*, 190.

31. Rüger, *Heligoland*, 195–96.

32. Rüger, *Heligoland*, 199.

33. Rüger, *Heligoland*, 200–202.

34. One means of power projection was a series of US Supreme Court cases between 1901 and 1922, known as the Insular Cases, that limited constitutional rights of the citizens of American Samoa, the Republic of the Marshall Islands, the Federated States of Micronesia, the Commonwealth of the Mariana Islands, the Republic of Palau, Puerto Rico, Guam, and the Virgin Islands. The justifica-

tion was explicitly racial and was akin to a colonial projection of power. In 2022 the US Supreme Court declined to consider a challenge to these laws. See Jess Zalph and Nina Totenberg, "Supreme Court Declines to Consider Challenge to Racist Citizenship Laws," National Public Radio, October 17, 2022, https://www.npr.org/2022/10/17/1128918500/supreme-court-insular-cases.

35. International Institute for Strategic Studies (IISS), "The GIUK Gap's Strategic Significance," Strategic Comments, vol. 25, comment no. 29, October 2019, https://www.iiss.org/publications/strategic-comments/2019/the-giuk-gaps-strategic-significance.

36. Quoted in IISS, "GIUK Gap's Strategic Significance."

37. IISS, "GIUK Gap's Strategic Significance."

38. Craig L. Symonds, *World War II at Sea: A Global History* (Oxford: Oxford University Press, 2018), 270–74.

39. Evan Andrews, "5 Attacks on U.S. Soil during World War II," History.com, August 30, 2018, https://www.history.com/news/5-attacks-on-u-s-soil-during-world-war-ii.

40. Symonds, *World War II at Sea*, 272.

41. Ian W. Toll, *Pacific Crucible: War at Sea in the Pacific, 1941–1942* (New York: W. W. Norton, 2012), 476.

42. Toll, *Pacific Crucible*, 476.

43. James D. Hornfischer, *The Fleet at Flood Tide: America at Total War in the Pacific, 1944–1945* (New York: Bantam Books, 2016), 397–402.

44. Sasha Davis, *The Empire's Edge: Militarization, Resistance, and Transcending Hegemony in the Pacific* (Athens: University of Georgia Press, 2015), 1–3.

45. John W. Dower, *Embracing Defeat: Japan in the Wake of World War II* (New York: W. W. Norton, 2000), 22–28.

46. Takashi Yamazaki, "The US Militarization of a 'Host' Civilian Society: The Case of Postwar Okinawa, Japan," in *Reconstructing Conflict: Integrating War and Post-war Geographies*, ed. Scott Kirsch and Colin Flint (Farnham: Ashgate, 2011), 257.

47. Yamazaki, "US Militarization," 266.

48. Robert Dallek, *Franklin D. Roosevelt and American Foreign Policy, 1932–1945* (New York: Oxford University Press, 1979), 147–52.

49. James I. Matray, "Dean Acheson's Press Club Speech Reexamined," *Journal of Conflict Studies* 22, no. 1 (Spring 2002): 28.

50. Michael A. McDevitt, *China as a Twenty First Century Naval Power: Theory, Practice, and Implications* (Annapolis, MD: Naval Institute Press, 2020), 73–74.

51. Dean Acheson, "Excerpts from Dean Acheson's Speech to the National Press Club, January 12, 1950," https://web.viu.ca/davies/H102/Acheson.speech1950.htm.

52. Matray, "Dean Acheson's Press Club Speech," 28.

53. Gillard, "Salisbury's African Policy," 631. "Zanzibar to Benefit from 7 China-Sponsored Projects," China.org.cn, April 13, 2013, http://www.china.org.cn/world/2013-04/13/content_28533136.htm; "Masato Masato, "Tanzania: Zan-

zibar, China Sign 14bn/-Agreement," AllAfrica.com, March 18, 2021, https://allafrica.com/stories/202103180736.html.

54. Wilson VornDick, "China's Reach Has Grown: So Should the Island Chains," Asia Maritime Transparency Initiative, Center for Strategic and International Studies, October 22, 2018, https://amti.csis.org/chinas-reach-grown-island-chains/.

55. Matray, "Dean Acheson's Press Club Speech," 28.

56. Toshi Yoshihara, "China's Vision of Its Seascape: The First Island Chain and Chinese Seapower," *Asian Politics and Policy* 4, no. 3 (July 2012): 293–94.

57. VornDick, "China's Reach Has Grown."

58. *The Economist*, "China Wants to Increase Its Military Presence Abroad," May 5, 2022, https://www.economist.com/china/2022/05/05/china-wants-to-increase-its-military-presence-abroad.

59. Rory Medcalf, *Indo-Pacific Empire: China, America and the Contest for the World's Pivotal Region* (Manchester: Manchester University Press, 2020), 3–5; Dennis Rumley, *The Geopolitics of Australia's Regional Relations* (Dordrecht: Kluwer Academic Publishers, 1999), 265–66.

60. Michael McDevitt, "Becoming a Great 'Maritime Power': A Chinese Dream," Center for International Maritime Security, July 19, 2016, https://cimsec.org/becoming-great-maritime-power-chinese-dream/; Julian Borger, "US, UK and Australia Forge Military Alliance to Counter China," *The Guardian*, September 16, 2021, https://www.theguardian.com/australia-news/2021/sep/15/australia-nuclear-powered-submarines-us-uk-security-partnership-aukus.

61. Joshua Espena and Chelsea Bomping, "The Taiwan Frontier and the Chinese Dominance for the Second Island Chain," Australian Institute of International Affairs, *Australian Outlook*, August 13, 2020, https://www.internationalaffairs.org.au/australianoutlook/taiwan-frontier-chinese-dominance-for-second-island-chain/; Vikas Pandey, "Quad: The China Factor at the Heart of the Summit," BBC News, May 24, 2022, https://www.bbc.com/news/world-asia-india-61547082.

62. Council on Foreign Relations, "China's Maritime Disputes, 1895–2020," accessed September 28, 2022, https://www.cfr.org/timeline/chinas-maritime-disputes; McDevitt, *China*, 125–43.

63. See the Asia Maritime Transparency Initiative, Center for Strategic and International Studies, China Island Tracker, accessed September 28, 2022, https://amti.csis.org/island-tracker/china/.

Conclusion

1. Quoted in Edward Wong and Steven Erlanger, "NATO Nations Grow More Receptive to U.S. Pleas to Confront China," *New York Times*, November 30, 2022, https://www.nytimes.com/2022/11/30/world/europe/nato-china-biden.html.

2. "How to Avoid a Third World War," *The Economist*, March 11, 2023, 7.

3. "How to Avoid a Third World War," 7.

4. "How to Avoid a Third World War," 7.

5. "Briefing: Defending Taiwan: Storm Warning," *The Economist*, March 11, 2023, 16.

6. "The World According to Xi," *The Economist*, March 25, 2023, 7.

7. "World According to Xi," 7.

8. Just as all politics is local, so are the everyday experiences of global warfare. Living in the US, I am very aware which side my bread is buttered on. I know that the economic and military pattern is one that I benefit from. But that does not mean I should see the world through a national lens. It is hard to resist the power of nationalism and militarism even when one is aware of their insidious nature: I still find warships "cool"! But deeper reflection can move one away from nationalism. Understanding geopolitics is best done through the recognition that for every action there is an opposite reaction. Simply labeling actions and reactions as good or bad on the basis of us/them allegiances makes us part of the problem and not the solution.

The book is critical. But critical of what? Not the individuals making key decisions. Not even the countries: it's not an anti-US or anti-British treatise. It's not a pro-China treatise either, though I suspect the "us versus them" assumptions of geopolitics will mean that asking readers to consider the history of China's near waters will provoke accusations of naïveté and bias. The book is a reflection on the nature of something bigger, a global system of profit seeking (capitalism, in other words). If the Dutch in the 1600s, the British in the 1700s and 1800s, the US in the 1900s, and the Chinese in the 2000s have all been doing pretty much the same thing, then this suggests the cause is not to be found within national agendas. Nor are seapower conflicts defined by historical epochs of "discovery," "empire," "development," or "South-South cooperation." The behavior of power projection in near and far waters is behavior driven by the imperatives of national competition within a global economy. The book's criticism is directed toward the social system that provides the context for the decisions of countries and businesses. Though we can, and should, be critical of the choices being made (are they overly aggressive or too exploitive, say), the choices can be understood only within the broader context.

What about whataboutism? I suspect that I will be accused of naïveté in my criticism of the US, and of a likely perceived sympathy for China. That would miss the point of the book, which is to argue that today's geopolitical tensions are a moment in a constant and historic process of economic dynamics that result in competition over the control of near and far waters. I am no supporter of Chinese island-building, dubious territorial claims, or military buildup. But neither am I a fan of the US militarization of the seas, and many continents, that began well over a century ago. The book is not an exercise in "whataboutism" to excuse China's actions. Rather, it is an awareness of a constant global dynamic. It is not an exercise in vilifying the military actions of one country to justify the military actions of another country. Instead, it is an attempt to recognize that the way the world works has, in the past, produced periods of near-waters/far-waters contests. Today seems beyond the beginning of another such period. By understanding the similarity to past moments I hope we can learn how to stop escalation into another global war.

9. I have taken an approach of historical comparison organized by identify-

ing the long-standing geopolitical imperatives of primary-subsidiary relations and the dynamics of competition between primary countries. The historical approach eschews much of contemporary scholarship by historians, with a focus on nuance and contingency. Rather, my approach sits within the Annales school of history in which long-term changes and continuities are the underlying structure in which actions, such as the conquering of a fort or the formation of an alliance, may be interpreted. See Fernand Braudel, *The Perspective on the World* (London: Collins, 1984). For a discussion of integrating large and small geographical-historical scopes in geopolitics, see Colin Flint, *Geopolitical Constructs: The Mulberry Harbours, World War Two, and the Making of a Militarized Transatlantic* (Lanham, MD: Rowman and Littlefield, 2016), 30–33.

Two major criticisms can be leveled at my approach. One is the use of hindsight. But as statements are often qualified with the phrase "the benefits of hindsight," why not exploit those benefits? Learning from history is not cheating, it's wise. I have identified regularities in geopolitical relations. Though each period of history is unique in its specifics, certain imperatives, and the tensions of competition that they create, keep cycling through history. To ignore those regularities seems like embarking on a pathway of willful ignorance. I prefer learning from hindsight to try to avoid the disaster of another round of global war.

The other criticism is that using a historical approach that emphasizes global relations and the persistence of geopolitical patterns diminishes or ignores the ability of countries to make decisions. Such criticism is put forward by those who see the importance of policymakers' decisions rather than the weight of contexts. For example, would the world be different if, say, the British had built a base at Singapore large enough to host the size of fleet necessary to patrol the Pacific? Or what if the vagaries of war had meant that the Battle of Midway had been a tie or even a Japanese victory? The historical contextual approach of this book suggests that the course of the war might have altered, but that the reasons for war and the eventual outcome would not have altered significantly.

Such are the different ways of looking at the world that intrigue academics and lead to lively debates. For example, see the discussion in James Sidaway, Michiel Van Meeteren, and Colin Flint, "Through Troubled Times: Reflections on Ron Johnston's *Geography and Geographers: Anglo-American Human Geography since 1945* (1979) and Peter Taylor's *Political Geography: World-Economy, Nation-State, and Locality* (1985)," *Geojournal*, May 7, 2020, https://doi.org/10.1007/s10708-020-10199-z.

As with nearly all theoretical frameworks in social science, there are advantages and disadvantages to any approach. The proof of the pudding is in the eating, or the set of lessons that a particular framework helps us to consider when thinking about contemporary geopolitics.

10. Geoffrey Till, *Seapower: A Guide for the Twenty-First Century*, 3rd ed. (London: Routledge, 2013), 17.

11. Michael McDevitt, "Becoming a Great 'Maritime Power': A Chinese Dream," Center for International Maritime Security, July 19, 2016, https://cimsec.org/becoming-great-maritime-power-chinese-dream/.

12. W. W. Rostow, *The Stages of Economic Growth: A Non-Communist Manifesto* (London: Cambridge University Press, 1960), 4–16.

13. For example, Geoffrey F. Gresh, *To Rule Eurasia's Waves: The New Great Power Competition at Sea* (New Haven, CT: Yale University Press, 2020), 206, who echoes Mahan's claims that there is a right and wrong way to conduct maritime commerce. Gresh claims China is doing it the wrong way through "more aggressive EEZ protection and defense of territorial waters." In other words, China should let the US remain powerful in Chinese near waters that are US far waters. Can we imagine a US policy statement arguing for a limited aggressiveness that is suitable for defending its near waters?

14. Isaiah Bowman, *The New World: Problems in Political Geography*, 4th ed. (World Book: New York, 1928), iii.

15. Peter J. Taylor, "Understanding Global Inequalities: A World-Systems Approach," *Geography* 77, no. 1 (1992): 10–21; Immanuel Wallerstein, *The Capitalist World-Economy* (Cambridge: Cambridge University Press, 1979), 66–94; Christopher Chase-Dunn, *Global Formation: Structures of the World-Economy* (Oxford: Blackwell, 1989), 23.

16. Immanuel Wallerstein, *World-Systems Analysis: An Introduction* (Durham, NC: Duke University Press, 2004), 7–8.

17. Colin Flint, "Putting the 'Geo' into Geopolitics: A Heuristic Framework and the Example of Australian Foreign Policy," *Geojournal* 87, no. 4 (December 2022): 2577–92.

18. "Briefing: China and Its Neighbours," *The Economist*, July 8, 2023.

19. John Vasquez, *The War Puzzle Revisited* (Cambridge: Cambridge University Press, 2009), 344.

20. "Special Report: China in Africa," *The Economist*, May 18, 2022.

21. Charles Hauss, *From Conflict Resolution to Peacebuilding* (Lanham, MD: Rowman and Littlefield, 2020), 10–11.

22. Colin Flint, *Introduction to Geopolitics*, 4th ed. (London: Routledge, 2022), 4–5.

23. Jason Dittmer and Daniel Bos, *Popular Culture, Geopolitics and Identity*, 2nd ed. (Lanham, MD: Rowman and Littlefield, 2019), 1–2.

24. Chad Ford, *Dangerous Love: Transforming Fear and Conflict at Home, at Work, and in the World* (Oakland, CA: Berrett-Koehler, 2020), 17–22.

INDEX

Abu Dhabi, 103
Acheson, Dean, 80, 152, 154, 155
Afghanistan, 48, 101
Africa, 52, 104, 109, 120, 135, 145; and China, 169; East 59, 78, 118, 145; east coast, 93, 154, 156; Equatorial, 118; as generative sector, 156, 157; and geopolitical competition, 167, 168, 169; Horn of, 24, 58, 156; interior of, 146; North, 15, 69, 73, 74, 75; northwest, 74, 75; pre-capitalist, 180n19; South, 94; southern, 48; West, 74, 75, 110, 118; west coast, 73. *See also* China-Africa community; Forum on China Africa cooperation (FOCAC)
African French Empire, 74
African Great Lakes region, 118
African Union, 104
Agenda for Sustainable Development. *See* United Nations
Alaska, 51, 70
Aleutian Islands, 70, 152, 154
Algiers, 47

almonds, 64
Amboina Island, 66, 143
American-British Conversation (ABC) Plans, 73
American Military Mission to China (AMMISCA), 76
American Revolution, 48
American Revolutionary War, 90
Amsterdam, 90, 111; and Baltic trade, 89; as entrepôt, 46, 88–90, 107, 117; and manufacturing, 107; and spice trade, 46
Amur River, 56
Anglo-Afghan War (1878–1880), 48
Anglo-Dutch War (1618), 66
Anglo-Dutch Wars (1652–1674), 47
Antwerp, 66, 90
Arbenz, Jacobo, 134
Archangel, 89
area denial, 81, 83, 149, 152, 158
Argentia, 74
Argun River, 56
Armstrong, William, 129
artificial intelligence, 102, 114

Asia: and British empire, 69, 76, 93, 96–97, 109; Central, 57; and Chinese power, 82, 120, 135, 154; and the Cold War, 152, 156; as Dutch Republic far waters, 89, 143; East, 50, 99, 154; and European colonies, 112, 113; as Great Britain's far waters, 76, 93, 98; and Japanese empire, 69, 86, 93, 113; Southeast, 50, 82, 86, 93, 156; as United States far waters, 96, 98, 99, 118; and United States power, 79, 83, 86, 96, 97, 118

Asian Infrastructure Investment Bank (AIIB), 37, 125

Atlantic, Battle, of, 2, 71, 74, 149

Atlantic Islands, 75, 77

Atlantic Ocean: African coast of, 75; and the Caribbean Sea; 100, 141; and the Dutch Republic, 43, 89–90; as far waters, 68–69, 71–72, 90, 110, 150; and Germany, 52, 73, 98; and Great Britain, 9, 52, 71–76, 109, 110; and Guatemala, 134; and islands, 77, 141, 148; and Mahan, Alfred Thayer, 183n14; and Mediterranean Sea, 74, 76; as near waters, 52, 68, 70, 73–75, 150; North, 73, 148, 150; and the Pacific Ocean, 76, 98, 100; and ports, 118, 134; and primary-subsidiary relations, 98, 100; and Russia, 149; and Sea Lines of Communication, 148; and seapower, 43; and the Second World War, 52, 68–76, 98, 141, 148; South, 9, 74, 109, 110; and the United States, 50, 52, 68–76, 98, 118, 141, 150. *See also* Atlantic, Battle of; Greenland-Iceland-United Kingdom (GIUK) gap

Attlee, Clement, xiv

Auerstedt, 144

AUKUS alliance, 83, 156

Australia, xii, 15, 24, 176; and Great Britain, 93, 109, 134, 168; and the Second World War, 74, 93, 134, 150; and the United States, 134, 168. *See also* AUKUS; Operation Ocean Shield; Quad, the

Axis of Evil, 14

Balkans, 112

Baltic Sea: as Dutch Republic near waters, 64, 65 fig 4.1, 66, 89, 142; and Dutch Republic power, 45, 143

Banda Island, 66

Bank of England, 47

banking, 36, 64, 107, 115

Barbary coast, 50

Bay of Pigs, 100

Belgium, 41, 91, 94

Belt and Road Initiative (BRI), 30, 31 fig. 2.1, 59; and China's far waters, 101, 140; and China's near waters, 140; corridors of, 102; and Europe, 59; geography of, 137; as geopolitical project, 30, 60, 62, 87; and primary countries, 140; and primary-subsidiary relations, 140; and railways, 59, 102, 103

Berger, General David, 122

Biden, Joseph, 31, 116

biotechnology, 114

Birmingham, 48, 109

Black Lives Matter, 34

Black Sea, 47, 149

Blake, William, 109

blockade, 8, 35, 85; and China, 161; and choke points, 19; and Great Britain, 147; and Greenland-Iceland-United Kingdom gap, 150; and near waters, 39, 82, 142, 147; and South China Sea, 82

Boer War, 48. *See also* South African War

Bolshevism, 100

Bombay, 109

Bowman, Isaiah, 163, 164

Brazil: and Dutch Republic power, 89, 101; and Great Britain, 110; and

INDEX

the Second World War, 73–76; and Thirty Years War, 66
Bremen, 144
Bretton Woods Agreement, 133
BRI (Belt and Road Initiative), 30, 31 fig. 2.1, 59; and China's far waters, 101, 140; and China's near waters, 140; corridors of, 102; and Europe, 59; geography of, 137; as geopolitical project, 30, 60, 62, 87; and primary countries, 140; and primary-subsidiary relations, 140; and railways, 59, 102, 103
Bristol, 109
Britain. See Great Britain.
British. See Great Britain.
British Commonwealth, 73, 74
British Empire. See Great Britain
British Expeditionary Forces, 69
British India Company, 134
Brunel, Isambard Kingdom, 111, 129
Burma, 15, 56, 93, 129, 151, 168

Calcutta, 109, 130
California. See Ellwood Airfield; Long Beach
Cambodia, 56, 155
"cannon shot rule", 9
Canton, 49
Cape of Good Hope, 75
Cape Navarino, 47
Cape Verde Islands, 74
Caribbean (region), 81; and the Second World War, 71, 76, 141, 148; and Thirty Years War, 66
Caribbean Sea, 8, 47, 61–62, 70, 100; as Dutch Republic's far waters, 64, 66, 89–90; as Great Britain's far waters, 47, 76, 81; as United States near waters, 51, 70–71, 76, 100, 148
Cartesian philosophy, 126
Castro, Fidel, 100
Celestial Empire, 53
CENTO (Central Treaty Organization), 32

Central America, 135
Central American Isthmus, 68, 183n14
Central Intelligence Agency (CIA), 50, 99, 101, 133–34
Central Treaty Organization (CENTO), 32
Ceylon, 44, 66, 150. See also Sri Lanka
Chabahar, 103
chaebol, 119
Chamberlain, Neville, 91, 111
"Chestnut" program, 57
China: and Africa, 103, 104, 166–67, 169; and blockade, 19; and "Chestnut" program", 57; China 20, 25, 30, 37, 115; and the Cold War, 56, 79–80, 152–53; and the Dutch Republic, 90; and far waters, 10, 40, 77–78, 101, 102, 134; and "freedom of navigation", 82; "Global Civilisation Initiative", 161; "Global Development Initiative", 161; "Going Out", 59; and Great Britain, 31, 40, 80, 92, 110; and Hong Kong, 81; island building, 153–54, 158; island chains, 156–57; and Japan, 54, 92, 96–97, 167; and Korean War, 80; as land power, 159, 162; Made in China 2025, 115; maritime power, 77–78, 162, 164; and the Middle East, 103, 167; as the Middle Kingdom, 82; and NATO, 160; naval power, 58, 83, 122, 156; and near waters, 9, 23, 40, 77–78, 82, 118, 123, 160, 162, 165; and the nonvirtuous cycle of seapower, 163; and "Open Door Policy", 51, 97; Opium Wars, 48, 54, 92; Overseas Investment Industrial Guiding Policy, 59; and the Pacific Ocean, 5, 9, 62, 78, 81, 122, 153; and Permanent Court of Arbitration, 82; and ports, 118, 120; as primary country, 28, 114; and rare earth minerals, 87; rise to global power, 55–56, 100, 162; Sea Lines of Communication,

China (cont.)
103, 154, 157, 167; and the Second World War, 54, 79, 81, 97, 140, 150, 162, 168; silk trade, 44; and the Soviet Union, 54, 56, 80; and subsidiary countries, 121, 136, 137; as subsidiary country, 53–54, 78, 110; and Taiwan, 81–82, 157, 160; and United Nations, 104; and the United States, 6, 23, 31, 34, 46, 80, 116, 123, 139; and Vietnam War, 56, 80; and the virtuous cycle of seapower, 18, 163; and War on Terror, 57; and Washington Agreements, 95. *See also* Belt and Road Initiative; China-Africa community; Chinese Communist Party; Cultural Revolution; Doctrine of Peaceful Emergence; Forum on China-Africa cooperation (FOCAC); *South-South cooperation*

China-Africa Community, 103. *See also* Forum on China-Africa cooperation

China-Pakistan Economic Corridor (CPEC), 102–103

Chinese Civil War, 54, 80

Chinese Communist Party, 80

choke point, 21, 103, 142–43

Christian proselytization, 51

Churchill, Winston, 69, 71, 132

CIA (Central Intelligence Agency), 50, 99, 101, 133–34

CM Ports China, 120

coal, 48, 115, 170

Cold War, xii, 13, 116, 152; and developmentalism, 132, 134, 138, 152; and seapower, 148, 152, 153; and United States power projection, 32, 49, 101, 119; and US-China relations, 57, 79, 80

colonialism, 5, 30, 50, 101, 107

Colombia, 99, 183n14

Columbus, Christopher, 78

commodity, 110, 131

commodity chains, 86

computer chips, 29

Congo, 118

Congress of Europe, 77, 109

consumption, 2, 59, 131

context. *See* geopolitical context

continental-oriented countries, 7

Copenhagen, 142, 164

copper, 64

Corbett, Admiral Sir Julian, 2, 87, 117

Corliss, John B., 99

corridors, 101–103, 120

Corsica, 145

Coromandel coast, 44

Cosco Shipping, 120

cotton, 110

COVID, 104

Cuba, 99, 100

Cultural Revolution, 55

culture, 91, 110, 144; and China, 114; and geopolitics, 184n32; as modernity, 203; popular, 48; and seapower, 7

Curaçao, 89

currants, 64

Dakar, 73–76

Damansky Island, 56. *See also* Zhenbao Island

Danish Sound, 142–43

Danzig, 142

D-Day landings, 68

Defense Intelligence Agency, 57

Denmark, 45, 66, 142, 144

Descartes, René, 126

Destroyers for Bases deal, 71, 73, 76, 148

developmentalism, 130, 131, 137–38, 152, 162

diamonds, 107

Dickens, Charles, 110

Diego Garcia, 118, 156

Dietrich, Marlene, 16

Djibouti, 32, 58–59, 122, 156

Doctrine of Peaceful Emergence, 122

Dokdo Island, 157. *See also* Takeshima Island
Dominican Republic, 51, 100
Dominions (British), 71, 93–94, 96, 130
Doolittle, James, 150, 152
Downs, Battle of, 45
Dulles, Allen, 134
Dunkirk, 66, 69
Dutch. *See* Netherlands, the. *See also* Dutch Republic
Dutch Brazil, 89, 101
Dutch East Indies, 97, 113, 151
Dutch Republic: and the Atlantic Ocean, 43, 89–90; blockade of, 82; and chokepoints, 142–43; and Denmark, 142; diplomacy of, 45; and England, 44–45, 90, 108, 143, 189n26; and the Enlightenment, 126, 127; as entrepôt, 88, 90; and far waters, 66–67, 89, 143; and geopolitics, 25; and the Hanseatic League, 142; and hegemony, 4, 42, 44, 60, 127, 210n8; and islands, 142–43; and Japan, 93; and liberalism, 128; and Mahan, Alfred Thayer, 196n12; manufacturing, 107; and the Mediterranean Sea, 64; mercantilism, 108; merchants, 46; and near waters, 64–66, 89, 143; and the Pacific Ocean, 43; and ports, 117; pre-capitalist, 180n19; and primary-subsidiary relations, 30, 40, 44, 66, 84, 87, 93; and projection of force, 5, 40; as seapower, 5, 41, 60, 66–67, 169, 175, 179n13, 210n8; and Spain, 41–45; and Sweden, 142–43; and a Third World War, 164; and trade, 43–44, 66, 84, 87, 90, 142–43; and violence, 43, 66; and the virtuous cycle of seapower, 18. *See also* Amsterdam; Anglo-Dutch War; Anglo-Dutch Wars; Dutch Brazil; Dutch East India Company; Dutch East Indies; Dutch Republic; Dutch West India company; *Pax Neerlandica*; United Dutch East India Company; United Provinces
Dutch East India Company, 46, 48, 78, 108
Dutch West India Company, 46
Duqm, 103
dyes, 64, 107

East China Sea, 24
East Indies, 46, 51, 64, 90, 143. *See also* Dutch East Indies
economic development, 28, 166; and China, 54–55, 59, 137, 162, 164, 169; and the Dutch Republic, 107–108; and geopolitical representation, 27, 34, 35, 37, 203; and Great Britain, 109, 145; and innovation, 30; and ports, 118, 120–21; and seapower, 41, 210; and the United States, 116, 134–35. *See also* developmentalism
economic geography, 2, 48, 60, 114
Economist, 161,
Egypt, 40, 47, 52
Eighty Years' War, 143
Elba, 145
El Salvador, 100
Ellwood Airfield, 150
energy, 29, 55, 103, 115; renewable 9, 24, 86, 87, 114
Engels, Friedrich, 128
England, 189n26; and Dutch Republic near waters, 44–45, 143; and Dutch Republic trade, 90,108; as seapower, 43, 47, 90, 158. *See also* Great Britain
England, Bank of, 47
English Channel, 52, 69, 71, 147
Enkhuizen, 46
entrepôt, 117; active, 88–90, 107; Amsterdam as, 46, 88, 90, 107, 117; Antwerp as 90; Chinese ports as, 114; Great Britain's ports as, 109, 110, 117; Gwadar as, 103; Heligoland as, 144; Japanese ports as, 113; Salt Lake City as, 117; Zanzibar as, 118

Española, 66
Eurasia, 12, 15, 49, 59
Europe, xii, 15, 23; and Asia, 54; and the Belt and Road Initiative, 59; central, 32, 49, 91, 112; and China, 51, 78, 120, 139, 153; and the Dutch Republic, 65, 108; eastern, 32, 91, 112; and empires, 113; exploration, 25; and far waters, 44, 98, 139, 140; and France, 109; and Great Britain, 47, 77, 91, 94–95, 109, 112, 145, 158; and Japan, 64, 86, 150; and Mackinder, Sir Halford, 12; and Mahan, Alfred Thayer, 68; and the Marshall Plan, 119; and near waters, 92, 145; northern, 144; Northwest, 69, 70; and ports, 120; pre-capitalist, 179n19; and seapower, 47, 158; and the Second World War, 52, 69, 72–74, 96, 111; southern, 73; and a Third World War, 168; and the United Nations, 50; and the United States, 49, 52, 57, 70, 73–76, 148, 163
European Union, 41, 176
Ever Given (ship), 19
Exclusive Economic Zone (EEZ), 9, 10, 181n33, 212n13

Falkland Islands, 9
Far East, 73, 96, 180n19
far waters: and Africa, 118; and China, 40, 77–83, 101–102, 114, 120; and the Cold War, 119, 152; definition, 2–3, 8; and the Dutch Republic, 64, 65, 67, 88, 90, 107; and the East China Sea, 24; and the First World War, 92; and the generative sector, 107; geography of, 5, 10, 24, 38, 61; geopolitics of, 62, 164–65; and Great Britain, 47, 52, 69–71, 90, 92, 94, 96–98, 109, 112, 118, 145, 147; and islands, 141, 158; and Japan, 92, 96, 113, 119; and Mahan, Alfred Thayer, 10, 68; and naval power, 6; and peacebuilding, 171; and ports, 117, 120; pre-capitalist, 179n19; and primary-subsidiary relations, 6, 8, 40, 85, 92, 99–100; and projection of force, 6, 7, 9, 13, 39, 41, 73, 117; and seapower, 5, 30, 104, 106, 112; and the Second World War, 69, 71–76, 97–98, 151; and a Third World War, 168; and the United States, 13, 50, 51, 68, 70–71, 73–76, 96–100, 119, 135, 150; and Washington Agreements, 95
Fiery Cross Reef, 158
figs, 64
finance, 110, 115,
Finland, 32
"First War of Indian Independence", 48
First World War: and China, 54, 79; and classic geopolitics, xii; and the Dominions, 93, 94; and far waters, 92; and France, 79, 94; geopolitical context of, 170; and Germany, 146, 147; and Great Britain, 79, 90, 92–94, 111, 112; and Japan, 79; and the Mediterranean Sea, 94; and naval arms race, 176; and near waters, 92; Town class destroyers, 71; and the United States, 71, 163
flax, 64
Foggo III, Admiral James G., 149
Ford, Gerald, 57
Ford, Henry, 111
Forster, E.M., 128
Fort Geldria, 44
Fort Maurits, 89
Fort Zeelandia, 89
Forum on China-Africa cooperation (FOCAC), 103, 104
France: and Africa, 118, 169; and China, 79, 153; and Djibouti, 58; and the Dutch Republic; 43, 45, 126, 143; and the First World War, 79, 94; and Great Britain, 47, 49–50, 73–74, 90, 91, 94, 110, 112,

144–45, 164, 169; and Mahan, Alfred Thayer, 196n12, 206n2; and Russia, 47; and the Second World War, 73–76, 91, 96; and the United States, 73–76, 99; and Washington Agreements, 95. See also African French Empire.
"freedom of navigation" operations, 61, 82, 85–86, 125, 127, 143
"freedom of the seas". See Mare Liberum
Fuenen, 143

G7, 30
Gandhi, Mahatma, 124
Gates, Bill, 129
Gdansk, 89
generative sector, 8, 10, 86–88; Africa as, 103, 146, 156, 158; and China, 97, 103, 154, 163; and the Dutch Republic, 88; and geopolitics, 87; and Great Britain, 129, 146; and hegemony, 106; and islands, 143, 157; and Japan, 98, 113; the Middle East as, 158; and ports, 117; and seapower, 38, 163, 165; and subsidiary countries, 107; and a Third World War, 167, 168, 170; and the United States, 97, 100
geography: of area denial, 81; of the Belt and Road Initiative, 137; and borders, 56; as deterministic, 13, 14, 68; as dynamic process, 32, 61, 158; economic, 2, 24, 30, 42, 48, 60; of the generative sector, 88, 98, 103; and geopolitics, xiii, 3, 11, 14, 18–19; of hegemony, 44–45, 128; of islands, 140, 144, 148, 153; and Mahan, Alfred Thayer, 13, 68, 182n35; of near and far waters, 5, 10, 62, 67, 71, 79, 118; physical, 13, 19, 21, 24, 38, 41, 61, 156; political, xii; of ports, 114, 118, 120; of primary-subsidiary relations, 17, 153, 160–61; of production, 86; of seapower, 2, 7, 8, 162, 164; of trade, 19, 64, 67, 67, 109, 140
geopolitical context, 19, 22–24, 164, 210n8; and China, 57, 79, 103; of the Cold War; 57, 119, 133, 152; current, 154, 156, 162, 166; and the Dutch Republic, 42, 127; and East Africa, 118; and economic growth, 112; of the First World War, 170; Germany, 32, and Great Britain, 40, 49, 50, 69–75, 91–92, 112, 154; and Heligoland, 144, 147; and Heligoland-Zanzibar Treaty, 145–46; and islands, 158; as middle power, 176; and "national socialism", 138; as near waters, 146, 147; and the Philippines, 99; and seapower, 82, 113; of the Second World War, 52, 69–75, 91–92, 97, 112; and the United States, 69–75, 134, 148
geopolitics: of area denial, 158; and the Belt and Road Initiative, 30, 60; building blocks, 15–21; and businesses, 17, 165; and cities, 116; classic, 3, 6, 7, 12–13, 19, 26, 160, 170–71; Cold War, 13; Continental, 158; definition, xii, 11, 21; and geography, xiii, 3, 11, 14, 18–19; as historical process, 19, 48, 94; and infrastructure, 122; of innovation, 107, 113; of islands, 141–42, 144, 153, 156; lessons, 166–67; and Mahan, Alfred Thayer, 182n35; and near and far waters, 10, 39, 62, 77, 135, 146, 153, 165; oceanic, 158; and peacebuilding, 170; political economy approach to, 3, 17, 160, 165; and ports, 117; of primary-subsidiary relations, 7, 8, 17, 85–87, 95, 157; relations, 15, 18–19, 36, 38; representations, 125, 138; and seapower, 1, 7, 18, 26, 107, 113, 140; threats, identification of, 28–35. See also geopolitical context
Ghana, 168,

Gibraltar, 144, 145
Glasgow, 48, 109, 128
glass, 107
"Global Civilisation Initiative." *See* China.
"Global Development Initiative" (China), 161
Global Development Initiative (United Nations), 104
global production networks, 86
gold, 30, 48, 64, 175, 196n12
grain, 64, 89, 142
Great Britain: and Africa, 118, 146, 154; and the Atlantic Ocean, 9, 52, 71–76, 109, 110; and the Caribbean Sea, 62, 71, 90; and Ceylon, 150; and China, 40, 54, 79–80, 92, 101, 153; and classic geopolitics, 12; and the Cold War, 80, 134; and the Commonwealth, 73; and Denmark, 142; and Diego Garcia, 156; and the Dominions, 94; and the Dutch Republic, 90; and Egypt, 40; and England, 189n26; as entrepôt, 109, 110; and far waters, 8, 47, 69, 70, 73, 92, 95–96, 98, 112, 146; and the First World War, 79, 90, 92, 94, 112; and France, 47, 49–50, 82, 90, 144–45, 164; and geopolitics, 31; and Germany, 52, 69, 82, 92, 111, 113, 144, 146–47; and hegemony, 4, 48–49, 64, 124, 128; and Hong Kong, 115; and India, 40, 52, 90; and islands, 9, 141, 144, 158; and Japan, 52, 92, 93–94, 96, 111, 112; and liberalism, 128, 130; and Mackinder, Sir Halford, 12; and Mahan, Alfred Thayer, 70, 183n14, 196n12; manufacturing, 48, 109, 110–11, 129; and the Mediterranean Sea, 52, 69–70, 74, 94, 98, 110, 112, 134, 145; merchants, 48–49; and near waters, 8, 47, 52, 69, 73, 92, 146, 165; and the Pacific Ocean, 74, 93–95, 97–98, 109, 134; and ports, 118, 129; pre-capitalist, 180n19; and primary-subsidiary relations, 40, 92–93, 145, 165; and projection of force, 68, 145; and Sea Lines of Communications, 70, 93; as seapower, 5, 46–47, 49, 95, 112, 145, 158, 169; and the Second World War, 68-69, 71, 73–76, 92, 112, 132, 141, 147–48; and South Africa, 94; and the Soviet Union, 91, 132; and a Third World War, 168; and trade, 50, 90, 109; and the United States, 50–52, 56, 62, 73–76, 94, 96, 98, 111–12, 156; and violence, 30, 43, 66; and the virtuous cycle of seapower, 18, 109, 112; and Washington Agreements, 95; and Zanzibar, 154. *See also* American-British Conversation (ABC) Plans; British Empire; British India Company; Destroyers for Bases deal; England; English Channel; Royal Navy
Great Famine (China), 55
Greater East Asia Co-Prosperity Sphere, 98, 113
Greenland-Iceland-United Kingdom (GIUK), 148–49
Grotius, Hugo, 44, 127, 128
Guam, 81, 151, 154, 155
Guangzhou, 120, 153
Guantanamo Bay, 99
Guatemala, 100, 134
Gulf countries, 28
Gulf of Guinea, 74
gum, 64
"gunboat diplomacy", 49, 86
Gwadar, 103, 122, 156

Hague, The, 9, 82, 157
Hainan Island, 80
Haiti, 51, 100
Halifax, Lord, 91
Halifax, Nova Scotia, 71

Hamburg, 144
Hammann, USS, 151
Hanover, 144
Hanseatic League, 43, 45, 142
Hart, Sir Basil Liddell, 112
Hawaii: and the Second World War, 74, 150; United States annexation of, 31, 51, 68, 70; and United States far waters, 154, 155; as United States near waters, 70, 154; and Washington Agreements, 95
hegemony: and China, 54, 59, 101; definition, 8, 44; and the Dutch Republic, 42–44, 46; and the generative sector, 8; and Great Britain, 47, 49, 90, 92, 145; and modernity, 124, 128, 159; and near and far waters, 64; and ports, 118; and seapower, 163; and the Soviet Union, 57; transition, 87, 90; and the United States, 47, 49, 54, 57, 90, 101
Heligoland, 144, 145, 146, 147
Heligoland Bight, Battle of, 147
Heligoland-Zanzibar Treaty, 119 fig 6.1, 145
hemp, 64
Henderson, Sir Nevile, 91
high-value goods, 41; and China, 115; and the Dutch Republic, 43, 64, 66, 107; and Japan, 113; and ports, 117
High Seas, 9, 10, 57, 61, 102, 181n34
Himalayan mountains, 19, 24, 103
Hindmarsh, Sir John, 144
hinterland, 117, 145, 146, 153, 183n14
Hitler, Adolf, 91–92, 111–12, 134, 138, 147
Hokkaido Island, 157
Holmes, Sherlock, 48
Honduras, 51, 100
Hong Kong, 31, 81, 95, 115, 120
Honshu Island, 154
Hoorn, 46
Horn of Africa, 24, 58, 156
Hornet, USS, 150

Houston, 118
HPH, 120
Hull, 144
Hull, Cordell, 71
Hyundai, 119

Iceland, 73, 74, 148, 149
imperialism, 5, 107; anti-, 152; as development, 34, 125; Great Britain's 92, 101, 137; Japanese, 92, 151; as modernity, 130; as form of primary-subsidiary relations, 30, 34
India, 15; and China, 56, 78; and the Dutch Republic, 44–45, 66, 89–90; and Great Britain, 40, 47, 48, 52, 69, 110, 129; and Operation Ocean Shield, 57; and Russia, 94; as seapower, 176; and a Third World War, 168, and the United States, 40, 47, 156, 168. *See also* Indo-Pacific region
"Indian Mutiny." *See* "the First War of Indian Independence"
Indian Ocean, 43; and China, 59, 77, 78, 83, 154, 158; and Great Britain, 93, 94, 109; islands of, 156; and ports, 118; pre-capitalist, 180; and the United States, 83, 134. *See also* Operation Ocean Shield
Indo-Arab trade, 118
Indochina, 73, 76, 113
Indo-Pacific region, 24, 83, 117, 156, 166, 176
infrastructure, 29, 103, 159; and China, 114, 121–22, 137, 154; and the Dutch Republic, 64, 88, 107; geopolitics of, 106; and Great Britain, 48, 110–11; innovation, 4; and Mahan, Alfred Thayer, 183; and trade, 110–11; transport, 30; and the United States, 133–34
Institute of Boundary and Ocean Studies, 77
Insular Cases, 207

"insular empire," 145, 147–48
International Monetary Fund (IMF), 34, 37, 50, 133
Ionian Islands, 145
Iran, 14, 36, 101, 103
Iraq, 14
Irish Sea, 158
iron, 64, 97, 113
islands: and Chinese far waters, 157; and Chinese near waters, 80, 153–54, 157–58; and Dutch Republic's far waters, 66, 143, 156; and Dutch Republic's near waters, 142; and Exclusive Economic Zone, 9, 140, 157; and geopolitics, 21, 147, 158; and Great Britain's far waters, 71, 92, 118, 145; and Great Britain's near waters, 144, 145; and Sea Lines of Communication, 140, 157; and seapower, 6, 7, 140–41, 144; and the Second World War, 75, 141, 154, 157; and United States far waters, 77, 150–52, 154; and United States near waters, 70–71, 75, 148
Israel, Jonathan, 88, 176
ivory, 64

Jambi, 90
Japan: and China, 51, 53; and the Cold War, 119, 152; and the Dutch Republic, 64; economic growth, 112; and far waters, 92; and the First World War, 79; and Great Britain, 49, 50, 69, 71, 94, 95–96; and islands, 151, 152, 157; and the Mediterranean Sea, 94, 98; navy, 93; and near waters, 9, 97, 113; and the Pacific Ocean, 9, 93, 95, 97, 119, 150, 151, 154; as primary country, 91; and Russia, 76, 157; and the Second World War, 54, 69, 71, 74, 79, 81, 86, 92, 94, 96, 113, 150–51, 154, 157, 168; and the United States, 32, 51, 72, 74, 81, 94–96, 118, 135, 168; and Washington

Agreements, 95. *See also* Greater East Asia Co-Prosperity Sphere; Hokkaido Island; Okinawa
Japanese Co-Prosperity Sphere. *See* Greater East Asia Co-Prosperity Sphere
Java Island, 66
Jena, 144
Jobs, Steve, 129
Johnson, Lyndon B., 130

Kadena Airbase, 151
Kai-shek, Chiang, 54
Kamchatka Province, 157
Karakoram Highway, 103
Kattegat, 142, 143
Khalifa, 122
Kiel Canal, 146
Kipling, Rudyard, 125, 131
Kissinger, Henry, 57, 80
Knox, Frank, 75
Kobe, 113
Korean peninsula, 56, 101
Korean War, 50, 56, 80, 152, 156
Kuomintang, 54, 56, 92
Kuril Islands, 93, 157
Kuwait, 103

landpowers, 7, 13, 184n16
Lawson, Jack, xiv
Leeds, 48, 109, 128
LeMay, Curtis, 135
Lend-Lease Agreement, 76
Lewis and Clark expedition, 51
liberalism, 126; and China, 136; and the Dutch Republic, 127–28; and Great Britain, 128, 130; and the United States, 49, 53
Libya, 36
Lisbon, 44
Liverpool, 109
London, 109, 117, 144; peace conference, 97. *See also* London, City of
London, City of, 48, 110, 129
London conferences, 97

Long Beach, 120
Louisiana Purchase, 51
low-value goods, 41, 55, 64, 131
Luxembourg, 41

Mackinder, Sir Halford, 12, 13
Magruder, Brigadier General John A., 76
Mahan, Alfred Thayer, 10, 51, 71, 212n13; and Chinese naval policy, 182n36; as classic geopolitician, 12, 13, 182n35; and colonization, 100, 196n12; and geographical determinism, 13, 183n14; and islands, 206n2; and near and far waters, 68, 70, 100; and seapower, 13, 178n9, 183n14
Malabar coast, 44
Malacca, 90
Malacca Dilemma, 19
Malacca Straits, 19, 103
Malaya, 76, 113, 150
Malaysia, 90, 152, 157
Malta, 145
Manchester, 48, 109, 128
Manchukuo, 168
Manchuria, 53, 92, 168
Manila, 89, 143
Manjoo, Farhad, 116
Mao Zedong, 54, 80, 135
Mare Liberum, 44, 127, 142
Mariana Islands, 154, 207n34
maritime-oriented countries, 7
Maritime Silk Road Initiative, 59
markets: and China, 49, 54, 59, 78, 102, 116, 120–21, 157; and the Dutch Republic, 42, 43, 45, 64,107; and far waters 7; and Great Britain, 49, 54, 68, 145; and Mahan, Alfred Thayer, 182n35; and ports, 117, 120–21; and primary countries, 29, 35, 86, 107; and the United States, 50–51, 68, 116
Marquesas Islands, 76
Marshall Islands, 207n34
Marshall Plan, 119

Marx, Karl, 111, 128
McCarthy, Joseph, 79
McCarthy, Kevin, 116
McKinley, William, 99
Mediterranean Sea: and the Atlantic Ocean, 73, 76, 98; and the Dutch Republic, 64; as far waters, 61, 70, 76, 98; and the First World War, 94; and Germany, 69–70, 73, 112; and Great Britain, 52, 69–70, 74, 94, 98, 110, 112, 134, 145; and the Indian Ocean, 94; and islands, 145; and Japan, 94, 98; and NATO, 149; as near waters, 70; and the Pacific Ocean, 76, 94, 98; and primary-subsidiary relations, 98; and Russia, 149; and Sea Lines of Communication, 70, 112; and the Second World War, 69–70, 73–74, 76, 98, 112; and the United States, 69–70, 74–74, 76, 98, 134
Mediterranean strategy, 70, 112
Mehmet Ali, 47
mercantilism, 108
Mexico, 100, 183n14
Miami, 118
microprocessors, 36
Middle East: and China, 103; as generative sector, 102, 157; and Great Britain, 69, 74, 94; and near and far waters, 140; oil 24, 52, 87; and ports, 120; and Sea Lines of Communication, 83, 120, 157; and a Third World War, 167
Middle Kingdom, 82
Middle Sea. *See* Mediterranean Sea
Midway, Battle of, 2, 151, 164, 211n9
Mississippi River, 50
modernity, 124, 125, 138
Moluccan Strait, 143
Moluccas, 66
Mombasa, 109
Monroe Doctrine, 75, 183n14
Moore, Blake, 116, 117
Moscow, 54

Nagasaki, 113
NATO (North Atlantic Treaty Organization), 27; and China, 31, 160; and the Cold War, 32; and Great Britain, 76; and the Netherlands, 41; and Operation Ocean Shield, 57; and Russia, 149, 150; and the United States, 76
naval power, 176; and China, 10, 37, 58, 81, 83, 122, 156, 163, 182n36; and the Dutch Republic, 142; and far waters, 6, 10, 31, 68, 70, 156; and geography, 11; and Germany, 146, 147; and Great Britain, 47, 91–92, 95, 109, 112, 147; and hegemony, 4, 106, 125; and islands, 141, 150, 156; and Japan, 93, 95; and Mahan, Alfred Thayer, 12, 13, 68, 178n9, 182n36; and near waters, 6, 10, 31, 68, 146, 147, 156; and ports, 117; and primary-subsidiary relations, 105, 112; and Russia, 149; and the Second World War, 73, 75, 150; and trade, 43; and the United States, 68, 70, 73, 97, 99, 149, 156; and Washington Agreements, 95, 97. *See also* Mahan, Alfred Thayer; seapower
navy: blue-water, 82, 162, 164, 182n36; and China, 78, 81, 82, 103, 164; and the Dutch Republic, 142; and Japan, 94; and Mahan, Alfred Thayer, 100, 182n36; merchant, 7; military, 7; and ports, 117; and power, 178n4; and Roosevelt, Franklin, D., 97; and the United States, 47, 50, 71, 75. *See also* Mahan, Alfred, Thayer; naval power; Royal Navy; seapower
Nazism, 132
Near East, 109, 110
near waters: and China, 40, 77–83, 114, 118, 120, 153–57; definition, 2–3, 8; and the Dutch Republic, 64, 66–67, 89, 90, 141–43; and the East China Sea, 24; and the First World War, 92; geography of, 5, 10, 24, 38, 61; geopolitics of, 62, 164–65; and Germany, 92, 146–47; and Great Britain, 47, 52, 69–71, 91–92, 94, 96–98, 112, 144–45, 147; and islands, 141, 153, 155–56, 158; and Japan, 96–97, 113, 117, 150; and Mahan, Alfred Thayer, 10, 68; and naval power, 6; and peacebuilding, 171; and ports, 117; and primary-subsidiary relations, 6, 8, 40, 92, 99–100; and projection of force, 6–7, 9, 31, 39, 41, 117; and Russia, 149; and seapower, 5, 30, 178n4; and the Second World War, 69, 71–76, 97–98, 154; and Taiwan, 161; and a Third World War, 168; and the United States, 48, 50–51, 68, 70–71, 73–76, 96–100, 135, 148; and Washington Agreements, 95
Napoleon, 47, 49, 82, 109, 144, 145
Napoleonic Wars, xi, 47
Nasir-ud-Din, 129
Nelson, Admiral Horatio, xi, xiii, 47
neoliberalism, 126
Netherlands, the. *See* Dutch Republic
New Caledonia, 76
Newcastle, 48, 109, 128
Newfoundland, 71, 74, 148
New Guinea, 151, 154
Newton, Sir Isaac, 16
New York, 51
New Zealand, 93, 154, 168
Nicaragua, 51, 100
Nigeria, 36
Nile, Battle of, 164
Nile River, 145
nine-dash line, 77, 82, 83 fig. 4.5; 155 fig. 8.2
Nixon, Richard, 57, 80
nonvirtuous cycle of seapower, 163. *See also* seapower; virtuous cycle of seapower
North America, 50, 183n14
North Atlantic Treaty Organization (NATO), 27; and China, 31, 160; and

the Cold War, 32; and Great Britain, 76; and Netherlands, 41; and Operation Ocean Shield, 57; and Russia, 149, 150; and the United States, 76
North Cape, 74
North Carolina, 32
North Korea, 14, 36, 56, 132
North Sea, 52, 71, 144, 147
Northern Ireland,73, 74, 189n26
Nova Scotia, 71
Nuclear Non-Proliferation Treaty, 27
nuclear weapons, 13, 36, 56–57, 148, 165

Obama, Barack, 83
oil, 88; and China, 82, 102, 103, 157; as generative sector, 28, 102, 158; and geography of, 24; and Great Britain, 69, 97; and Japan, 86, 97, 113; and the Middle East, 28, 87, 102, 103, 158; and primary-subsidiary relations, 28, 102; and Sea Lines of Communication, 157; and the United States 51, 97, 115
olive oil, 64
Okinawa, 118, 135, 151–52, 155
Oman, 103
"Open Door policy", 51, 97
Operation Barbarossa, 96
Operation Bolero, 73, 148–49
Operation Ocean Shield, 57–58
Operation Torch, 69, 75
opium, 48, 78
Opium Wars, 31, 47–48, 54, 92, 153
Orwell, George, 129
Osaka, 113
Ottoman fleet, 47

Pacific Ocean: and the Atlantic Ocean, 72, 74, 76, 98; Central; 93; and China, 5, 9, 62, 78, 81, 122, 153; and the Dutch Republic, 43; eastern, 70; as far waters, 9, 74, 81, 98, 109, 119, 150, 156; geography of, 19, 24, 156; and geopolitics, 167; and Great Britain, 74, 93–95, 97–98, 109, 134; and Indian Ocean, 93; and islands, 141, 153; and Japan, 9, 93, 95, 97, 119, 150, 151, 154; and Mahan, Alfred Thayer, 183n14; and Mediterranean Sea, 76; as near waters, 9, 70, 78, 81, 97, 150, 152, 154; and ports, 118, 134; and primary-subsidiary relations, 100; and Sea Lines of Communication, 155; and seapower, 167; and the Second World War, 9, 72–76, 97–98, 148, 150–52, 154; South, 93, 122, 151; and the Soviet Union, 150, 156; and the United States, 50, 51, 68, 70, 72–76, 81, 95, 97–98, 117, 119, 122, 134–35, 148, 150, 154, 156; and Washington Agreements, 95; western, 5, 9, 62, 77–78, 81, 83, 110, 135, 153. See also Indo-Pacific region
Pakistan, 103, 156. See also China-Pakistan Economic Corridor
palm oil, 118
Palmerston, Lord, 49
Panama, 99
Panama Canal, 68, 99, 183n14
Pan-Asianism, 98
Papua New Guinea, 154
Paracel Islands, 157
Paris Climate Accords, 27
Passchendaele, Battle of, 94
Pax Americana, 101
Pax Neerlandica, 142
peacebuilding, 170, 171
Pearl Harbor, 51, 70, 74–75, 96, 150
Pearl River, 153. See also Zhujiang River
Pelosi, Nancy, 116
People's Republic of China. See China
pepper, 64
Permanent Court of Arbitration, 9, 82
Perry, Commodore Matthew, 51
Persia, 129
Persian Gulf, 78, 103
Peters, Carl, 146

Philippine-American War (1899–1902), 99
Philippines, 23; and China, 40, 142, 157; and the Dutch Republic, 66, 90; and Japan, 113; and South China Sea, 9, 157; and the United States, 31, 51, 76, 81, 99, 100, 150–52, 155, 157
pitch, 64, 89
Platt Amendment, 99
port power, 117–18, 120
ports: and China, 103, 114, 120, 122, 154; and Destroyers for Bases deal, 71; as entrepôt, 88, 110, 114, 117; and Great Britain, 110, 111, 129; and "Open Door policy", 51; and primary-subsidiary relations, 29; and seapower, 12; and the Second World War, 74, 76; and the United States, 133. *See also* port power
Portsmouth, xi
Portugal, 30, 42, 44, 46, 66, 175
power, 4; arc of, 42, 60, 62; and China, 53–60, 77–79, 136–38, 154; cultural, 184n32; and the Dutch Republic, 42–46, 126–28, 142; economic, 21, 30, 35–36, 114, 163; and geography, 21, 24, 32; and Great Britain, 46–49; 128–30; and hegemony, 42, 44, 46, 107, 113, 124; imperial, 34; material, 178n4; military, 17, 31, 32, 35–37, 163, 183n14; and modernity, 125; political, 21, 114; and primary countries, 27, 35; and primary-subsidiary relations, 87, 98; relations, 16, 165, 178n4; and a Third World War, 170; and trade, 43; and the United States, 49–53, 130–36. *See also* naval power; port power; power projection; seapower
power projection, 4–6, 9; and China, 156; and the Dutch Republic, 64–67; and economics, 23, 26; and far waters, 30, 39, 64, 77, 81, 85, 210n8; and geopolitics, 15, 17, 28; and Great Britain, 68, 145; and hegemony, 8, 85; and islands, 141; and primary-subsidiary relations, 40, 98; and trade, 61; and the United States, 13, 81, 148, 152. *See also* naval power; seapower
primary countries: and the Belt and Road Initiative, 140; definition, 7, 27, 36, 181n27, 185n3, 211n9; and far waters, 39, 62, 78, 107, 166; and the generative sector, 8, 86; and geopolitics, 28–29, 35; and entrepôts, 90; and imperialism, 53; and NATO, 160; and near waters, 39; and the "Open Door policy", 97; and peacebuilding, 171; and ports, 118; and seapower, 66, 84, 87; and the Second World War, 91–93; and strategy, 31; and violence, 43, 45, 129. *See also* primary-subsidiary relations
primary-subsidiary relations, 8, 27, 29, 211n9; and the Belt and Road Initiative, 140; and China, 37, 55, 59, 114, 136–38, 161; and commodity chains, 86; as development, 34, 131; and the Dutch Republic, 43–44, 127; and the generative sector, 86; and geopolitics, 28; and Germany, 113; and Great Britain, 48, 113; and hegemony, 42; as imperialism, 30, 34; and islands, 142, 158; and Japan, 112–13; and NATO, 160; and peacebuilding, 170; and ports, 118; and power projection, 40, 45; and seapower, 87, 104, 164–65, 169; and Taiwan, 161; and a Third World War, 168; and the United States, 100, 131; and violence, 129; and Washington Agreements, 95
production, 23; and China, 59, 103, 116; energy, 9; and the generative sector, 87; and Great Britain, 109, 111; industrial, 21; and infrastructure, 29, 30; and Mahan, Alfred

Thayer, 68; of primary countries, 28; and Roosevelt, Franklin D., 98; and seapower, 163; of subsidiary countries, 55; and trade, 2, 86; and the United States, 116
Protestantism, 126
Prussia, 144, 146
Pulicat, 66

Qingdao, 120
Quad, the, 83, 156
"Quasi-War" (1798–1800), 50

railways, 29; and the Belt and Road Initiative, 59, 102, 103; and Great Britain, 110, 129; and Guatemala, 134; and Japan, 113; and Russia, 54
raisins, 64
Rama V, King of Siam, 129
rare earth minerals, 24, 29, 87
Red Sea, 58
Rembrandt, 127
Rhodes, Cecil, 48
Rimland, 184n
robotics, 37, 115
"rogue state", 27
Roosevelt, Franklin D., 75, 76, 97, 98, 132, 152
Roosevelt, Theodore, 99, 112, 183n14
Rostow, Walt Whitman, 130–33, 135, 137, 152, 162
Rotterdam, 46
Royal Marines, xii
Royal Navy, xi, xiii, 49, 94
rubber, 51, 86, 113,
Russia, 32; in the Arctic, 167; and the Atlantic Ocean, 149; and China, 53, 54, 55, 103; and classic geopolitics, 12; and the Dutch Republic, 66; and Great Britain, 12, 94; and Greenland-Iceland-United Kingdom gap, 150; and India, 94; and Japan, 92, 93, 112, 157; and the Mediterranean Sea, 149; near waters of, 149, 165; and Sea Lines of Communication, 167; and seapower, 176; and the Second World War, 76; and subsidiary countries, 36, 47; and a Third World War, 167; and the United States, 70, 149. *See also* Soviet Union
Russia-Ukraine War, 32, 160
Ryukyu Islands, 152

Salt Lake City, 117
San Francisco, 57
Santa Maria, 78
Saudi Arabia, 103
sea: attributes, 1. *See also* choke points; Exclusive Economic Zone; far waters; High Seas; near waters; Sea Lines of Communication; seapower; United Nations Convention of the Law of the Seas
Sea Lines of Communication (SLOCs), 19, 20 fig. 1.1, 61
seapower: and China, 60, 77–78, 82, 121, 138, 154, 162; and classic geopolitics, 13, 26; definition, 1, 7; and developmentalism, 138; and the Dutch Republic, 41–43, 64, 90, 108, 127, 142, 169; force projection, 3, 85, 87, 104; and the generative sector, 8; geography of 2, 24; geopolitics of; 3, 15, 19, 21, 30, 84, 87, 104, 165, 167, 170; and Germany, 146; and Great Britain, 46–47, 68–69, 90, 92, 100, 112, 130, 144, 146, 158, 169; and hegemony, 5, 8, 85, 92; and islands, 140–41, 143, 146, 154, 158, 206n2; and Japan, 50, 112; and Mackinder, Sir Halford, 13; and Mahan, Alfred Thayer, 12, 13, 69, 178n9, 182n35, 183n14, 196n12, 206n2; and near and far waters, 8, 38, 52, 62, 90, 166; and the nonvirtuous cycle of, 163; and ports, 121; and Portugal, 42, 44, 66, 143, 175, 196n12; pre-capitalist, 179n19; and primary-subsidiary relations, 7,

seapower (*cont.*)
26, 85, 98, 113, 165, 170, 181n27;
and projection of force, 40, 66,
88, 98; and Sea Lines of Communication, 38, 61, 93, 160; and the
Second World War, 68; and Spain,
42, 44–45, 66, 99, 175, 196n12; and
Taiwan, 161; and a Third World
War, 167; and trade, 2, 114; and the
United States, 49–50, 68–69, 71,
95, 100, 155, 161, 169; the virtuous
cycle of, 18, 27, 41, 43, 84, 106, 112–
13, 117, 122, 138, 152, 162, 178n4;
and Washington Agreements, 95
SEATO (Southeast Asia Treaty Organization), 32
Second World War, 2; Asian-Pacific
theater, 68, 72, 150, 151; and the
Atlantic Ocean, 52, 68–76, 98, 141,
148; and Australia, 74, 93, 135,
150; and Brazil, 73–76; and the
Caribbean, 71, 76, 141, 148; and
China, 54, 79, 81, 140, 150, 162,
168; and classic geopolitics, 13, 14;
and Destroyers for Bases deal, 148;
and developmentalism, 34, 125,
133, 137; Euro-Atlantic theater,
72, 148; and Europe, 52, 69, 72–74,
96, 111; and far waters, 69, 71–76,
97–98, 151; and the generative
sector, 86, 168; and geopolitical
context, 52, 69–75, 91–92, 97, 112;
and Germany, 79, 147; and Great
Britain, 68–69, 71, 73–76, 92, 94, 96,
112, 132, 141, 147-48; and Hawaii,
74, 150; and hegemony, 113, 116,
118; and islands, 75, 141, 154, 157;
and Japan, 54, 69, 71, 74, 79, 81, 86,
92, 94, 96, 113, 150-51, 154, 157,
168; and Lend-Lease, 76; and the
Mediterranean Sea, 69–70, 73–74,
76, 98, 112; and naval power, 73,
75, 150; and near and far waters, 9,
69, 71–76, 97-98, 148, 154; and the
Pacific Ocean, 9, 72–76, 97–98, 148,
150–52, 154; ports, 74, 76; post-, 32,
56, 77, 100–101, 116, 118, 125, 137,
154; and primary countries, 91-93;
and Roosevelt, Franklin, D., 152;
and Russia, 76; and seapower, 68;
and Singapore, 76, 93, 151, 211; and
the Soviet Union, 49, 91, 96, 132;
and the United States, 9, 51, 52, 68,
69–77, 81, 86, 96, 113, 116, 118, 134,
141, 150, 151, 154, 163
September 11, 2001, xii
Shamian Island, 153, 157
Shanghai, 120
Shanghai Cooperation Agreement, 55
Sheffield, 48, 109, 128
Shenzen, 120
Siam, 129
Siberia, 97
Sibley, David J., 99
Sicily, 145
Sierra Leone, 118
silk, 44, 64
Silk Road, 137
Silk Road Economic Belt, 59
silver, 30, 175, 196n12
Singapore, 109, 168; and the Second
World War, 76, 93, 151, 211; and
Washington Agreements, 95, 97
Sino-Japanese War (1894–1895), 54
Sino-Soviet border conflict, 56
slavery, 30, 34, 130
Smith, Adam, 126
soap, 107
Solomon Islands, 121, 122
Somalia, 168
Somme, Battle of the, 77, 94
South African War, 48. *See also* Boer
War
South America, 66, 75, 100, 118
South China Sea, 6; and islands,
140–41, 153, 157; and near and far
waters, 62, 77–78; and the nine-
dash line, 82; and Permanent Court
of Arbitration, 9; and Sea Lines of
Communication, 59

INDEX 229

Southeast Asia, 82, 86, 93, 118, 156
Southeast Asia Treaty Organization, 32
South Korea, 119, 135, 156, 157
South-South cooperation, 34, 37, 125, 136, 137, 210n8
Soviet Union, 32; and Atlantic Ocean, 150, 156; and Bolshevism, 100; and China, 54, 56, 57; and the Cold War, 57, 156; and the Greenland-Iceland-United Kingdom gap, 148, 149; as landpower, 13; and the Pacific Ocean, 150, 156; and the Second World War, 49, 91, 96, 132; and the United States, 49, 132, 152; and the Vietnam War, 156
Spain, 30, 42, 175, 196n12; and the Dutch Republic, 41–43, 44, 45, 64–66, 90, 142; and the Eighty Years War, 143; and Great Britain, 47; as seapower, 30, 42, 43, 45; and the Thirty Years' War, 126; and the United States, 78, 81, 99. *See also* Spanish-American War
Spanish-American War (1898), 51
spices, 64
Spice Islands, 66, 143
Spratly Islands, 157, 158
Spykman, Nicholas, J., 184n4
Sri Lanka, 150, 156
Stalin, Joseph, 132
Stanley, Henry, 146
Stimson, Henry L., 97
St. Lucia, 71
strong countries. *See* primary countries
Subi Reef, 158
Subic Bay, 155
subsidiary countries: and commodity chains, 86; definition, 7, 27, 36, 181n27, 185n3, 211n9; and economic change, 55, 60; and far waters, 75, 84, 96; and the generative sector, 8, 86, 112; and geopolitics, 28, 29, 35, 112, 161; and

hegemony, 42, 85, 104, 107, 124, 128; and infrastructure, 121; and islands, 158; and NATO, 160; and near waters, 84; and peacebuilding, 170; and ports, 118; and seapower, 40, 64, 66, 87, 130; and strategy, 32; and violence, 45, 66. *See also* primary-subsidiary relations
Sudan, 48
Suez Canal, 19, 52, 58, 110, 118, 145, 183n14
sugar, 64, 107
Sun Tzu, 16
supercomputing, 23, 37, 102, 114
supply chains, 19, 29, 30, 55, 82, 160
Sweden, 32, 45, 66, 142, 143
Syria, 32, 36

Taiwan, 36; and China, 82, 156, 157, 160; and Chinese nationalists, 54, 56, 80; and the Cold War, 80, 81, 152; and the Dutch Republic, 89; and Japan, 54, 93; and near and far waters, 156, 160; and a Third World War, 161; and the United States, 81, 82, 156, 157
Takeshima Island. *See also* Dokdo Island, 157
Tanzania, 154, 168
tar, 64, 89
technology, 25, 114; and China, 59, 103, 114, 115, 162; and far waters, 167; and the generative sector, 167; and geopolitics, 21, 135, 160, 162; nuclear, 57, 148; and primary-subsidiary relations, 104; and seapower, 59, 135, 149, 167; and the United States, 115
telecommunications, 103, 114
Ternate Island, 66, 143
terrorism, 104. *See also* War on Terror
Texas, 115
The Hague. *See* Hague, The,
Third World War, 161, 167, 169
Thirty Years War (1618–1648), 66, 126

Thornton, Edward, 144
Tianjin, 120
Tibet, 56
Tidore Island, 66, 143
timber, 64
tobacco, 107
Tokaido line, 113
Tokyo, 111, 113
Tokyo Bay, 51
Top Gun, 171
Town class destroyers, 71
trade: arms, 29; bulk, 64, 89; and China, 30, 44, 54–58, 78, 80–82, 92, 101, 104, 114–16, 137; and choke points, 142; and developmentalism, 133; and the Dutch Republic, 41–44, 64–67, 88–90, 107–108, 142–43; and far waters, 5, 66, 77, 98; free, 6, 28, 29, 50, 52, 89, 96, 98; and geopolitical context, 23–24; and geopolitics, 17–19, 21, 28, 42, 61, 85, 167; and Germany, 112–13; and Great Britain, 47–49, 68, 77, 92, 94, 96, 109–13, 145; and hegemony, 44–45; high-value, 66, 107–108; and islands, 140–41, 145; and liberalism, 126–27; and Japan, 94, 97; and Mahan, Alfred Thayer, 68; 178n9; and near waters, 64–66, 89, 143; and the nonvirtuous cycle of seapower, 163; and ports, 119–20; pre-capitalist, 179n19; and primary-subsidiary relations, 26, 29, 85–86, 92, 137; and Sea Lines of Communication, 148; and seapower, 1–4, 7, 21, 39, 61, 85, 167; silk, 44; and the Soviet Union, 148; spice, 44, 46; and a Third World War, 167; and the United States, 50–52, 97, 115–16, 133, 148, 163; and violence, 30, 125; and the virtuous cycle of seapower, 18, 109–10, 178n4
Trafalgar, Battle of, 2, 144, 164
Trinidad, 71

Truman Doctrine, 135
Truman, Harry S., 80
Tsuruga, 113
Turkey, 134
Tyneside, 129

Ukraine, 28. *See also* Russia-Ukraine war
Union of Utrecht (1579), 41
United Arab Emirates, 122
United Dutch East India Company, 46
United Fruit Company, 134
United Kingdom. *See* Great Britain; *See also* Greenland-Iceland-United Kingdom gap
"united nations" 79
United Nations, 50, 76, 80, 81. *See also* Agenda for Sustainable Development; Global Development Initiative.
United Nations Convention of the Law of the Seas (UNCLOS), 9
United Provinces, 41, 42, 44, 46, 65, 126. *See also*, Dutch Republic; Netherlands, the
United States of America: and Africa, 58, 73–74, 166; and the Atlantic Ocean, 50, 52, 68–76, 98, 118, 141, 150; and Australia, 122; and the Caribbean Sea, 61, 71, 141; and China, 5, 34, 46, 51, 54, 55, 57, 78, 79, 82, 83, 103, 115–16, 120, 122, 135, 150, 156, 157, 160, 162; and classic geopolitics, 13; and the Cold War, 13, 56, 57, 79, 80, 101, 119, 135, 149, 152; and Cuba, 99, 100; and Dakar, 73, 74, 75, 76; and developmentalism, 125, 130, 132, 137; and Diego Garcia, 156; and the Dominican Republic, 51, 100; and El Salvador, 100; as entrepôt, 117; and far waters, 5, 9, 52, 61, 64, 68–77, 78, 81, 82, 83, 95, 98, 152, 160, 166, 167; and the First World War,

71, 163; and France, 73–76, 99; and "freedom of navigation" operations, 82; and the generative sector, 100; and geopolitics, 23; and Germany, 52, 70; and Great Britain, 40, 46, 47, 49–50, 52, 62, 70–77, 91, 94, 95, 96, 97–98, 112; and Guam, 81, 151; and Guatemala, 100; and Haiti, 51; and hegemony, 4, 34, 36, 49, 59, 91, 114, 123, 164; and Honduras, 51; and Hong Kong, 95, 115; and India, 40, 47, 156, 168; and islands, 140, 148, 149, 150, 154; and Japan, 51, 74, 81, 94, 96, 97–98, 113, 119, 135, 151; and Korean War, 50, 56, 80, 152, 156; and liberalism, 53, 126, 130; and Mahan, Alfred Thayer, 10, 13, 51, 68, 178n9; 182n35; 183n14; manufacturing, 111, 114, 115–16; and the Mediterranean Sea, 69–70, 73–74, 76, 98, 134; and the Middle East, 103; and near waters, 9, 48, 52, 61, 68, 78, 100, 148; and Nicaragua, 51, 100; and the nonvirtuous cycle of seapower, 163; and North Korea, 56; and Okinawa, 118, 135, 151, 152, 155; and Operation Ocean Shield, 58; and the Pacific Ocean; 50, 51, 68, 70, 72–76, 81, 95, 97–98, 117, 119, 122, 134–35, 148, 150, 154, 156; and peacebuilding, 171; and the Philippines, 81, 99, 151; and ports, 109, 117, 118, 120; and primary-subsidiary relations, 30, 32, 34, 40, 100, 101, 134, 140; and projection of force, 5; and Sea Lines of Communications, 58, 103, 148, 169; as seapower, 5, 50, 51, 64, 95, 100, 164, 166, 169, 175; and the Second World War, 9, 51, 52, 68, 69–77, 81, 96, 97, 113, 116, 118, 134, 141, 150, 151, 154, 163; and South Korea, 119, 135; and the Soviet Union, 57, 80, 150; and Spain, 78, 99; and Taiwan, 36, 80, 81, 157, 160; and a Third World War, 161, 165, 167–68; and trade, 50, 97, 109, 115, 133; and the United Arab Emirates, 122; and the Vietnam War, 13, 50, 56, 80, 119, 135, 152, 155–56; and violence, 31; and the virtuous cycle of seapower, 18; and Washington Agreements, 95. *See also* American-British Conversation (ABC) Plans; American Revolution; American Revolutionary War; Central Intelligence Agency; Spanish-American War; US Congressional Research Service

US Congressional Research Service, 115

Ussuri River, 56

Utah, 116, 117

Uyghur Muslims, 57

Venezuela, 66

Verenigde Oost-Indische Compagnie (VOC). *See* United Dutch East India Company

Vermeer, 127

Viborg, 89

Vietnam, 40, 135, 142, 152, 155, 157

Vietnam War: and China 56, 80; and South Korea, 119; and the Soviet Union, 156; and the United States, 13, 50, 56, 80, 119, 135, 152, 155–56

virtuous cycle of seapower, 1, 17–18, 41, 178n4; and China, 122, 162; and the Dutch Republic, 43; and far waters, 84; and Great Britain, 109; and hegemony, 84; and innovation, 106–107; and Japan, 112; and the nonvirtuous cycle of seapower, 163; and port power, 117; and power projection, 122; and primary-subsidiary relations, 27, 113. *See also* nonvirtuous cycle of seapower; seapower.

Vladivostock, 150

Wang, Yi, 58
War of 1812, 47, 50
War on Terror, xii, 14, 57
Washington Agreements, 95
Washington Conference, 95, 97
Washington, D.C., 74
Watson, Dr., 48
weak countries. *See* subsidiary countries
Western Hemisphere, 42, 73, 75
West Indies, 71, 72 fig. 4.3
West-Indische Compagnie (WIC). *See* Dutch West India Company
West Virginia, 115
whale oil, 89, 107
White Man's Burden, 35, 125, 131
White Sea, 89
Whitsun Reef, 23
Wilhelm II, Kaiser, 146, 147
Wilhelmshaven, 147
Wilson, Woodrow, 100

wool, 64,
World Bank, 34, 37, 50, 124, 133
Wuhan University, 77, 82
Wyoming, 115

Xi, Jinping, 59, 81, 104, 137
Xinjiang Province, 56, 57, 137

Yokohama, 113
Yorktown, USS, 151

zaibatsu, 113
Zanzibar, 118, 146, 154, 156. *See also* Heligoland-Zanzibar Treaty
Zealand, 142, 143
Zhenbao Island, 56. *See also* Damansky Island
Zheng, He, 78, 79 fig. 4.4
Zhujiang River, 153. *See also* Pearl River

The authorized representative in the EU for product safety and compliance is:
Mare Nostrum Group
B.V Doelen 72
4831 GR Breda
The Netherlands

www.ingramcontent.com/pod-product-compliance
Lightning Source LLC
Chambersburg PA
CBHW020835160426

43192CB00007B/663